For my brothers, Mark and Jim

i-brainmap

Freeing your brain for happiness

Rita McInnes

ISBN: 978-0-9924519-0-5

Copyright © Rita McInnes 2014

This publication is protected by Australian and International copyright laws. Other than as permitted by law, no part of this book may be reproduced in any way whatsoever including online without specific permission of Rita McInnes. Enquiries should be addressed to ibrain@ibrainmap.com.au

With thanks to Michael Leunig for permission to use his cartoons.

The cases and characters described in this book based on real events or people have been changed to protect their privacy.

As every individual is different, these materials are intended as a guide only. They should not be used or relied upon as a substitute for professional medical or psychological advice. If you have a physiological or psychological condition, we recommend that you seek professional advice tailored to your specific needs.

Contents

- ix   Preface

1   Tracking brains in the wild

Part 1 gives the inside stories and context of i-brainmap and introduces the characters.

- 2   Say hello to the wolf in your brain
- 15   Meeting my yellow-eyed wolf
- 30   Introducing the i-brainmap
- 46   How i-brainmap works and when it doesn't work
- 60   Meeting Mary

69   The brain and the map

Part 2 outlines each section of the i-brainmap in detail.

- 70   Brain basics
- 74   Fight, flight, freeze and appease
- 88   Triggers
- 98   Stuck in old memory maps: hippocampus lost in action
- 110   The gesture of integration
- 120   Primary activation
- 129   Secondary activation
- 145   Making meaning
- 153   The integration Zone or i-Zone
- 170   Orientation and the AND pathway

185   AIR(s) flow

Part 3 explains how to apply the AIR(s) technique to encourage integration and flow and move towards happiness.

- 187   Introducing AIR(s): Applying the i-brainmap
- 198   AH! = Awareness as it Happens
- 208   Interrupting the pattern
- 221   Reorienting
- 232   Soothing the lower brain
- 239   Finishing i-brainmap with AIR(s)
- 255   Sustainable happiness

- 266   *Epilogue*
- 269   *Further reading*
- 276   *Acknowledgements*

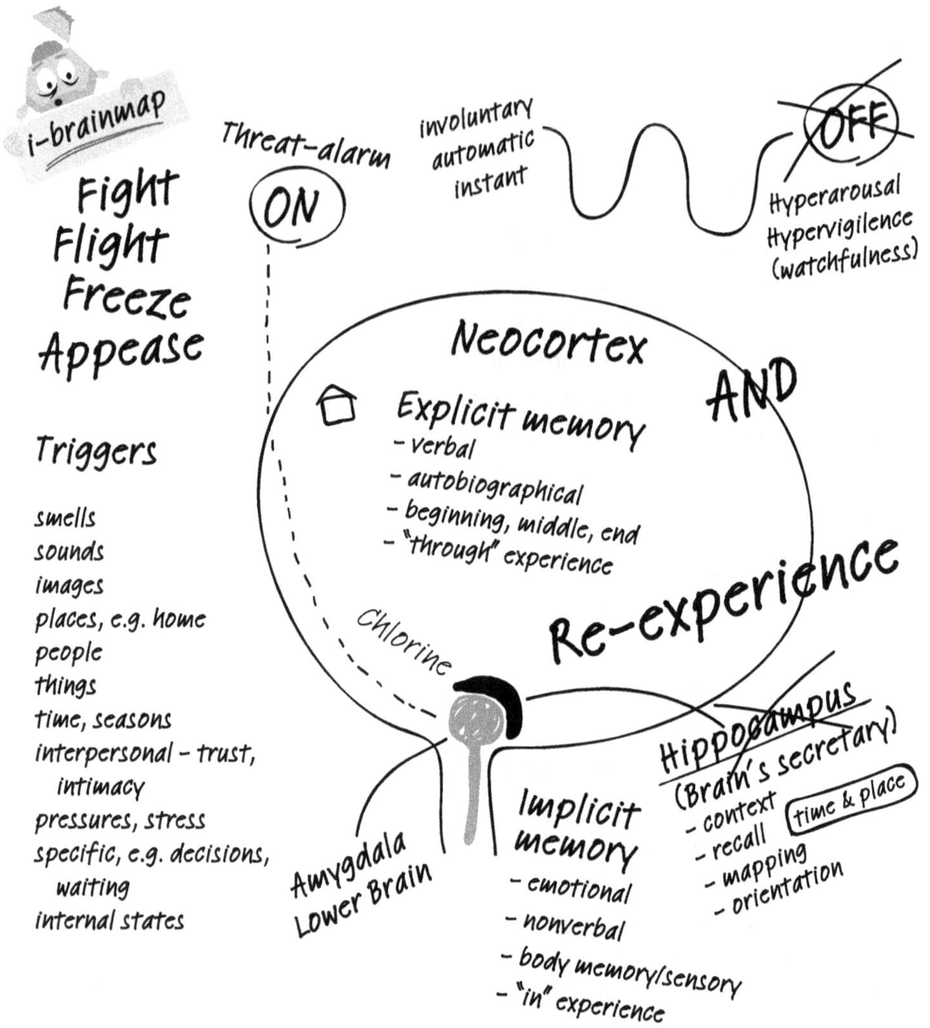

i-brainmap

Threat-alarm **ON** — involuntary automatic instant — ~~OFF~~ Hyperarousal Hypervigilance (watchfulness)

Fight
Flight
Freeze
Appease

Triggers

- smells
- sounds
- images
- places, e.g. home
- people
- things
- time, seasons
- interpersonal – trust, intimacy
- pressures, stress
- specific, e.g. decisions, waiting
- internal states

Neocortex
- Explicit memory
  - verbal
  - autobiographical
  - beginning, middle, end
  - "through" experience

AND

Re-experience

Chlorine

Amygdala / Lower Brain

Implicit memory
- emotional
- nonverbal
- body memory/sensory
- "in" experience

Hippocampus (Brain's secretary)
- context
- recall — time & place
- mapping
- orientation

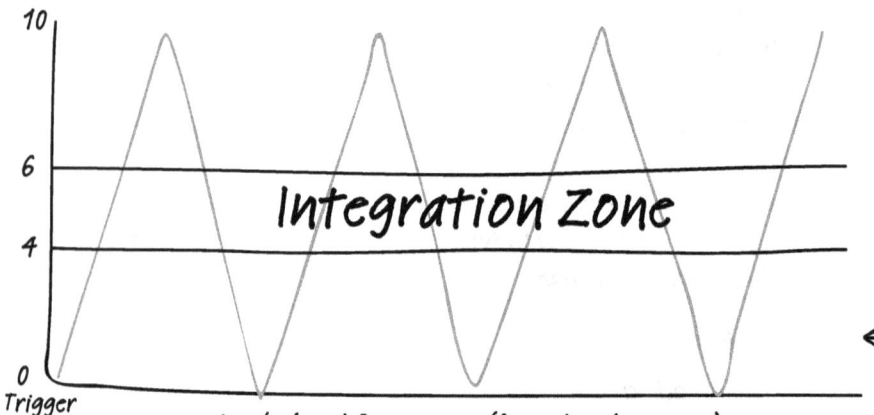

Activation / Overwhelm

10 — 6 — 4 — 0

Integration Zone

Trigger

Numb, Avoid, Dissociation (Secondary Activation)

© Rita McInnes

Primary Activation
(symptoms)

Anxiety

Anger – Defend

Dissociative Experiences

Splitting/Disconnect

Isolation/Loneliness

Shame

Powerlessness / Overwhelm

Stuck Sadness

Safety–Danger

Trust–Mistrust

Physical Symptoms

Sleep disturb

  Concentration

  Memory

Wired & Tired

Exhaustion

Hopelessness

Depression

Secondary Activation
Adaptations–Misadaptations

<u>Avoid – Escape</u> reactions

<u>Control</u> Reactions
Perfectionism
"fix it", "gotta get it right", driven,
  high achieving

<u>Struggle</u>

<u>Over</u> – reactions (disprop)
over thinking, over-identification

<u>Stuck Thinking Patterns</u>: either-or
repetitive, right-wrong, all or nothing,
  catastrophic

<u>Storied-mind</u> – stuck
always, never, can't, "victim myth",
  "blaming", "wishing & hoping", "if only"

<u>Relationship (R) Patterns</u> – others

<u>Identity</u> – R with self

<u>Body</u> – R with body

<u>Food & things</u> – R with food & stuff

For a full colour i-brainmap go to
http://www.ibrainmap.com.au/images/i-brainmap.jpg
or scan this QR code with your smart phone.

Meaning making

I have to be in control, etc...

I can't trust myself or my body

I can't trust anyone

I can't / I'm hopeless-powerless

I'm not OK / I'm crazy / I'm ....

I'm not safe / World isn't safe

Preface

As you read these words your brain lights up like a Christmas tree, sending messages, neuron to neuron, chatting noisily amongst itself like the local knitting club catching up on gossip after the summer break. So efficient is your brain that you can sit there in your chair and sip a cup of tea while you read, and perhaps keep an eye on the kids in the other room or wonder how you can get out of the family reunion next month.

Your brain is a wizard, a maestro. Even as the frontier of science shows some small part of the brain's capability, including the greatest feat of wizardry – that the brain can change itself – there is so much we don't know, and may never know, about that lumpy grey quivering mass between your ears.

But what does brain change mean for you? Can you change your brain to feel happier, more peaceful, less stressed, or stop yelling at the kids? Can you learn to become a brain whisperer and talk yourself out of that burning desire to fling yourself at the fridge to grab that lonely piece of chocolate cake that seems to be calling out to you through the night, and hold it to your lips? Can you teach your brain to down-regulate your nervous system when your boss is raging around the office red-faced, stabbing a finger at the air, while your heart pounds in your chest and your fists clench ready to hit something, or someone?

These are the questions that i-brainmap addresses.

Entering these pages is an invitation to curiosity – about your experience and about your brain. Along with Jack and Mary, characters I've created from a conglomeration of real clients and issues arising in real therapy sessions, I will guide you through the complex personal experience of the brain and how it can change. Why do you need a guide? Because if I'd written a book and just *told* you how the brain changes, only your big brain, your brain's cortex, would join us on the page. But to catch the attention of the lower, the subcortical, regions – and some other less well known parts – of the brain, I need to *show* you, through experience and interaction, how the brain changes. If you want to change your brain you need your whole brain engaged, especially the subcortical areas, or lower brain.

In these pages you'll meet Jack's and Mary's brains, though they're all wrapped up in the usual way, behind a face and stories and experiences from their lives. Jack and Mary get stuck and struggle with problems just like you and me. I discuss Jack and Mary's role in more detail in chapter 1.

But this book isn't about Jack and Mary; it's about you. About your brain and how it, like every other brain, can get stuck in old pathways so that you feel like you're on a never-ending loop going nowhere. Through my interactions with Jack and Mary in session I invite you into curiosity about your own brain: about how it gets stuck but also how it can get unstuck. Through watching and listening to Jack's and Mary's stories (and mine) you may see some of your own experience mapped out in these pages, so your brain can make new connections, create new pathways and maps, create an integrated brain map (i-brainmap), because that's the key to brain changing.

You don't need to bring anything with you on this trip with Jack and Mary and me; just your brain and as much curiosity as you can muster. Your brain will do the rest.

Because no one else can know your brain from the inside, i-brainmap invites you to step into your own brain-science lab – the one between your ears – and see what is going on, through your personal experience. Even brain science can only observe the brain from outside experience. You get a front row seat in your own science lab from inside your own brain.

 In any moment the brain can create and perpetuate misery, but in that same moment it can delight in the sound of a magpie singing across the dawn or a child laughing at a beetle.

About the book

The book is divided into three parts. Part 1 takes you through how i-brainmap was developed and some of the significant personal and professional influences. In part 2 each section of the i-brainmap is explained in detail. Part 3 illustrates the mindfulness-based technique used to guide your brain towards integration. Part 3 also shows i-brainmap in the larger context of sustainable happiness.

About the author

I am a registered psychologist. I've worked face to face with clients experiencing a broad range of issues for more than twenty years.

The first seeds of the i-brainmap were planted almost ten years ago when I was working with people experiencing symptoms of post-traumatic stress. Since then, these seeds have grown and taken over my practice to become central to my work and this book. The story of i-brainmap is offered in chapter 3. In chapter 2, I tell my personal stories of trauma, which underpin my dedication to this work.

There are also deep tracks of knowledge and practice, the long lineage of my profession, running through my work. These are the great minds and therapists who have gone before me, giving us all new maps of the territory of the human psyche, and human suffering: Freud, Jung, Adler, James, Janet, Maslow, Satir and Rogers, to name a few.

Now there are so many neuroscientists opening doors into the brain and mind each week they are too numerous to mention. Clinicians and neuroscientists who have particularly inspired i-brainmap are mentioned throughout the book.

There are others who have had a more obvious or personal influence on my approach, such as Roberto Assagioli, Gregory Kramer, and the Buddha, through my experience in the monastery in Sri Lanka, which is talked about in chapter 2. Then there have been my supervisors, my supervisees and trainees, and colleagues who have gently added tone and depth to my practice.

But my greatest teachers have been my clients. They have made me honest and kept i-brainmap practical and real. They tested it at every stage of its development. Their courage to face and move through their pain and trauma was my greatest teacher and the fertile ground in which i-brainmap evolved.

Preface

All of these influences have changed my maps in the field of psychology in which I work, and have therefore contributed to what I have discovered. This is the solid and privileged ground on which I stand as I hold out my discoveries to you.

Part 1

Tracking brains in the wild

Chapter 1
Say hello to the wolf in your brain

When something dreadful happens your body remembers

The memory lives under your skin and in your bones and breath like a yellow-eyed wolf ready to pounce. A look, a sound, a touch or a leaving can snap your body into remembering quicker than a finger click. The old terror crashes in, and your body goes into alarm with hormones flashing and chemicals spilling through your nervous system as if the threat is right here, right now. You reach for a drink or turn and run back into your busy day, and the wolf retreats back under your skin and into your bones and breath, lying in wait for another chance to pounce.

Your partner sits across from you at the kitchen table reading the newspaper while you're telling him about Beth's latest catastrophe. He doesn't seem to be listening to you, and yet your body reacts as if it's life or death and triggers a murderous rage in you.

Or your boss raises his voice in a meeting, pointing at you and wagging his finger. You feel the hard grip of panic in your chest, your words dry in your mouth as you choke down the bile. Your hands tremble as you fumble to find an elusive document. You are a child again cowering before your drunken father.

Or your child is only ten minutes late home, but your heart pounds in your chest while your mind fills with catastrophe.

In that moment, all your skills and resources go out the window

You revert to a three-year-old. You want to stamp your feet. You *do* stamp your feet and run from the room screaming. You throw a plate across the room. You collapse in tears. The techniques you discussed with your psychologist are nowhere to be seen. Your breathing and mindfulness practice shrivel into hard nuts in the front of your brain, and you feel yourself winding up and tightening into a ball of rage or terror, or to the point of collapse, or some other familiar sticky emotion.

A few minutes later, a friend phones and you're laughing and talking as if everything is fine. And you *feel* fine – now. Your heart rate slows, your breathing is rhythmical, your mind settles. And it's over. Till next time. And you wonder, 'What was all that about?'

How your brain is behaving

Actually, your brain is behaving exactly as it should in a threatening situation. But there is no current threat. Instead, your brain is working from a map or neural network that was created perhaps twenty, thirty or fifty years ago, based on an experience of powerlessness. Like when your teacher ridiculed you in front of the class, or your mum told you to 'get outside' because you tore your sister's doll's dress. You felt overwhelmed by your teacher's ridicule. And although you wanted to tell your mum that your sister bit the toe off your doll, she wouldn't listen. This is the same map your brain uses when your boss asks you to review your report or your partner suggests that you've been a bit tough on little Chloe.

Enter the memory maps

Our brain is an amazingly sophisticated network of memory maps, and it uses these maps to make sense of and respond to the world and the array of ever-changing situations that arise moment-to-moment throughout the day. Most of the time, we hardly notice all this mapping and recalling and interconnectivity; the brain does its thing seemingly without effort, and mostly it works well enough for us to respond effectively.

But what if the brain keeps opening an old map that's outdated, or uses the *wrong* map in a situation? What if it makes you furious at your partner for ignoring you at the kitchen table because, without even knowing it, the situation reminds you of when your dad left, and you missed him most at breakfast because he'd made it fun? After he left, Mum turned into a grouch, always crying and needing to lie down a lot, in her darkened bedroom. Sitting at the breakfast table alone each morning when you were seven made you want to cry and run away. But you've forgotten all of that. Well, your mind has forgotten, but your body remembers – quietly, each morning – then when your partner gives all his attention to his newspaper or iPad you feel like you're alone again. Instead of asking him to talk to you, you bite your lip and withdraw, or you yell at him that he never listens and storm out slamming the door as you leave for work.

Those are the *wrong maps*, and they live in all of us like time bombs that can go off at any moment. For those of us who've experienced traumatic events in life, these maps can explode and drop us into terror at the sound of a car backfiring or a raised voice. Some of the wrong maps the brain uses can be more subtle, less explosive, but they can still keep you stuck or stop you enjoying the intimacy of a relationship or taking a risk in your work or creativity.

Maps are stored in the body

It seems obvious that the solution is to *change the maps*, or *get the right map*. But the problem is that these maps are held in the body and are mostly inaccessible to the thinking or deciding mind. Just deciding to do something different won't necessarily change anything. If you've ever tried to change an old habit, like giving up smoking or coffee or chocolate, you probably know how hard it can be.

Take dieting, for instance. You decide to go on a diet. You get the books, find the latest diet and perhaps even get a coach. You might do some mindfulness groups because you've heard that helps. For six months, you work really hard at losing the weight. You record what you eat, and you exercise, and you make healthy choices; you eat mindfully. You lose some weight. You buy some new clothes, and you're feeling good. Now you just want to lose another five kilos and you'll be your perfect weight. Feeling confident and hopeful, you buy an expensive garment in a size that will fit when you reach that perfect weight, and you hang it with ceremony in the end of the wardrobe.

Then you go on a holiday. You relax. You tell yourself it won't matter if you have dessert while you're away, an extra glass of wine or two, or make a platter of nibbles with drinks each night as you sit on the balcony and watch the sun set over the tropical ocean. You relax and breathe out, and so does your body.

When you get home you get back on track, but as soon as you relax there's that old habit dragging you back. You struggle between dieting and giving up, giving in. And this goes on and on and on. Your expensive garment hanging at the end of the wardrobe goes out of fashion.

The reason it's so hard to change these old habits is that they live in the body-brain, or subcortical areas of the brain, connected with the body as automatic reactions to stimuli, like a trip wire. Your moment-to-moment response to the world is dictated by what's happening in your body, by body maps that direct how you respond. Food is especially complicated, as it hooks into one of the oldest networks of body-memory maps each of us carry. It was the first way we were comforted by our parents, so food has many other maps connected with it: food and comfort, food and love, food and enough or not enough, food and deserving, food and happiness, food and family. You name it, food can have an association with it.

When you try to change your eating habits, or any other long-established habit, you can try doing it in a 'top down' way, using your big brain or intellectual function to try to change things, like trying to *think* or *manage* your way through it. But that won't necessarily access the memory maps about food that are stored in your body and driving those habits. Dieting is like trying to impose a new map over the old one you're still following, or you could say it's like trying to reason with a two-year-old while they're screaming and snot-nosed in the middle of a supermarket aisle. Reasoning isn't the language that will get through to them when they're distressed. When the body-brain is operating from an old map you need to use the language that it understands. Talking and reasoning just won't cut it and are likely to get you into a push-me-pull-you fight with yourself.

Brain-body-mind and memory maps

What is happening in the present moment, right now, is interpreted through established memory maps, while the brain, being quite lazy, often ignores contradictory evidence suggesting this may be the wrong map. The *lazy brain* will use a near-enough map for whatever is going on. 'Oh yeah, that's the map for *food, love, being touched* or *not being touched, the boss* or *someone telling me what to do*,' or any other map for making sense of and responding to stimuli or experience. Most of this happens outside your awareness, and trying to change just your thinking may not change the established maps that are interconnected and running through the body. If the map is an intellectual one, like a maths equation, with no associated emotional or physiological connection, then changing your thinking will work just fine. But if there is some emotional association, trying to think your way out of it may not help.

Going back to our friend who gets upset about her partner not listening to her at the kitchen table: she has a memory map operating that was established thirty years ago when her father left, and it's triggered each time her partner checks his iPad or reads the newspaper while she's trying to tell him something at breakfast time. Her mind races, she overthinks, saying to herself, 'He always ignores me; he never listens,' or perhaps even 'He doesn't love me.' But her thoughts are repetitive and disconnected from the current situation or from other times when her partner *did* listen, or when he's been attentive and loving. She is operating from a scrap of map that is stuck on a body reaction of distress, and she can't access it through her usual reasoning and other resources to help her make sense of the current situation. In other words, her body and mind are operating independently, stuck on separate loops, not interconnected, and therefore she can't integrate the two and change.

When the brain is operating in an interconnected way it is constantly updating and integrating maps, based on new experience and evidence. But because some maps are fragments, like a mummified body part found under ice, and not connected to the rest of the system, they remain frozen free-floating lumps in the system. And until we can re-establish interconnectivity in the brain these maps remain frozen in disconnected loops.

A whole-brain map for sustainable brain change

To change an established pathway in a sustainable way you need a map for the whole brain.

When the brain is overwhelmed by an experience it can't integrate it. Then whenever something in the environment triggers the memory of that experience the lower brain (the subcortical functions associated with survival) is activated as your system drops into survival mode, disconnecting from other functions in the brain. This disconnection repeats every time an association with that experience occurs. It is this disconnection that results in a split-brain system that stops the brain integrating. The brain is reading fragments of memory maps instead of an integrated memory map and it can't make the necessary connections with other maps of current or other experience.

The split-brain system is how the brain is designed to function in an emergency, so that the lower (survival) brain can override every other function until you're safe. But if split-brain functioning continues it can become a permanent orientation, like a blueprint for all experience, and the world is seen as divided between *either–or*: black–white, right–wrong, us–them, with no *and*. Instead of interpreting experience as black *and* white with different shades of grey, every experience is *either* black *or* white, or right *or* wrong; experience and the world are compartmentalised and segregated.

Imagine this split-brain system as a company, with management on the top floor. But management never communicate with people on the ground. Everyone is doing their own thing independently, each department operating as a closed circuit (or neural loop), disconnected from each other. And what if management speak Spanish and the people on the ground speak English but there's no interpreter? That's how a split-brain system functions: isolated operations with no communication between. This split, or lack of interconnectivity, affects every aspect of the company.

To help the brain recognise how it is disconnected we need to speak to all its functions in their own language. To do this we need a map that *everyone* can make sense of and use for common orientation, a whole-brain map. And we need a mediator or interpreter between all these segmented brain functions.

i-brainmap and this book

The whole-brain map I've developed for this purpose I call the 'integrated brain map' or 'i-brainmap'. It's an experiential and functional map *of* the brain, and *for* the brain. It provides the whole brain with a map explaining how the brain can get stuck in split-brain following an overwhelming or extreme event or experience.

The i-brainmap uses the different languages of brain function to explain to the whole brain why and how it gets stuck, which can kickstart interconnectivity so that the brain can integrate the overwhelming experience or fragments of memory maps.

It is a bottom-up map that starts by acknowledging and naming the experience of the body-brain, especially what happens when the brain is overwhelmed. It also speaks to the intellect because we need to engage the big brain: if we leave out any brain functions the brain is likely to continue operating from a split-brain system. And of course we need to engage an interpreter, or mediating function, of the brain. This is the aim of i-brainmap.

This book explores i-brainmap: its principles; the techniques it uses to encourage brain integration; and why it works, and when it doesn't work, to change the brain.

Big-Braining

One of the biggest inhibitors to brain integration that I've observed when working with i-brainmap is what I call *Big-Braining*. Big-Braining is when your big brain dominates all other brain functions. It is endemic in our society so is rarely considered problematic. But understanding the brain only through the intellect, while ignoring personal and sensory experience, won't catalyse integration. That's not a problem when you're an academic and need to understand weather patterns. But when it comes to understanding the brain, you need to factor in experience, especially body-sensory experience, because this changes the brain. If you leave your personal and sensory experience out of the equation – *no brain change.*

The propensity for Big-Braining in our culture is the main challenge I've faced in developing i-brainmap, but even more so in writing this book. In therapy sessions when I use i-brainmap I can monitor and engage different functions of the brain through questioning or reorienting attention. So if a person is stuck in big brain, intellectualising everything, I can invite them to notice how they are breathing as they describe an event. If they are lost in their body experience with no understanding we can explore how they've made meaning of that experience, or the story they tell themselves about it. Moment-to-moment we can move between the different functions of the brain so it has a different experience of an old pathway or map.

But reading is predominantly an intellectual or big-brain exercise, unless you engage your imagination and personal experience. For this reason I have invented two characters, Jack and Mary, so that you can have a more direct experience of i-brainmap. I also share some of my own very personal experiences to speak more directly to your own experience rather than your intellect.

An invitation to curiosity

This book is not intended as an intellectual discussion of facts and information, but as an invitation to curiosity. Curiosity keeps your big brain or mind open. Because as soon as you think you know, the brain-mind has just locked onto an old memory map, because it's lazy, and the mind wanders off to think about what's for dinner or the fight you had with your partner last night.

Curiosity is a particular quality of attention: your brain is engaged and open and uncertain – this is the space where creativity breathes. And creativity is the experience when the whole brain is interconnected, dynamic and engaged with focused attention – the curious brain.

Brain change needs curiosity and attention

I don't want you to believe what I say but to discover what makes sense for you, based on your experience, as we explore the ideas that I've uncovered in working in close contact with many brains using i-brainmap.

Because your brain is unique in the way it takes in information, the best way for you to read this book is by drawing on your personal experience and particular curiosities. Only you know what engages your brain. Follow your curiosity. *The invitation to curiosity begins with your direct experience.*

If you think you already know, or compare i-brainmap to something you already know – that is, you let your lazy brain take charge – it will fall half asleep, thinking it has done its job by finding an approximation of the current experience (an old map). Then there will be no chance of integration or change.

The i-brainmap is not intended to be a map of what you know or even what I know, but more a map of 'unknow', a map of 'maybe' or 'what if' wondering, to keep your mind open and curious. Sometimes you might feel as if you're at the Mad Hatter's tea party, as I get very silly. Silliness and play are a handy way to upset the big brain's *I think I know everything* attitude or map, and can open the mind again to the ridiculous and laughter. So silly away, I say.

This is not a book of answers; it's more like travelling through a strange yet familiar land. Because once you think you know what will happen next, like believing you'll find an answer, your brain has already grabbed onto a specific map, the *find the answer* map, which will limit how and what you discover.

A bouncy ride

Dialogue with Jack and Mary is used to capture some of the experience – the dynamic and interactive quality – of i-brainmap as I use it in my work. The dialogues demonstrate some of the ways people react to this material and some of the pitfalls we each encounter. Although I've invented Jack and Mary, they have similar problems, ideas and memory maps to real clients.

At times the dialogues may seem disjointed; that's because I didn't want to get bogged down in the lead-up to crucial interactions. I invite you to leap with me. You may feel like Alice in Wonderland at times: one moment a giant staring down at the action from far off, the next as close as a mouse whisker. Or you might find yourself rushing along behind the white rabbit, who seems to know where she's going ... but maybe she only knows where she's going once she arrives.

Definitions and language

Words are limited constructs of an idea; they can kill curiosity because your big brain thinks it already knows. Therefore, at times, I deliberately change the words or metaphors I use to describe something – not to confuse you but to remind your brain not to get locked onto a particular perspective, and to keep your brain engaged. I hope to surprise your brain occasionally; to keep it on its synaptic toes.

What is true of words in general is also true of labels given to the brain. They can assume certain things that may be misleading or limit our understanding of brain function, which is still very limited. Therefore I will sometimes use words or metaphors for brain function that are different to the accepted labels. At other times I will name the parts of the brain that neuroscientists suggest are involved in certain functions. But sometimes I deliberately leave ideas about the brain vague, because most of what we know about the brain is limited, and how the brain behaves in the lab may not be the same as an unwatched brain in the wild.

Some words I deliberately leave loose because I've observed that people have different experiences of these brain processes. For instance, words like 'activation' and 'integration' I leave undefined. I invite you to discover your own understanding as you read about Jack's and Mary's experiences, and check in with your own brain-body-mind experience.

Because the brain is lazy I will avoid giving you certain definitions, because these could over-simplify them and close your mind or limit your understanding and access to your own experience to make sense of what I'm saying. The word *emotion* is an example. I will use the term and occasionally speak about the brain and emotions, but we can easily make assumptions when we use this term, or terms such as the *emotional brain*, that may be misleading and close the mind to further understanding and therefore brain change. Neuroscientist Joseph LeDoux explains why it's difficult to define emotions (www.youtube.com/watch?v=tjh-CPhhzBqQ, 14:12–17:21). As Fehr and Russell put it, 'Everyone knows what an emotion is, until asked to give a definition'.[1]

References and definitions

The i-brainmap is an experiential and functional model, not a theoretical one. It is a bottom-up approach founded on direct experience with research and psychological approaches linked in later. Over the years in which I've been developing i-brainmap these aspects have become interwoven. But the most important element is the experience – your experience and how you make sense of this information – because the brain changes from bottom up, experience first.

Often I will change the term I use to refer to a particular brain function. Each of these terms has a different orientation, which cues the brain differently. Take the terms *lower brain, survival brain, body-brain* and *child brain*, for instance. I may seem to use these interchangeably but each term has a different orientation. *Survival brain* focuses on the brain as it functions in survival mode, fight–flight response, while reminding us of the evolutionary perspective. *Lower brain* refers to how these subcortical structures operate in memory, specifically implicit memory. *Body-brain* refers to the innate connection between brain and body, and reminds you that the action or expression of brain function is *in* the body. And *child brain* refers to the direct emotional experience that people describe when the brain is stuck on alarm. One reason I don't use the term *limbic system*, which will be discussed in more detail in chapter 6, is that the orientation is a structural one and a static rather than interactive model of the brain.

Because this journey started more than ten years ago, it's hard to know exactly where some of the ideas came from. My clinical observations have been interwoven with brain science. With a few early exceptions most of the evidence on which the i-brainmap is built comes from

---

1 B. Fehr and J. Russell, 'Concept of Emotion Viewed from a Prototype Perspective', *Journal of Experimental Psychology: General*, 113 (1984): 464.

my experience and observation. In general I won't reference ideas that are in the public domain, unless they are derived from specific sources.

For ease of reading and to keep your lower brain engaged I have avoided littering the pages with references. Your lower brain is likely to get distracted and bored if I give you too many facts, stats, definitions and references, so I have focused on the experience and brain function rather than overloading the book with brain science. If your intellect is left reading the book like some lonely old academic in his corduroy trousers surrounded by shelves of thick dusty volumes, it's probably the end of any brain integration.

The other problem with referencing specific research is that brain science is changing even as I write. By the time you read this, a definitive explanation for a particular brain function may have changed as new evidence and another explanation is discovered. For instance, a number of brain scientists are challenging the idea of localisation of brain functions, suggesting that all brain functions are interconnected.

Most of the brain science and psychological approaches that have informed my thinking are available in the public domain. There is also a list of further reading at the back of the book of particular books and researchers who have influenced my thinking and my work.

For a quick, clear and simple understanding of any brain function or structure discussed in the book, Wikipedia is excellent. When I read the description of the HPA-axis and the hippocampus on Wikipedia each was explained coherently, in accessible language, by people who know much more about the brain than I do. So instead of writing in-depth explanations, except when I think it is essential to what I am saying, I suggest you check out Wikipedia if you need more understanding. Just be careful not to get into Big-Braining.

Aside for therapists

If you are a therapist reading this book, you may be wondering how to use this approach with your clients. The best way to learn how to work with the i-brainmap is through your own experience. If you can use it as a model or map of the terrain of your own internal distress or stuck brain, and experiment with the techniques provided, you will have a better understanding of this approach than I, or anyone, can teach you. Learning through your own brain-body-mind experience is the most effective way to learn how to work with other brain-body-minds.

As this book is not intended as a handbook for therapists, I will offer only minimal information in working with i-brainmap as a therapeutic model, occasionally offering some suggestions or insight for those who are reading this book for professional purposes.

Post-traumatic stress

The brain dynamics described in i-brainmap, and throughout this book, were originally developed through understanding gained from working with clients with post-traumatic stress, and with how traumatic and overwhelming events impact on the brain. Over time I realised that the dynamics are similar for many kinds of chronic stress and stuck brain. So I'm writing about how any overwhelming event can impact on the brain-body-mind, although the intensity and dimension of impact will be different for every brain.

Post-traumatic stress is more intense and impacts more extensively on people's lives than other types of stress, but the same principles apply even though people may not always report or remember incidents that could have had a similar impact. What overwhelms a brain can be unrecognised or cumulative, such as work stress, and therefore invisible, yet may result in the same stuck-brain dynamic outlined in these pages.

If you have a history of trauma, it is highly recommended that you have access to a therapist as you read this book, because it could stir up established memory maps or open old wounds. Take care and tread gently.

Mary, Jack and me

My strongest reservation in writing this book is that it can't be interactive, that I cannot be with you as you read, as I have been in therapy with brains that have faces. The brain is interpersonal and interactive, so a lot happens in a therapy session with i-brainmap that won't be happening as you read this book. The main danger with reading is that your brain will intellectualise i-brainmap, which won't promote brain integration.

Through dialogue to animate the experience of i-brainmap I hope you will recognise your own experience as I speak to Jack or Mary. And I hope you can laugh and perhaps cry with Jack and Mary and me as we uncover some hidden memory maps through our conversations. You might see how our brains have held us hostage in old maps that no longer fit the territory of our lives, and also observe our brains integrating.

Together I hope we can uncover the common brain we share called 'humanity', and see how we each suffer and how we can also free ourselves from that suffering. But most of all, I hope that in the journey of this book your brain will learn how to put down fear for a while and remember how to play. Because that is what the brain wants to do when it is safe, and working at its best – to play.

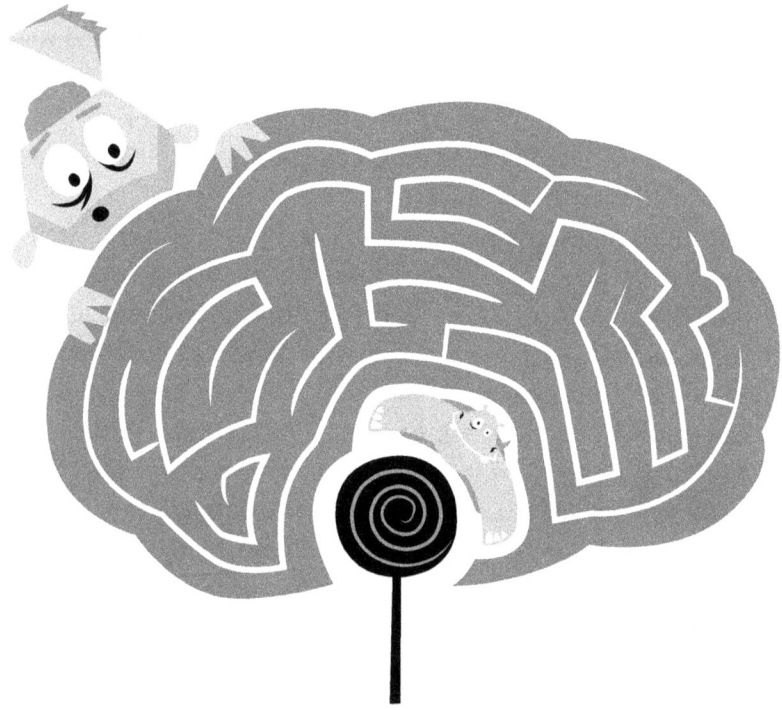

Chapter 2
Meeting my yellow-eyed wolf

The seeds for this book grew out of my counselling practice, but my passion and commitment for working with people experiencing the impact of trauma and overwhelm came from my own experience, my personal memory maps.

Three significant events have shaped my life and the way I work. While other traumas, sorrows, joys, successes and relationships have affected me profoundly, these three experiences underpin my dedication to this work. I will describe these stories for you as if they are happening now, as frozen memories of the events, because that's the way we tend to experience memories of traumatic and overwhelming events. I invite you in close to my direct experience.

First story: Meeting the wolf with yellow eyes

My first indelible experience of trauma came a month before my 18th birthday. My older brother Mark was killed in a car accident. The raw edges and sharp outline of that time pressed into the deepest terrain of my mind and body, and lived in me like a tormented beast in a dungeon. Here is my frozen memory of what happened.

It's June, midwinter. I am seventeen. I sleep a dreamless sleep until some sense of urgency pierces through my slumber, dragging me into that dread. I wake and listen as the night holds its breath. Then I hear hushed voices through the walls. Rubbing my eyes, I pull on my red dressing gown and stumble out along the hallway towards the light. When I slip through the crack of doorway and into the kitchen, the hard fluorescent light stuns me. Four faces look up. The picture has no context, and everything is strange, even the faces of my parents. My brain stumbles and my eyes blink. Words crack the silence between us, a stinging slap from reality that wakes me fully.

'There's been an accident.'

My breath holds itself like a frozen bird far inside the hollow of my chest, waiting.

One of the vaguely familiar strangers, a teacher from the high school, speaks into my thick fog of confusion. 'The car rolled. Mark was in the back seat ... thrown from the car ... stayed till the ambulance arrived.'

'They won't tell us anything over the phone. We'll have to go to the hospital,' says Mum.

The words are coming at me through thick glass, as if I'm watching a movie through a shop window. It feels as if the warmth inside me slips away with each word. Then suddenly all the people are gone, out the door and into the night, and I stand alone staring at the door that slams shut behind them. The friendly strangers are driving Mum and Dad to the hospital in Griffith, an hour away. I have to stay home in case my younger brother Jim, still sleeping his innocence in the far bedroom, wakes up.

This is the longest night. Waiting.

The cold night watches me. I light the fire in the kitchen to push back the chill at the window. Stepping out into the dark to fill the wheelbarrow with wood, I look up into the big night sky. Stars blink and wink, mocking my small misery. Is God up there watching me in his 'All's well with the world' heaven, I wonder? But I have to look away, filled with doubt. I stare at my feet walking, park the wheelbarrow at the back door and go inside, slamming the door, startling the still night. There is no response; no one and nothing stirs. Down the hallway, when I peek through the door into Jim's bedroom, I can see the halo of his blonde curls peeping out from his nestled bedclothes. For a moment, I stand and listen trying to hear him breathe before I walk back to the kitchen and put more wood on the fire.

The long moments are filled with busy nothings. I make a pot of tea. Pressing myself into each moment, slow and mindful, I watch my hand take the milk from the fridge then pour the tea. I stare at the dark amber liquid and hear the sound it makes as it fills the cup. My hand stirs slowly. I press the hot liquid to my lips to taste the comfort of familiar ritual and almost relax. Then I sniff the horror of fear at my elbow, so I grab a magazine and find a crossword. My mind bends to the words, focusing hard on the tiny squares. On the shelf, I find a dictionary and fascinate myself with words beginning with M, then S, then P, so many fascinating words. When the crossword is done, I read my novel for school, *Heart of Darkness*, but the words slip and slide and can't hold me.

Meeting my yellow-eyed wolf

And truth creeps into the silent waiting night, coming at me like a coal-black train, but I keep my mind pinned to the page trying to ignore what's coming. The clock watches overhead. Time slows to eternity, and each heartbeat holds a lifetime of questions, a bleak wondering, wanting to know and not wanting to know. Time melts my strange dream, each tick tolling a bell and peeling back the layers of my small humanity.

When everything else is gone, I pray. I bend my knees, bow my head and stare down at the fine golden threads crisscrossing the white linoleum on the floor. There are tiny black spots where embers have leapt from the fire. There's a row of breadcrumbs along the skirting board under the sink. I pray to the God of my childhood, the guy with the long white beard and white robes who hasn't spoken to me since I was fifteen and took up the hem of my skirt. At sixteen, I pulled down the blind on God's eye that glared down at me while I wriggled and writhed in the back seat of a dark car, with hard breath and hands and lips probing soft pink flesh under thin cotton. I call out to that God that I've abandoned. I hang my head and pray into the silence.

Terror scratches at the window and I'm a four-year-old again. My body trembles as I sense the wolf at the door who wants to come in; his yellow eyes stare in at me. Don't look up. Keep your head down, and maybe he won't see you, I whisper to my quivering heart. I can smell him, the wolf with the yellow eyes and foul breath. I can smell him coming for me, but I won't look up. I won't look into his face. I go back to reading the same page again and again: 'We live, as we dream – alone …'

I wait. There's not a sound in the world save the gentle crackle of the fire. I am the only one, the only one.

The wolf comes so close I can see my reflection in his yellow eyes, and the terror creeps in and fills my belly with rats, ferocious rats that nibble on my insides and eat my loveliness away. This day comes quietly with all the beasts of terror sniffing, their padded footsteps creeping closer, coming to eat me alive. With dread I look over my shoulder, but all is still, frozen. I'm in a child's game and turn to move forward. Again I hear the shuffle of soft feet and the sharp intake of breath. I turn quickly. 'What's the time, Mr Wolf?' But all is quiet and still behind me. I dare the beast, half turning. Ha! But nothing is there, only the empty chair, the painting of the man at the plough, the table scattered with newspapers, the phone silent and waiting. It all looks still, but I can hear them breathing.

And then he comes, not with a pounce but a slow circling.

There's a car outside on the road. I pull back the white lace curtain and stare out the window into the blackness at two beams of headlights. Mark's ute. *Mark's ute?* It's parked on the road just in front of the driveway. I'm at the window, watching, waiting, my mind cracks and bends. What's he doing? Who is it? Is it Mark? Is he all right? I want to scream the madness in me and let it out, but I stand at the window and look out into the night, silent. Bile burns my throat, and I swallow. My body trembles like a dry leaf in a chill wind. My knees buckle. What's happening? Stop this. Stop. But the hard night won't let me scream my words, and I swallow down the bitter taste of silence. I kneel at the windowsill like a four-year-old waiting for her big brother to come home from school. The madness of waiting closes in around me, the ute moves slowly, turning into the driveway, and parks, the engine is silenced. I grip the window ledge to pull myself up because my knees still tremble like leaves with no bones.

I go to the door and stand waiting. There's a soft knock. The terror of what's on the other side is nothing compared to this agony of waiting, so I open the door. It's one of the familiar strangers who were in the kitchen. I stare at him and then out at Mark's ute parked in the yard.

'I saw you at the window,' he says. 'I was waiting till your parents got here first … I brought Mark's ute …' He stumbles for words.

'What happened? Is he okay? What … ?' My own words can't find themselves and fall flat in the silence between us.

'Wait till your parents get here. They need to tell you.' The man steps out of the night and in through the door, turning to close it gently. My sobbing begins, and my body collapses around me. The man catches and holds me against him. Strange sounds come out of me. I want to say something, but a wailing sound comes out instead. The wolf howls inside me.

Then the stranger says the words that end the waiting. 'Mark died at the scene.'

He rocks me until I am still.

The slow dawn comes like sour milk spilt across the horizon. The truth fills the frozen morning, while the beasts sniff and breathe foully around the kitchen. My brother, not yet twenty-one, lies dead and cold in the hospital.

My parents return and stand in a huddle under the fluorescent lighting like two small children on a stage in the wrong play. I stare at my parents' tears with fascination, my own tears already dried and sucked back into my belly. The thin thread that held me to normal has snapped, and I float overhead watching down from a great height.

It's time to make a pot of tea, so I bustle and step around the dead rat lying at the sink. The wolf with the yellow eyes licks my face when I take the milk from the fridge. It tickles, and I smile and wipe away the slimy stink clinging to my lips.

The rooms fill with weeping and warm casseroles. I walk through them, between beasts and neighbours, like a somnambulist. No one can see me. No one can hear me coming. I am invisible. Only the ferocious rats and the wolf with the yellow eyes know me. They lie down with me at night, foul breath and itchy hide close and warm.

Three days after the funeral I'm back at boarding school. No one mentions death. I am invisible here too, but I know they all watch me out of the corner of their eyes. My friends don't know what to say to me; they tiptoe around me, watching from a distance, not laughing too loudly or sharing their small concerns of boyfriends and lumpy thighs and zits and untamed hair that had been the mainstay of our friendship. I am alone with my beasts. The ferocious rat has a wicked sense of humour, and the yellow-eyed wolf a hunger for love that keeps him prowling the edges. I suck them into me and let them fill me. I am the beast. I learn to smile back at the world and hold in the dread in my belly. I am nearly eighteen.

Second story: Finding the path, losing the path and being pathless

I'm twenty-five years old and all I own is a backpack full of grey clothes that were once white or coloured. I've been travelling for several years when I fall into a jungle monastery in Sri Lanka, called Kanduboda. I walk in with my ignorance clinging to me like a fat skin; my Western values jingling like a million bangles on my wrists and ears and legs and hips. I sit listening with my mind jangling so loudly I can't hear the silken silence held soft between thick green-dark walls of jungle surrounding the monastery. But within days I know that I know nothing, and so it begins.

At 4 am the bell rings. Meditation. We sit. Silent. We stand. Walk. Sit. Then eat salty porridge, silent. We walk, silent. We wash. We meditate.

We eat. We walk. Meditate. Meditate and meditate again. Then we sleep. At 4 am the bell rings and we meditate again. A routine so familiar it becomes a second skin, tight around me, holding me together. A routine so plain and unadorned there is nowhere to go, nowhere to hide.

The only contact I have with the world beyond myself is my talk each day with Big Bhunte (head monk), my teacher. In a small white-walled room I sit on the cool checked floor. He speaks to me through an interpreter. Big Bhunte's words are sparse, but his eyes and heart are larger than the world, and I fall in. He brings me back to the path with *annicca, dukkha, annatta*; always *annicca, dukkha, annatta. Annicca-dukkha-annatta* becomes my mantra.

Every day I watch. I find wonder in the ordinary. My breath becomes my new friend; I get to know it intimately. Walking is a close encounter with the senses. One foot lifting, the other solid on the ground, gravel prickling, heel lifting, leg bending, soft fabric against skin, warm air on my face. I have never known walking before. And I meet my curious tongue and smile. I watch my mind and get lost in the tangle. The wolf with the yellow eyes comes to meet me, and the rats are there too.

'Every mind is the same,' Big Bhunte tells me. 'Only the contents differ because of our experience. And the way to free the mind is the same.' I wait until the interpreter tells me his words. *Annicca-dukkha-annatta* need no interpretation. And he brings me back to the path again and again.

'Observe your thoughts as they arise and pass away,' he says.

'Ha. Pass away nothing,' I want to tell him. 'They stay. My brain is stuck.' My mind chatters in my head making it hard to hear what Bhunte is saying.

'Don't give them your attention,' he tells me. 'Come back to the breath.'

I don't believe him. Mine is a mad mind; if I don't battle with it, it must surely win. It always wins. 'It's a demon,' I want to tell him, but I just sit and listen to Bhunte's eyes.

'Monkey mind,' he laughs. 'If you rage against it, the monkey gets madder. If you chase him you will never catch him. Be gentle, and he will settle and eat from your hand. He is your servant.'

I press my lips tight so I don't laugh out loud. 'I think I am his servant, Bhunte,' I say, and we both laugh.

I sit and meditate trying to remember his words and be gentle when the mad monkey grabs me and drags me off for minutes that are hours.

I smile when I can. And slowly the monkey grows quieter and rolls over and lets me scratch his soft belly.

And slowly, like a small child's Christmas, understanding comes. Each morning I take my great insights to Bhunte and excitedly explain what I have discovered, then wait fidgeting while the interpreter tells him, sure that she can never express the depth of my insight. He smiles and accepts my small gifts graciously like a grandfather holding a child's small treasures – a dead beetle, a twig, a speckled leaf – and lays them gently aside, calling me on into the great living forest of the *Dharma*.

Then Big Bhunte leaves on pilgrimage, and I am alone. I have another teacher, but he is not *my* teacher, and my mind and ego rebel. I go on alone and speak to no one. I cling to *annicca-dukkha-annatta*. Everything is meditation. In meditation I am the sound of chopping and the mosquito buzzing. I am the warm breeze on my skin. Life breathes me. Resting into each moment as it arrives, all my hard edges soften and dissolve the little self with all its stories of yesterday and tomorrow and what might be.

And I watch.

I come back to the gentle breath when I'm lost, the breath breathing me. I watch with a child's curiosity, the breath moving through me, in and out and in and out, like soft waves kissing white sand then slipping away in a gentle blush, only to return and kiss again the sweet white flesh.

Then the breath dissolves too, and I open into the vastness where there are no boundaries. The bell sounds in me like a wide song across the alps on a clear morning, and the world vibrates with melody. The heart rocks my body in soft rhythm of bird wing in flight, and I glide on a horizon of freedom beyond, awake in every sense, more awake than I've ever been. Nothing holds me. What had once bound me now frees me.

Words melt in the vast silence. Thoughts crumple like leaves in autumn, blown before a wide and gentle wind. Sensations crawl like ants across my body.

The vast space of my mind lights the darkening, and I see beyond what I can grasp or name or understand, yet I know it all in my heart's opening. The moment stretches like an eternal fountain filling me, yet not me. Some might call it Love, some God, but I have no words for this. To name it is like offering my filthy sandal at the foot of a great master. Instead I prostrate myself and kiss the ground of being and watch in wordless wonder.

Then I am done. It's time to go. The Sri Lankan authorities refuse to renew my visa yet another time. I think I know something and have attained something, but I can't see the spiritual pride swelling in me, bursting the gold buttons on the stained white vest of my spirituality. I leave the monastery.

I leave and walk back into the world. Within days I arrive back in India like a rabbit unskinned. India crowds in on me, my senses burning like needlepoints under the too bright sun. The filth and stink of so much humanity after the silken silence of the monastery eat into me. Each day is acid; it stings and burns. My mind screams for silence, for space. My body wails for the gentleness of the jungle monastery.

I have no words for the feelings that come with the experience of hate and rage that surge through me towards the dark-eyed men and women who touch me or speak to me and want to haggle with me. Last week I loved the mosquito trying to bite into my skin, and now I hate these people who won't leave me alone, who press in so close I can't breathe. Every sense shrieks and rages.

I don't know what I want to eat, how to be, where to go; the dissolution of self has dissolved my desires. I stare down at my hand when I eat or feel the rupee lying sticky in my palm, but I can't find the meaning or any reason for these ordinary things.

Despair blows in like tumbleweeds banking up against the old contours of my mind and fragments of ego, blocking out the infinity that had been so close I could feel it in my skin and bones when I was in the monastery.

I walk then run from the sensory world crashing in on me. I whirl in circles and stand still, disoriented with nothing to guide me, nothing to hold onto. I am angry at everything including my real teacher, who a week ago was my beloved, the *Dharma*, the Buddha and everything I've learned. I'm stripped and alone with my rage burning me.

I go to sit in meditation, wanting relief from my fierce mind, and the bright memories of the vast stillness come so close I can almost taste them, almost touch. But the 'almost' is an abyss of longing that aches in my heart, with a sorrow deep and wide as an ocean. I stop meditating and try to live in the world. But the old comforts and distractions of blame or disgust or arrogance, and even food, the old stories, turn on me laughing. I writhe and twist like a blind snake, furiously flicking my tongue at the empty space.

Inside something cracks. I turn to grab hold of a scrap of certainty, but my mind closes around nothingness. The sea of dark eyes watches me. I hear them laughing behind me, and I turn quickly but there's no one. I jump at shadows and call out through my dreams. I curse and rage until there is only shattered glass left inside me. Then I crawl into a room and lie there curled around myself trying to keep out the world. I don't cry, I don't think, I feel nothing. The sounds from the street are far away. I'm underwater, deep down in a dark place where no one can reach me. I don't want to breathe, I don't want to live, and I don't care.

A knocking floats through the deep-cool ocean of silence. The knocking comes louder, and someone is calling from far off. But it's quiet and peaceful down here. Now someone is pulling me, dragging me up. 'Leave me alone. Let me rest, go away,' I say without words. Someone keeps tugging at me. I keep my eyes shut, but hands drag me away from the dark peace. My body moves without my permission, remembering some forgotten pull to survive hiding beneath the skinless skin. I feel myself coming back. The hands on my arm are gentle and warm through the deep coldness. The voice is gentle too, calling me. 'Rita, Rita, wake up.' I can hear the words now. The darkness is clearing.

I open my eyes to find dark eyes looking into mine. My teacher? Such kind eyes. I close them again, glad that my teacher is here. The tugging continues. I want to rest. I'm so tired, so tired.

'Come back, Rita.' I open my eyes. Those black eyes are so close they are all I can see. 'Rita, wake up.' It's a man I've seen before. 'Rita, are you alright?' The man is Indian. I'm in India. Everything rushes back in a flood of remembering. I blink. The man is still there in front of me. 'I was worried that you didn't come out for so long. Sorry for unlocking your door. Are you alright, Rita? Sorry for disturbing you, Rita. I was worried.' He keeps saying my name. How does he know my name? My body moves me. Blinking, I raise my head. The man steps back. I feel alone without his warm hand on my arm, so I cling to the black eyes. My body is heavy and strange, and he helps me sit up. He puts a pillow behind my head.

'Will I bring you chai, ma'am?' He doesn't say my name now, and I miss it. I nod. 'Wait here. I'll get chai.' When he goes to the door, I see other dark eyes looking in at me. I feel my skinless humanity stinging with those stares, and I watch my hands as if this is the first time I've seen them. The man closes the door as he leaves, and now he's shooing them off, those other eyes.

He returns and stands watching me sip the milky sweet liquid. 'Sorry for disturbing you, ma'am,' he says again. 'I was worried that you didn't come out for so long.' His English is neat at the edges.

'It's okay,' I croak, my voice unfamiliar. 'Thank you.'

'I'll bring you some food.'

'I'm not hungry.'

'You must eat, ma'am. I'll bring you food.'

'Okay, thanks.' It's easier.

For the next week this short man with the dark eyes and rice-white teeth feeds me – thick yellow curries nestled in mounds of perfect white rice, delicacies dripping in sweet syrup and rose water, clotted mountains of fresh yoghurt tangy on the tongue, and sugary warm chai. And I eat my way back into the world. I pull up my tattered ego and move on again, the laughter and staring dark eyes watching from the doorway fading behind.

Weeks later, I'm in a Sri Aurobindo community near Pondicherry in southern India. In the round clear days that follow I come back to the ordinary. I work in the garden and cycle around the large community on a rusty bicycle that makes a rhythmical clacking sound as I pedal. I eat food plucked straight from the garden and walk the sandy paths alone. I sleep in a tree house with a snake. The black plastic roofing sags with his weight above my head as he curls into the comfort of himself each night.

In the ordinary of every day I pull on my skins. I step back into all the layers that had peeled away in the monastery. Skin after skin I pull around me, wrapping myself into ego and curling into myself. I sew myself a misfit-self, covering over the nothingness. The sting of the world grows less each day, and each night I dream my skins in.

When I finally get home to Australia all my old habits rush up to meet me. From a distance, I had loved everyone and been free of old addictions. Now, up close, the old faceless demons of fear and loneliness, anger, aching hunger and desperation creep in and crawl under my skin, skulking into my bed and feeding on the scraps of tormented dreams that I toss and turn in every night. Within days of my return, I'm drinking and smoking again, and my old addictive habits in relationships have grown back like a cancer. Briefly I struggle against it all, but soon I surrender as the old ways crash in around me, erupting over my life like a great wave. Always there is a voice in me, an arrogant voice mocking my ignorance and my stupidity, a voice that knows better than this, that remembers how to be free. So I drink another glass of wine to drown it.

I turn my back on what I knew in the jungle in Sri Lanka. I set off to university to study English and Psychology and build myself a life and an ego in the traditional way, to grow myself a career and learn how to live in the world. I'm twenty-eight.

Third story: Into the yellow eyes of the wolf

It's the end of October 1996.

The first call comes as I'm about to walk out the door for a dentist appointment. Cursing, I drop my bag and run to beat the answering machine.

'Hello?' It's my sister. Funny time for her to ring, the thought flashes past before my mind can grab it.

'Jim's missing.' The words drop like rocks into my belly. I wait in silence, my breath narrow. 'Mum's worried. She said to ring you.'

'Oh.'

'She thinks something's wrong.'

'Mmm.' My thoughts won't move to form any words in my sticky throat.

'Gotta go, Rit. Talk soon.'

'Let me know if there's any news,' I say, words coming in a rush as if there's a wolf at their heels.

'Of course.'

I put down the phone, stare into the bright sky outside and shiver. Now I don't want to go to the dentist. My tongue runs over my teeth, pushing into the familiar groove of the rough tooth that's been niggling for weeks. I've already put off the dentist twice. I pick up my bag and pull the door shut behind me.

'Should I come home?' I ask later on the phone to Mum. Home is a six-hour drive. 'Wait. Just wait,' they say, every time I ask the question.

While the day is bright I don't hear the wolf scratching, but at night he's there again. I drink red wine and find an old packet of tobacco and roll thin dry cigarettes, smoking and coughing and gulping red wine from a giant tumbler. I talk to my friend on the phone; he's busy cropping five hours away. He says, 'Wait. Jim's probably gone fishing.' We laugh, and he distracts me from the wolf for a while. But then the world grows silent. I am alone, waiting. I pour another glass of red wine and spill some on the table, looking up quickly at the door for the sound. It's them scratching. The ferocious rats and the yellow-eyed wolf and other nameless beasts have found me again. It's a long time since I've seen them, but there's the familiar rank smell of grey fur. I'm tired, but I don't want to sleep. The world sleeps, and I wait. The wolf scratches to come in. I pull the curtains and lock the door.

Other 'gone missings' creep into my mind, and I float around in old memories looking for signs, for hope, remembering times when Jim was found or never lost in the first place.

'Not this again. I can't do it. I can't. I can't do this again. Jim, please come home. For Mum's sake, come home, come home.' A mantra slurred in a whisper into the night.

The next morning, I wake crumpled on the sofa and sniff the rank air, the stale red wine and cigarette butts before I open my eyes. My body lies in disarray like items of clothes strewn in drunken haste across the floor. I lie still, waiting for my sluggish mind to catch up. Then memory crashes in, and my eyes split open and look around. The phone sits unemployed on the table surrounded by magazines and old post. My body is stiff and feels old, very old. My mouth tastes like grimy carpet on a pub floor on a Saturday morning before the cleaner has been. My tongue rests on the unfamiliar feel of new tooth, suspicious. Everything moves slowly. Light streams in when I open the curtains, and I shut my eyes against the hurt. I waddle to the kitchen and put the kettle on, then go to the bathroom and piss the dark yellow of last night's toxicity. With my sunglasses on, I stand and look out the window, sipping a cup of steaming tea that tastes like life.

The phone rings loudly, and I spill my tea. 'Hello?' Breathless. It's my friend Jane. She will come this evening and stay the night. 'Thanks Jane. See you then.' My voice sounds surprisingly cheery.

I shower, eat toast and Vegemite and drink more tea. The longest day has no seams. It is colourless and without contours, filled with grey moments that shift and slide into nothingness. I walk around the house searching but can't remember what I'm looking for. I read, but words don't stick. I drink cold tea and eat warm salad. The mail comes, and bills lie unopened on the table sneering through their little windows. In the afternoon, I walk on the beach, and the grey-green waves melt into the drizzling sky in one melancholy wet-on-wet.

In the evening, Jane arrives. We light the lamps and sit on the back veranda, eating pasta and drinking beer while I tell stories of Jim – 'Jimmy', as we used to call him when we were kids. I lay out the happy contents of my kid-hood, unpacking the small precious parcels of memory one at a time: small intimate stories of yabbying and drinking homemade ginger beer after a swim in the channel, his love of fishing and the river, Jimmy always grinning, so that Jane will know him as I know him. I don't share the dark stories of his later years, clouded with dope smoke and drenched in alcohol, or talk about how he lost his smile somewhere along the way. The friendly night holds us tenderly in velvet darkness, washed clean by the afternoon rain. Finally, we turn out the lights and go to our beds.

The ringing tears open the morning like a serrated knife-edge, ripping me out of my dreams. My eyes snap open as remembering smashes in. I run for the phone, banging my shoulder against the bedroom door. Breathless, I hold the phone to my ear and listen, rubbing my shoulder.

'It's happened.' My mother's voice is flat and matter-of-fact. The police have found Jim with his car. The local newspaper will read 'no suspicious circumstances'.

So I drive home to bury my other brother. We lay him gently in the warm red earth, five rows from his big brother, beneath the pine trees that whisper their lullaby to the wind.

Fourth story: The Earth, my home

There is one other thing that has shaped my life and my work and lives in me quietly as a deep current of peace and hope: my home, the Earth.

I grew up close to the Earth – a wide brown Earth under a brimming sky that stretched through to heaven, holding the fat round sun that drenches freckled skin and streaks hair gold. I drink Her in, this Earth – through my senses, my skin and my small brown body; her wonder so close it sings me awake each morning and holds me in gentle dreams each night. On bare-breasted summer mornings I can hear Her heart beating in my skin, She is so close; Her rhythm skipping in my brown legs.

Leaping into cool flowing water on hot, *hot* days in late summer, when the world is shimmering under the big sun, small sun-brown bodies jump and call out in joy. With a white strip of zinc on our upturned noses, we look like bronzed Aussie Indians screaming war cries of delight as we leap from the grassy bank. Big splash. We dive and duck and leap and splash until our teeth chatter in blue lips and our bellies growl, and we feel the tug of home.

I lie down on new-mown hay sniffing in Her sweet breath. I lay my cheek to Her breast so close I hear the creaking of Her bones, the rumble in Her belly and the beat of Her deep heart. Her big love lifts and carries me into bright daydreams, swinging in the white puff clouds where God is laughing. Her love pierces me and makes my heart big and round and fat like a ripe peach warm from the tree.

Dad brings the steaming milk bucket home from the golden cow, and we drink warm milk on our porridge. Sometimes I watch the milking; Dad's hands move like a drummer grabbing and stroking the teats, milk squirting into the silver bucket and making a happy white sound like a soft drum beating time in the morning mist. When I am alone I pick a thick pod from the bush creeping up the trellis. My fingers push into the green line down the pod, and it splits open to show five small round peas nestled in their little green boat. I pick one out and put it to my mouth, biting into the sweetness, the taste of the Earth and the rain and sun in its skin.

I walk on Her skin and find small miracles of lacy tracks in sand made by some tiny creature I can't see. Each tree is a map of the universe, and I can read a whole story of far-off lands of giants, goddesses, dragons and knights in their daring rescuings. In Her arms, I can be whoever and whatever I want, and She holds me close to Her skin and breathes Her sweet breath into me and laughs and sings with my imaginings.

When I am lonely or sad or have a fight with my sister, She hears me and dries my tears and shows me some small miracle to make me laugh: a small beetle on his back and I help him up, or the tracks of a tiny bird on the soft sand. She hears me when I'm scared and I don't know what to do. She holds me and listens to my sad song and sings with me until our harmony makes something new and bright and lovely.

And now, every day, I walk with Her and hear Her beating heart through my feet. Her song is the song of my soul, and Her beauty the bright of my eye. She is my greatest love and lives in me and with me my whole life until the day I will lie down in Her and with Her forever: my Earth, my mother, my home.

I won't refer back to these stories throughout the book or in session with Jack and Mary because that is how it is in real life. Each of us carries our own pain hidden from the world, usually in the bottom drawer of our psyche, which is why we need to tread gently in the presence of every human heart.

Nor will I describe my own journey through integration because that may suggest that my experience of integration is the right way. But every brain is different, and therefore your journey through integration will be unique.

My emergent experience of integration is embodied in i-brainmap and this book.

Chapter 3
Introducing the i-brainmap

In this chapter I introduce you to Jack and to the i-brainmap, and give you some of the backstory of how the map was developed. In the next chapter I explain the nuts and bolts of i-brainmap, why it works and when it doesn't work. Then in subsequent chapters I unpack each section for your brain. Note that the i-brainmap is a map of the impact of traumatic and overwhelming events on the brain but is not about physical brain trauma.

Introducing Jack and the map

Jack is thirty-four. He is married to Katie, and they have a two-year-old son, Ted. Jack is experiencing stress at work because of his conflicted relationship with his boss. Jack has had warnings about his angry outbursts and has been told that another incident will result in his dismissal. His GP is concerned about his drinking, though Jack doesn't see it as a problem.

In the first session Jack was reluctant to discuss his family of origin, but he eventually described his childhood with a violent alcoholic father and a mother overwhelmed with taking care of a household of five children, constantly trying to keep the peace to avoid angry-violent outbursts from Jack's father.

The following dialogue between Jack and me occurs in our third session and shows one way I might introduce the i-brainmap to clients.

Rita: Have you ever been really lost, Jack? I mean lost where you thought you could die, or never-get-out lost?

Jack: Yeah, I got lost in the Blue Mountains once with a friend. We were seventeen, a bit macho, and made out we knew more than we did. It came in cold suddenly and we weren't prepared.

How did you feel when you realised you were lost and didn't know if you'd get out?

Terrified. I pretended I was cool, but I freaked out. I thought I was going to die. Lucky we found some shelter for the night.

Yes, when we're lost and disoriented we feel frightened and distressed, and we panic and go around in circles.

Yeah, we did start going round in circles. But we couldn't find any signs or markers. Everything looked the same.

We look for signs or markers to work out where we are in relation to where we want to get to. We try to orient ourselves. What do you need when you're lost, Jack?

A warm jacket, even if it's summer.

Anything else?

A good map. We had a crappy old map, not enough detail and out of date. There'd been a flood that had washed out paths and markers, but we didn't know that till later.

Yes, a good map that's up to date and sufficiently detailed. And that's why I want to give your brain a map, because essentially it's working on old maps or maps that don't fit together or have enough detail of the territory of your experience.

Old maps? Try *no* maps. I don't think I have a map for any of this stuff. I'm just going round in circles with no way out. Like a dog chasing its tail.

How is it to go round and round and not know where you're going, feeling like you'll never get out?

Horrible. Frustrating. Pointless. Frightening. Confusing. I feel like an idiot. Do you want me to go on?

No, Jack, I get the picture. That's exactly what I'd expect. When you drop into those old maps, what we call 're-experiencing' because it feels like a current experience even though the old map you're running might belong to an experience from twenty years ago, the part of the brain that orients, the hippocampus, goes offline. Your experience of being lost is neurobiological.

The hippocampus is a structure in the brain involved in memory. The function of the hippocampus is at the heart of orientation and mapping, which is the cornerstone of i-brainmap. The function, and malfunction, of the hippocampus will be discussed in detail in chapter 9.

Well, something goes off, usually me when I'm in a rage. I might as well be a mad man lost in the mountains.

That's why I'd like to give you a map of what's going on, so your brain has something to orient to when it's lost in the old terrain of fear, frustration or rage.

Worth a try, I s'pose.

I'll also give you some strategies to help you bring your attention into the here and now or, in orienting terms, find your current position. The main two things the brain needs when it's lost are a map and knowing where you are now. The brain can pretty much do the rest, and we can fill in the gaps as we go.

So can I have the map now?

I'll do the map with you in the next session.

But couldn't you just give me a copy now?

No, I actually need to explain it in a way that engages the whole brain. The physical map that I'll give you is only the representation of the map. Something else happens as I describe, explain and provide an experience of the map with you. If I just give you a nice coloured map, instead of unpacking it with you and working with you to discover what's relevant for you, there won't be much integration. Just giving you a ready-made map would give you some cognitive understanding but it wouldn't catalyse integration.

Say what?

Catalyse. Yeah, I know it sounds a bit neurobum – that's another term for being up my own ... bottom. But 'catalyse' is the best word because it seems to be how the brain map works for most people; it is a catalyst for integration. Forget neurobum, I made that up!

Neurobum works for me ... Catalyse. Like the way my boss catalyses my rage when he does his rant in the meetings?

Perhaps. We can talk about where the boss is in your map later. Doing the map with you is like inviting your brain to pull out its relevant maps of experience to make some adjustments as we go, because some of the maps you're using you picked up as a kid and they're no longer relevant.

Yeah, makes sense. Like you said before, when my boss starts misbehaving I pull out the map of my dad I drew up when I was four years old. Right?

Yes. But you can't just change these maps by thinking or trying to talk yourself out of your reactions, because the relevant part of the brain uses a different language; it's nonverbal. But we'll talk about this when I do the i-brainmap with you. It's this unfolding of the map through describing the experience of what's happening in the brain that allows it to travel the terrain of how trauma impacts, and that can kickstart the integration process, allowing the brain to weave together the old map with this new information and experience. At the moment, these maps are all operating separately.

Sounds like a lot of work, Rita.

Well, a lot of it relies on the brain's capacity to integrate, and the brain can do that in its sleep, quite literally.

The tunnel

When an old body-memory map is activated it's like suddenly finding yourself lost in a dark tunnel – you freeze with fear because you can't find a way out. It seems endless, 'frozen in forever'. When you are lost in the tunnel you will do almost anything to get yourself out of there or avoid it ever happening again.

The i-brainmap gives you a different orientation, an experiential map of what is happening when you're trapped in the tunnel. It helps you reconnect with what's beyond the tunnel, with the possibility of getting out. It's likely that having a map engages the hippocampus (because this is the mapper and navigator of the brain) so it can orient to the map in the context of distress and begin to navigate you through the tunnel. This is an important point: the brain needs a map that can be accessed during activation, so the map needs to include sensory detail to engage the lower brain, because that's the brain region associated with the alarm.

Between avoidance and overwhelm is the sweet spot called 'integration', where the brain is able to update old maps of experience that are still running. Not just any new map will do the trick. It needs to be a map grounded in direct experience that the brain can recognise when it's stuck. Giving the brain a new map based on its own experience (not just on fact and science, which speak the language of the big brain) invites the brain to make new connections.

Rather than *what* you see, i-brainmap changes *how* you see.

A brief history of i-brainmap

The integrated brain map or i-brainmap started life more than ten years ago, while I was working with clients with post-traumatic stress. At the time, a lot of research was emerging about the impact of trauma on the brain, and about brain science generally. Like a bowerbird I collected together all the scraps of research I found, my clinical observations and personal experience, and used these to create the i-brainmap.

The first major piece of the puzzle appeared at a seminar by John Briere, a Californian professor of psychiatry and psychology. Briere had developed a treatment model, which he called the 'self-trauma model'. This explains that hyper-arousal and flashbacks (what I refer to as re-experiencing or activation) are the brain's attempts to integrate the trauma memory. The self-trauma model suggests that the brain is continually trying to integrate the traumatic memories experienced as symptoms of arousal and intrusive memories. But when a trauma memory is triggered it trips the wire for the alarm system that's hooked up with the memory, and the brain goes into threat-alarm-survival mode.

Briere explained that the role of the practitioner is to regulate the client's level of arousal and distress in a certain 'window of tolerance', which he later called 'the therapeutic window' and what I refer to as the *integration Zone*, for integration of the trauma material or memory map to occur. Once I understood this principle I began explaining it to the people I was working with.

At the same time, I became fascinated with the work of Bessel van der Kolk, Babette Rothschild and, later, Peter Levine. Their work indicates that the trauma memory is stored in the body, and to work successfully with trauma you need to work with the residual body experience of the trauma. I also explained that to my clients.

As new neuroscience emerged I read broadly, distilled the information and integrated it for myself, finding metaphors and analogies, and then explaining it to clients. I kept adding and adjusting information, depending on how people responded to what and how I was explaining it to them. I also closely observed my own experience and reactions and experimented with the techniques and new insights personally.

In the beginning, the reason I explained the impact of psychological trauma on the brain was twofold: so clients could understood why I might need to stop them (*put on the brakes*, as Babette Rothschild calls it) if they were getting too distressed, and also to prepare them for exposure therapy (for a description of this therapy see Jane's story below).

To avoid or minimise the possibility of re-traumatisation, I provided a lot of psycho-education on what was happening in the brain so we could monitor and ensure a safe passage through the therapeutic process, using any re-experiencing of body sensations that occurred therapeutically. I wanted to explain the purpose and effect of exposure therapy to establish an alliance, working *with* people, so they didn't feel like I was doing something *to* them, which replicates the dynamic of trauma.

I found that integrating all this information into a narrative based on experience elicited a stronger response from people and seemed to catalyse a process of integration. I observed, and people also reported, subtle changes that led me to believe that something else was occurring in the brain through this way of explaining the experience of brain overwhelm through a visual and narrative map. It appeared that the brain responded in ways beyond what happened when I simply explained the facts before I'd created a map.

As I don't have access to neuro-imaging equipment, I can only guess what these changes might be, based on the available science. I simply call it *integration* and, more recently, brain change. Perhaps we will never know exactly what goes on in the brain when it is unobserved, or engaged with another living, walking, talking brain in the world.

i-brainmap stories

Following are three stories of how people responded to the i-brainmap, which influenced the map's development. The names and details of these stories have been changed.

Sue's story – from overwhelm to understanding to choice

I was working with a young woman who I'll call Sue. Sue had a history of severe childhood abuse. Over several weeks following assessment, I discussed, and drew, the dynamics of the impact of trauma on the brain, describing the techniques I would use in session if she became distressed. This was all preparation for exposure.

But before I had a chance to start the process of exposure Sue came to session animated. She explained that she'd been driving and was activated for some reason. Instead of responding with her usual reactions: 'Why, why, why?' or 'What's wrong with you, Sue, you crazy bitch?' and becoming increasingly agitated, she had recognised that she was activated and was able to use a condensed version of the technique I'd recently given her. She pulled to the side of the road and brought her attention into the present through detailed sensory awareness. She described how she'd given it a '9' (out of 10) and felt her hand touching the steering wheel, listened to the radio and looked around at the scenery outside the car window then had a cigarette. 'It worked,' she said, grinning.

Through our discussion it became apparent that what was important about this for Sue was that through this brief experience she went from feeling powerless, overwhelmed and confused to understanding through direct experience what was happening, and everything I'd been explaining about the impact of trauma on the brain made sense.

This experience changed everything for Sue because she understood what was happening to her. She no longer felt so powerless or crazy and not just because someone said she wasn't, which she'd never believed, but because it made sense to her through her own experience. For Sue this was the beginning of having some choice.

Jane's story – gentle exposure

Jane had been raped two years prior to attending counselling. I was cautious about re-traumatising her and worked with her for several weeks preparing her for exposure therapy, telling her how it would work and explaining on the whiteboard how the brain gets stuck in overwhelm or numbing and how we needed to help her get into the 'window of tolerance'. Jane was sometimes distressed during session, although we didn't speak directly about the rape, only about the impact of trauma on the brain. At those times, I would bring her attention back into the room and help soothe her by introducing her to techniques to regulate the emotional distress.

When the agreed day to begin exposure therapy finally came, I was as nervous as Jane because there had been so much preparation, and it was the first time I'd taken someone through the process of exposure to a specific traumatic event. Firstly, I asked her to describe the experience of the rape as if from a distance or in 'headlines', as it's often described. Then gradually I directed her to move in closer and closer to the events with increasing detail. Although she could describe the details clearly she reported minimal activation. I checked for dissociation, but she said she felt fully present and could clearly remember and describe everything. As we got closer to the graphic details of the most disturbing part of the rape, she cried softly as she described what happened. For some time, I kept checking and thinking we'd missed something. I was wondering why she wasn't more distressed than she appeared, because she had been extremely disturbed by the rape when I initially assessed her. When she came in the following week, she'd had no flashbacks or nightmares, had slept soundly and said she felt great.

At the time I hadn't realised that all the preparation we'd done was a gentle form of exposure that allowed her system to integrate the traumatic events, but through a new map rather than having to enter directly into the terrain of terror, which could have overwhelmed and re-traumatised her. Over several sessions I had also been teaching her sensory soothing and self-regulating strategies so she was confident in monitoring and soothing her distress as it happened. I realised that explaining the map, including the experience of activation, could act as a gentle form of exposure.

Sam's story – a management strategy

A colleague approached me about a university student she was working with, Sam. She wanted ideas about how to help Sam manage his flashbacks and nightmares. I gave her Babette Rothschild's flashback and nightmare protocols and suggested she try those with him. A couple of weeks later my colleague informed me that they hadn't helped. A few months later that colleague left, and Sam became my client.

Sam was still having intense flashbacks, which were interfering with his attendance at uni because he was anxious that he'd have a flashback during a lecture or when he was with friends. We went through the flashback protocol again. It turned out Sam had never remembered to use the technique during a flashback. Because he was so anxious and activated in session, I used a similar technique to bring his attention into the present. We went slowly through how he could use the techniques when he was activated outside session, and I also explained what was happening in the brain.

That week I had a call from Sam, who was standing outside his lecture theatre as he was re-experiencing an intense body memory related to extreme childhood abuse. He said he was shaking and nauseous. I stepped him through the mindfulness-based technique (which I will outline later in the book) firmly and gently and also reminded him that this was the brain trying to integrate something. At the beginning of the call he reported the intensity of his distress as '8 or 9', and by the end of the phone call he said it was '3 or 4', and he joked that his lecturer had probably given him a fright because he was so boring.

The next time I saw Sam, he was much happier. We discussed that even knowing to call me when he was activated meant a light had come on for him. He said he 'got it' now; he understood what I'd been telling him about the brain. Together we developed some techniques that he could use to interrupt, reorient and soothe lower brain activation.

Working with Sam, I realised the importance of how something is explained. Even a great technique if delivered without some experiential component may be useless. The important learning for me was that I needed to find a way to introduce and explain things in a way that a person could access or orient to during activation, or high states of arousal.

From hodgepodge to narrative

These stories and many others happened over a period of several years, while I continued developing, adding and integrating information about the impact of trauma on the brain to make it easily accessible. If something worked it stayed, but if it seemed too complicated or theoretical it was changed or left out. Slowly the hodgepodge of ideas evolved into a visual and experiential map of the dynamics of the brain following extreme events. I saw that making it an experiential, visual and narrative map instead of lots of bits of information made it easier for people to take in and digest the large amount of information I was giving them. Gradually I realised I was talking more directly to the brain than to the person.

In the beginning, I wrote the map on a whiteboard in session. But later, when I was working in a room that didn't have a whiteboard, I started using A3 sheets of paper and coloured textas. On the front page was all the information and visuals about the brain and how it gets stuck when it's been overwhelmed, and on the back was a mindfulness-based technique (originally inspired by the work of Babette Rothschild) that I've continued to adapt and change, for clients to use during activation. And they could carry the map with them, which many people did, as a reminder of what was happening and what to do when they felt trapped in that 'fully and forever' dark tunnel.

In the early days, it was called the 'integrated trauma map' because it was based on what I knew about the experience of trauma and its impact on the brain. Over time, I realised that the same principles apply any time the brain is stuck or overwhelmed, and the same approach can be helpful to unstick the brain. That's when it became the 'integrated brain map' or 'i-brainmap'.

Although I occasionally change bits of the i-brainmap it has essentially been in its current form for more than two years at the time of writing. I expect it will keep changing and adapting; at least, I hope it will. Everyone who uses it seems to use it differently because, after all, it is just a map, and a map doesn't tell you where to go or how to go. It just shows you the way, or one way. But it's always *your* journey.

The i-brainmap is based on experience, my own and that of hundreds of people I've worked with over the years. It has also been influenced by brain science and the work of many researchers and clinicians. Some of the main influences are Antonio Damasio, Babette Rothschild, Bessel van der Kolk, Bruce Perry, Dan Siegel and Peter Levine, to name a few (more are listed in Further Reading at the end of the book).

Spontaneous integration

In the beginning I didn't set out to develop the i-brainmap; it evolved through my work with hundreds of people by trying different clinical techniques, based on current research, to help them manage their distress, as well as my personal experience and understanding of trauma and the brain. As the stories above illustrate, I began explaining the brain as preparation for exposure therapy, but I found that before I had a chance to do the exposure the brain had already started integrating. It is this spontaneous and innate integration process that I've been tracking like a bloodhound for years.

Integration is what the brain *does*, and we can assist it in this process of integration and change – that's what I've come to understand. Integration is difficult to explain and describe because it is a living process that emerges similarly and yet uniquely for each brain. I am much more a tracker or facilitator in this way of working than I am a director, though sometimes I am quite firm, like a mother holding a child's hand near a busy road, when people are lost in activation.

This approach works with the body reactions rather than the actual details of the trauma. So when I refer to integration I am referring to the brain's capacity to integrate or respond in new ways to the body reactions that people usually experience as intense and overwhelming. The i-brainmap explains the importance of working with the body as the most effective way to access these memory maps.

Therapeutic context

Because i-brainmap evolved in a therapeutic context, it is worth noting some of the reasons I developed it the way I did, because often it was a response to what people told me wasn't working for them. Following are some of the broad dilemmas that influenced the way I developed the i-brainmap.

Exposure and the trauma story

Exposure therapy could be likened to going into the dark tunnel again and again so that you become less afraid of it. This can work if a person has the resources to manage the distress and can remain oriented to the present and/or the therapist. But sometimes exposure can overwhelm a person's resources, replicating the traumatic experience. At best, it can reduce the distress around that particular trauma, but often it doesn't encourage generalised brain integration or teach a person how to respond when they experience lower brain activation outside of sessions.

Many people who came to me for treatment had told their story to numerous practitioners over the years, and some refused to tell it again, saying that talking about it didn't help. So we focused on the impact of the trauma rather than the event itself. My job, as I increasingly saw it, was to teach people techniques to interrupt and soothe lower brain activation as it happened.

Another issue is that most people are activated out of session and sometimes almost continuously, so I needed to teach something that would work outside, as well as in, sessions to reduce the feeling of powerlessness inherent in post-traumatic stress.

Complex trauma

One problem with trauma memory is that it is often disconnected and therefore not accessible through words or story, or there may be no conscious memory of the events. So we need to access the memory in a different way. Therefore the most troublesome aspects of the memory, especially in complex interpersonal trauma such as child sexual assault, can be difficult or impossible to access through *talking* therapies or techniques. In complex interpersonal trauma the violence is wrapped up with love and trust or contradictions that can't easily be untangled in any cognitive or behavioural approach.

Added to this, I found that the impact of trauma was extremely diverse with a myriad of symptoms that at first seemed unrelated, but always I found trauma or overwhelm lurking underneath. Could I treat fibromyalgia in the same way as panic attacks or Obsessive Compulsive Disorder? These were some of the questions I faced as I began to realise that it was all related to what happened when the brain was overwhelmed and unable to integrate experience.

Thinking, talking and telling tales

I found that cognitive and talking therapy was often not helpful for clients with high levels of distress. Challenging their unhelpful thinking often tied us both up in knots because they got into a struggle with their thinking, and their distress intensified. Often this was driven by a *fix it* mentality or *shoulds* and *shouldn'ts*, and working with changing cognitions only exacerbated this. In working cognitively or with changing behaviours, some clients reported a sense of shame at 'failing' to make the expected changes, changes that they wanted desperately.

Some people wanted to go over and over their story, while others worked hard to change the story. Telling the story or even creating a new, more insightful story didn't necessarily result in integration that allowed them to change their responses. Working on a narrative level often caught us up in the content of story while the deeper story remained inaccessible through words or thoughts because it was buried in the body, in a different language – that of the lower brain.

Some people remained trapped in the story by trying to work out its origin. For many people this didn't result in significant sustainable change in their life or even change associated with the impact of the trauma.

Leaving the treatment room and entering the world

Although i-brainmap began life as a therapeutic model, in this book I offer it to you as a personal approach to understand and respond to lower brain activation whatever it's form, including: anxiety, anger, agitation, overwhelm, freezing, and any other kind of distress that has a stuck quality. Different manifestations of activation are discussed throughout the book, especially chapters 11 and 12.

The i-brainmap, and its associated techniques, is intended for use in interrupting, reorienting and soothing lower brain activation as it happens, which can be anywhere, anytime. I outline these techniques throughout the book and invite you to experiment with what works for your brain. What I can't measure or even fully understand is that indefinable quality of change that many people describe when we work with this approach, and that I call *integration*. It's as if the brain is rewiring in ways that we can't predict or measure.

Interweaving the personal

It's easy to describe stories about people I've worked with and how, through intense observation of their responses to this work, I've adapted the i-brainmap to capture their experience and weave them in, drawing all the complex threads together. But it's hard to know exactly how much my personal experience has impacted on the development of the i-brainmap, because I'm inside this story.

The impact of my own trauma on this work is central; it's what has driven me to develop i-brainmap. But there are other less visible currents and threads that interweave the development of i-brainmap and this book. It has only been through writing the book that I've realised how powerfully my work has been influenced by my experience in insight meditation and the principles I learned through the guidance of my teacher when I was in the monastery in Sri Lanka. All these things I learned directly through close observation of my own brain-body-mind.

These direct insights, which are interwoven through the fabric of i-brainmap, are outlined below.

Interweaving with insight

Struggle keeps your brain stuck

The more you struggle with something the tighter the mind holds onto it, like a fly caught in a spider web. But if you observe with curiosity or find a different relationship (orientation) with it, over time it can soften and untangle.

The paradox of change

Trying to change something creates a struggle; it is non-acceptance. Until you can accept something as it is, you can't change it. This isn't a call for passive acceptance or an 'I don't care anyway, it doesn't matter' attitude, but an active, engaged acceptance – curious and attentive, like a mother watching her child learning to walk. The other thing about change, that we all know but rarely act as if we know, is that the only context we can change is the one we're in right now, and we can't change anyone but ourselves.

The body is the brain, and all experience is stored in the body

To know the mind, you have to know the body; the two are intimately interconnected and interactive. And when the body is distressed, in pain or discomfort or upset, it grabs our attention until we learn to observe gently without struggle, and then the distress can soften and lose its power over us. Through learning to watch instead of reacting, you develop a mindfulness of whatever is arising.

Interweaving the natural world

Another thick thread that runs through this work is my relationship with the natural world, especially through daily solitary walks in the forest. There is something about the rhythmical movement of the walking, the silence, the birds and the flicker of light through the trees that takes my brain into a state that doesn't happen anywhere else. I enter the walk with openness. My mind feels completely awake but not tethered to anything in particular; it's like an open door, and I never know what I'll discover. An idea flashes into my mind about something I've been stuck on for weeks; it's as sharp as mountain air – 'Oh, of course, that's it.'

Walking is like a poem for the brain-body-mind. It's as if the brain weaves together all the bits and pieces and comes up with something beyond what was known till now. The old is new, and something surprising emerges. Mihaly Csikszentmihalyi's term *flow* describes it well. I call it *integration*.

That makes it sound eloquent, perhaps even romantic, but sometimes my brain-body-mind is like a truck driving through a garden bed. At other times, it's like a trickle of rain down the face and into the mouth, or a flute across the clear morning. But no matter what emerges or where I get stuck, I keep walking through it, with it, in it.

Nature connects the brain to a poetic quality like integration or flow. In working with brains, I have often observed something ineffable, like the mystery of nature and walking through the forest in the morning. The quality of poetry, story and music impacts on the mind and body in ways that facts and information do not.

Brain-face

Every brain has a face, a brain-face, which is a complex individual, not just a point on a bell curve of normality. My work has been to take what brain science is offering and discover what it means for each brain-face I work with, including my own, and to watch for patterns to help me track and understand the brain in everyday interactivity, or *brains in the wild*.

Brains in the wild don't behave the same as brains in captivity. The brain-mind is connected to a body that is constantly moving and interacting with the world and giving us feedback. No matter how much we learn about brains in a laboratory, the lab situation is artificial and so is limited; it can only show us a small scrap of the reality we walk in every day.

Perhaps the most important question is: How does the brain decide what to focus attention on or orient to in the everyday when it's not directed? Because what we orient to or focus on dictates everything else. But in the laboratory that decision is made *for* the brain. Even being in a science lab, or being observed, is a particular orientation.

How the brain behaves in the wild – when it's frightened, lonely, expectant, in love, cranky, distracted, bored, hopeful, worried, unselfconscious, creative, praying, writing, talking, yelling, drinking a cup of tea, looking out the window and remembering a different summer, singing and dancing, or doing yoga or chi gong or anything else – is still a mystery.

Brain science tells us the brain can change itself, but what does that mean for you and me and our individual brain-face, and in our relationship with other brain-faces, like our boss or sister? Can Jack's brain change the legacy of his father's violence? Or can Mary (who you'll meet shortly) find peace with food?

A scrap of the holy

The brain is organic, a mystery of nature that we can never pin down completely, because dissecting the brain in order to know it doesn't allow us to see the interconnectivity that is the poetry of the brain-body-mind. It is far more than the sum of its parts. It's more than can ever be known, because we can only know the brain *with* the brain.

This mystery of interconnectedness of brain-body-mind singing in harmony (integrating) is like a moment of exquisite beauty, sunrise camping on a deserted beach, rain on a tin roof in the long dry, the first bite of a fat strawberry in summer, a lover's touch, children laughing, a line in a poem that reaches into the heart. It's that indescribable quality beyond the experience itself, an awakening.

I see it as a scrap of the holy; a small miracle that is much more than science or fact, which only point to its exquisite complexity. That poetry is also part of the journey of this book, through my encounters with the brain and the discoveries I've made. I can't write that wonder down; that would be like capturing the blue butterfly and pinning it to the page. But I hope you may glimpse a flicker of blue out of the corner of your eye occasionally as you step inside your own experience of brain in the wild.

Chapter 4

How i-brainmap works and when it doesn't work

In this chapter I explain why i-brainmap is effective in catalysing brain integration and some of the ways integration is inhibited. Then I describe what people report after the i-brainmap. I also outline some of my observations about working with i-brainmap that may be helpful in understanding your experience and avoiding pitfalls if you use this approach.

This chapter is like the handouts in a class, outlining some interpretations of the mechanisms behind i-brainmap and some of those main pitfalls. If you're the sort of person who throws the handouts in the bin without ever looking at them, or never reads instructions but leaps in, you might want to skip this chapter because it will possibly bore you.

The lazy brain

Because the brain is lazy – or efficient, depending on your orientation – it will use an old map, a *near-enough* map, if it can, so that it is able to turn its attention to something else. So if you know a lot about the brain or psychology you are more likely to orient to this material through existing maps. It's likely your mind will compare i-brainmap to something you already know and stop giving it your full attention (closed mind). That's a fine way to read the book, but not if you want brain integration. For that you need your brain's whole attention. This is why I've written the book (and developed the map) with the emphasis on your experience, and not as an intellectual exercise to simply add to what you already know, or think you know. This is best explained through a story.

Full cups of empty minds

There was once a man who spent his whole life in the pursuit of truth. He had read and studied for many years, but truth remained elusive. At last he heard of a great master who lived far away in the mountains who was said to know truth. The man packed up his house and belongings and set out on the long and dangerous journey to the mountains where the master lived. Many months later when he finally arrived, he explained to the young monk who greeted him that he was a great scholar and wished to become a student of the master. The man was shown to a cell, and there he waited for three days before he was summoned to meet the master.

The only person in the small room when he arrived for the interview was an old man making tea. The man sat down to wait for the master. When the tea was ready the old man asked if he'd like some. The man nodded without taking his eyes from the door, impatient to meet the master at last. Then the old man began pouring tea into the small cup. When the cup was full the old man continued pouring tea, and it overflowed across the table. Finally, as the steaming tea flowed onto the floor, the man looked up and said loudly, as if the old man might be deaf, 'The cup is already full.'

The old man looked up, smiling right into the eyes of the man who thought he knew so much, and said, 'And so it is with your mind. There is no room there for truth, my friend.'

And with that, according to one version of the story, the man's mind opened fully, a boundless truth pierced his heart and he was enlightened on the spot. In other versions, the man got angry and left the mountain and returned to his books, never realising he had met the master.

Invitation to curiosity

The best way to keep your brain's attention is to stay curious, because that's when your brain is most likely to make new connections to existing memory maps. To engage your curiosity as you read the dialogues with Jack and Mary it helps to check in with your own experience, asking yourself something like, 'How is it for me?', rather than approaching what you're reading as an intellectual exercise, which will only access the big brain. You could try checking in with your body responses now and then as you read, for instance, to discover what *sense* your body makes of what you're reading.

Why it's called 'i-brainmap' and 'the i-brainmap'

You may have noticed by now that sometimes I call it 'the i-brainmap' and other times just 'i-brainmap'. The reason for this is that it is more than just a physical map; it is also a dynamic or process. *The i-brainmap* refers to the physical map I draw for people, whereas *i-brainmap* refers to the dynamic process of brain integration.

Explaining i-brainmap is like trying to describe a journey that hasn't happened yet. Some signposts to watch for, and a direction – integration – to head towards, follow. But integration is different for everyone, so I don't know what you'll discover in this process. *Oh, I know! I'll give you a map and you can take the journey yourself!*

The 'i' in i-brainmap is you; this process is about *your* experience of brain mapping, or remapping what needs updating.

What the i-brainmap is and what it's not

Based on principles of brain integration, i-brainmap is primarily an experiential and functional approach to psychological stuckness. It communicates with the different functions in the brain using a range of devices, including story, gesture, colour, factual information and sensory experience. This is one of the reasons I call it an *integrated* brain map: it uses the different languages of brain function, working from the bottom up and the inside out of your brain. Especially important is that it describes sensory experience, which is an essential language of the lower brain or the body-brain (that connection between the brain and the rest of the body).

The i-brainmap is a generalised map; it is an approximation (like a mud map) of what's going on in your brain when it's stuck. You adapt the map to suit yourself as you make sense of it based on your experience so that, over time, you create your own unique, dynamic map. In other words you *integrate* the brain map. Eventually it becomes an interactive map that you continually update and adjust as your environment and your experience changes.

The i-brainmap is also a field map to help you make sense of and respond to difficult and stuck experiences as they happen; it helps you get your bearings.

It's also an experimental map, not the one-and-only true map.

The i-brainmap as orientation

Maps help us orient, and so orientation is one of the functions of the i-brainmap.

When you feel like you're trapped in a jungle, a tunnel or some other dark place inside yourself (in other words, when you are activated), the i-brainmap orients you to the experience in a way that helps you navigate through the distress. The map gives you a tangible starting point when you feel lost. By naming an overwhelming and frightening experience, and making it external and visible, i-brainmap provides a way for you to orient to the experience differently. Rather than being stuck *in* it, you can begin to find a way to be *with* it and move *through* it. Changing your orientation changes your experience, and changing experience changes the brain.

The map is about you. The eye (I) can't see itself; it needs something to reflect it back. But whatever reflects back needs to constantly change and adapt because, when it comes to the brain, seeing something differently changes the experience. That's why you need to keep adapting and updating your i-brainmap through curiosity.

The i-brainmap guides you towards a path of integration until your brain regains its self-organising, integrating capacity – because when the brain is functioning optimally it's integrative, interactive, interconnected, interpersonal and self-creating. Until the brain-body-mind can re-establish the necessary connections to integrate, i-brainmap is simply a guide.

The i-brainmap offers an outline of the brain's normal response and shows how it can get stuck as a result of extreme, chronic or overwhelming experience. Discovering that your brain is functioning as it should in response to extreme conditions, and understanding its behaviour, is, for many people, the first relief.

Fragmented maps

Post-traumatic stress can result in non-integration or disintegration. This feels as if the brain is working on lots of separate maps.

Imagine that each small map page on your iPhone is disconnected from the other maps, or fragmented so that there is no connection between them and you don't know how they fit together. Under these circumstances, each time you switch to a different map to work out where you are or where you're going you'll be disoriented and confused and eventually get lost. Or imagine that you have no maps, which would be closer to the experience of dissociation.

In short, in this state your maps – if you have them – don't fit the experience of the current terrain you're moving through, or they're so fragmented they are useless.

The foundation of i-brainmap is an interconnected map for all the brain, to help it put the pieces together and move through 'activation' towards 'integration' (terms which I progressively explain throughout the book). Using it is like finding the zoom-out on your iPhone maps, so you can see how the scraps of maps fit together.

The i-brainmap given in a therapy session is an actual paper map. Some people carry it with them to pull out of their bag or pocket and orient to when they drop into the distress of lower brain activation, which can happen anywhere, anytime, even in the frozen goods section of the supermarket or stuck in traffic on the West Gate Bridge!

After the i-brainmap

Giving people the i-brainmap is only the beginning of the process of integration.

Giving your brain a map can kickstart integration, but the brain can easily fall back into old patterns unless the map (or paradigm) is continually refreshed and the techniques practised consistently.

In the beginning most people notice the more intense and difficult aspects of activation such as anxiety, rage, paralysis or overwhelm. But as you continue discovering and rediscovering and reworking and integrating your maps, you will find deeper layers of disintegration or habits that have been established to protect you that are no longer helpful, at least not in the situations in which they're activated.

Tracking integration

After giving someone the i-brainmap, I track integration – except that integration is a process and can't be seen. So I watch for signs of integration and what feeds and catalyses it, just as you might track a small wild animal and try to discover its habitat and feeding patterns in order to protect it and ensure its survival so it can thrive.

Signs of integration can be hard to find because they're often not what you expect but are unique to each person. They are also rarely reported by people using the i-brainmap. When I first realised that people didn't report these changes following the i-brainmap, or only reported a few significant changes, or sometimes attributed changes to something else (from psychic readings to a new pair of glasses), it was confusing. But it happens so often that it appears to it be an aspect of brain integration.

I think the changes are so rarely reported because they happen bottom-up and inside-out – with the brain at the centre of the changes, so the person to whom they are happening is barely conscious of them. Also, integration happens so gradually that it's like cooling the water in the frog-pot: the frog doesn't notice it's happening. It's the same as not noticing wrinkles or weight loss or weight gain for a while.

We are so accustomed to effortful goal-driven change or focusing on a specific change, that few people have a strong experience of personal organic change from the inside. As with growing a garden or learning to play a musical instrument, the changes occur subtly and incrementally, and it's quite common for other people to see them before we notice them ourselves.

Brain integration is an organic process that emerges slowly and quietly, like the first signs of spring after a long, dark winter.

Reporting after the map

What follows are just some of the things that people have reported when questioned about their experience after i-brainmap. I call these changes 'subtle spontaneous differences' (SSDs). SSDs are indications of integration, like the random scats or tracks of that small, timid animal hidden in the wilds that I'm always on the lookout for.

- 'The same but different somehow.'
- 'More space.'
- 'I've (spontaneously) stopped biting my fingernails,' (although we never discussed nail biting in session).
- 'I'm not drinking as much.'
- 'I've enrolled in the design course I've been talking about for the last five years.'
- 'I can smell the Christmas tree.'
- 'The stove clock is so loud, I hadn't even noticed it before.'
- 'I feel more connected. I'm having lots of dreams.'
- 'I didn't realise so many things have changed until I started talking about them.'

- 'I was just washing the dishes and I realised I didn't have that awful feeling in my chest anymore. I don't know when it went, and I don't know when I stopped looking for it, but it's not there.'
- 'I can breathe.'
- 'I feel freer.'
- 'More peaceful.'
- 'I'm playing the guitar again.'
- 'I caught myself singing the other day.'
- 'I slept through the night. I can't remember the last time I did that.'
- 'I felt touched by their kindness. I cried.'
- 'I can see the colour of the autumn leaves. I didn't know that I wasn't seeing things before.'
- 'My partner says I'm not as angry.'
- 'I'm in my skin.'
- 'I feel real.'

Activation continues

In the beginning of the integration process there is only a very thin line between activation and integration. As I show throughout the book, one of the most difficult things to understand is that we're not trying to stop the activation. Activation is the brain trying to integrate some experience, so if we try to stop the activation we give the brain the message that the experience is still an active threat. Instead, we want to teach the brain, through changing our response to activation, and therefore the experience, that the experience (or the memory map of it) is no longer dangerous.

We all forget this because we don't want to be activated; it's uncomfortable, difficult, scary and embarrassing. We want the brain to change instantly. The challenge is to recognise that activation is the brain trying to integrate, and our job is to move through activation in a non-reactive way, again and again, changing the experience so the brain gets a different message. This is the path into brain integration.

Just using the techniques once won't change the brain pattern, which will quickly revert to the established pathway if you don't keep practising a different response. No one would expect to pick up a musical instrument for the first time and be able to play it. Yet when it comes to brain change, people often expect that just doing something once, or having a new map but never taking the journey, will change things immediately, and they get impatient and frustrated with their brain!

About avoidance

Avoidance of activation works in the short term because your nervous system feels like it's fighting for its life, and the system is trying to protect you. This includes protecting you from change, especially changing avoidance. Part of my job has been to find ways to teach the brain that it's now safe to put down avoidance and struggle.

One of the reasons I developed i-brainmap was to explain to people the impact of avoidance and how it keeps you stuck in the activation cycle. Understanding avoidance as part of activation in the context of being stuck, rather than viewing it as being wrong or *bad brain*, or calling it 'resistance', all of which can result in struggle, offers a different orientation to avoidance.

Approach gently, never with a whip, if you want to tame the brain.

Your brain is uniquely the same

While the same principles apply to every brain, your brain is unique because of your personal experience, and therefore some techniques will work better than others: i-brainmap isn't one-size-fits-all. It's an experience and an experiment, and the brain lab is the one inside your skull.

Some pitfalls of i-brainmap

Gotta get it right

Instead of encouraging integration, co-opting i-brainmap into existing maps – such as a *fix it* or *gotta get it right* one – uses the map and techniques to try to *fix the problem*, alerting the brain that there is something wrong. This alert-alarm reaction reduces the likelihood of integration.

Getting stuck in an activation cycle

Surprisingly we don't always recognise activation, because it has many faces. One of the hardest things in using i-brainmap is identifying activation as it happens.

Internal conflict

The integration process set in motion by i-brainmap can create an internal conflict between the old way and the new way. Once you see something, you can't unsee it. Once you understand how you entrap yourself or how the brain gets stuck you can't not see it. And if you understand i-brainmap you'll know that avoidance and other reactions can perpetuate the activation cycle. But sometimes you want to get mad and yell at your partner's 'ridiculous' behaviour, or you just want to have a Scotch or eat half a chocolate cake.

Occasionally people get angry at i-brainmap or at the person who explains it to them, because the integration process can take on a life of its own. The process of integration isn't always easy or comfortable because it can bring you face to face with what you've been avoiding or denying. But i-brainmap doesn't suggest stopping or changing anything, even avoidance or internal conflict. It's all just part of activation.

Familiar is safe, change is scary

Change is scary because it brings uncertainty. Change signals the brain to be on alert even when that change is positive or wished for. Whatever is familiar feels safe; even if it's dangerous, it's what you know. For instance, when depression or anxiety has been a familiar for many years it can feel like a friend; at least you know what to expect. Changing out of those patterns even when they are painful or unpleasant can be frightening, especially when you look beyond them and see into an abyss of the unknown.

The i-brainmap doesn't dictate what you do but invites more choice. So, if you choose to curl up in your doona all day, that's different to feeling as though you can never get out of bed. Finding the choices is a very different experience to powerlessness in which you don't believe you have any choice.

once new or different. This is significant because you need attention for integration and brain change.

If you want to continue integrating the brain (and not everyone *does* want to), you need to keep refreshing and changing the techniques and the map to catalyse brain integration, to keep noticing the subtle changes.

When the map becomes rigid

If your map isn't continually upgraded, it becomes rigid or just a concept. The brain will always try to use an established map without adapting it. As I've suggested, the brain is lazy/efficient. Your amazing brain can quickly take this experiential map and make it into a representational one that is disconnected from your ongoing direct experience. When it does this, there is no further integration.

Disconnecting the map from your experience turns it into a cognitive map, which is a top-down process, and top-down processing of the i-brainmap by the big brain (developing only 'intellectual understanding') is perhaps the biggest inhibitor of integration other than avoidance. As an experiential bottom-up map, i-brainmap is effective because it speaks the language of the lower brain, which is direct sensory experience. If that isn't part of your approach to i-brainmap it's unlikely your brain will integrate.

Some antidotes to the pitfalls

There are many pitfalls and stumbling blocks on the journey towards integration, and every antidote includes curiosity and attention.

Once you think you've *got* the i-brainmap you've probably stopped integrating. That's why I keep inviting you to be curious, telling you stories and finding new metaphors to keep your brain engaged. It's also why I use dialogue with Jack and Mary, to provide a direct experience of i-brainmap to illustrate some common pitfalls.

We're not looking for answers with i-brainmap but for a little bit of wondering. Being curious allows the edges of what you think you know, or rigid pathways in the brain, to soften and perhaps change a bit. We could call this approach 'the curious brain'.

Meeting yourself curiously

Giving you a map before we start using techniques allows the brain to take the lead, and we just follow. What happens with Jack and Mary in session will show you how I track the timid and untamed animal of the lower-brain–body, which is where the trauma and distress are held. The animal nature of experience is often vulnerable and afraid, hiding beneath layers of protection. So we lean in gently to contact and listen to the body-brain and how it responds to, and holds itself to protect against, change. We're not trying to do anything, change anything; we're intensely curious. These same principles apply as you read this book and try the techniques.

Go gently

It's easy to forget that our patterns of reaction, especially avoidance, are first and foremost protective. So to strip away any protective habits such as drug and alcohol use without developing other strategies to self-regulate can be harmful. Without protective habits you can become trapped in the original feelings you were trying to avoid, but now you have no escape. For this reason it's important that you approach this gently.

The i-brainmap isn't suggesting that you stop doing anything, but most people know what reactions are no longer helpful, and as integration progresses you will usually want to change old habits such as addictive behaviours. So don't stop doing something because you think you should; instead, become curious. Especially be curious about what message each reaction is giving your brain.

Go gently.

Clarification of terms

The main terms I will use throughout the book to describe different elements of i-brainmap are: AIR(s), inter-Active Mindfulness or i-AM, and mindfulness. These will be discussed in greater detail throughout the book.

AIR(s) – is the technique I provide as part of the i-brainmap. It was initially inspired by the work of Babette Rothschild but has undergone numerous transformations. It is based on the principles explained in the i-brainmap and is based on mindfulness.

inter-Active Mindfulness, or i-AM – is how I track activation and integration through body reactions in session. It is how I have always worked, but I hadn't given it a name until I wrote this book. i-AM is simply a way of tracking direct experience, especially body experience, during session and is based on principles of mindfulness and i-brainmap. It is an important part of i-brainmap because it grounds the principles charted in the map in direct body experience. i-AM will be discussed and demonstrated throughout the book.

Mindfulness – when I use this term I'm not referring to a particular technique but simply attending with curiosity. I find it difficult to define mindfulness, partly because it is tied to my experience of insight meditation in the monastery in Sri Lanka. I think we often try to make mindfulness simpler, or sometimes more complex, than it actually is.

There are many ways to define mindfulness, and each will orient you in a different way. I invite you to stay curious and attentive and see what else you uncover about mindfulness as you read and experiment with the techniques described in the book.

Chapter 5
Meeting Mary

In this chapter I introduce you to Mary, your other companion through the book. And our dialogue shows another way I might introduce the i-brainmap to a client.

Mary, first session

Mary is fifty-six. She was referred by her GP, who is concerned about her constant exhaustion, aches and pains, including frequent headaches. She has had a raft of tests, but so far nothing has shown up. Her GP has also referred her to a dietitian to help her lose weight, and has prescribed antidepressant medication. Mary has come to counselling because she is reluctant to take the antidepressant medication.

In the waiting room, she is sitting quietly, flicking through a *Home Beautiful* magazine. She looks up and smiles at me when I come into the room. We make our introductions then she places the magazine neatly on top of the pile of other magazines and pulls herself up out of the chair with some difficulty and follows me into my office. Her large frame fills the chair.

Mary calls herself a 'carer' and describes her childhood:

> I was the eldest of five. Mum would take to her bed for days and pull down the blinds to shut out the world including us kids. We hid it from everyone and pretended she was busy if anyone called. I can't remember how old I was when it started. It seems it was always like that. We'd fend for ourselves.
>
> I became the carer for the others. I had to, there was no one else. Dad was never around. He was either away working or at the pub. By the time I was in high school I was pretty much taking care of things at home. I took lots of days off school. I'd forge Mum's signature. But we always went to mass on Sundays. Mum would get up and drag us all to mass – rain, hail or shine. Maybe that's why no one suspected

anything. And she would put on a show for everyone. It was like she was another person, chatting and laughing even. It was strange, really, but normal for me. By the time we'd get home she was silent again.

Mary: When I was in therapy last time I talked about it a lot.

Rita: Was that helpful?

It helped to understand my 'attachment' issues. That's what the therapist called it. And why I'm the way I am now.

It's sometimes called 'early parentification' when a child takes on a parenting role before they have the resources to cope with the responsibility.

But I didn't have any choice. And Mum couldn't help it. She really was sick mentally, though I didn't understand that back then.

Yes, sounds like she was depressed, and we certainly don't want to blame anyone for what happened. But we do want to understand the impact on your brain and how it may be still impacting on you now. It's likely this early experience of responsibility was overwhelming for you as a little girl.

Yes, it was overwhelming. But I got used to it.

That early experience may have laid down a map that says, 'I must take care of everyone full-stop, no excuses ever.' Even if you're exhausted or they can easily take care of themselves. Does that fit, Mary?

Sounds about right. My brother still calls me 'little mother,' not so little these days though. Can you help me get rid of it?

We're not trying to get rid of anything but just give you more choice. Feeling responsible and taking care of people sounds like an automatic reaction.

I feel exhausted all the time lately. I find the grandchildren tiring. Sarah, my eldest daughter, is always off doing this or that and leaving the kids with me. I love the kids, but it's such an effort.

Have you ever said no to her, Mary?

Oh, I couldn't. I'm not good at saying no.

I wonder if it may be almost impossible for you to say no, because the reaction to care for others is tied up with your brain's survival response.

Really? My last therapist got really frustrated with me because she wanted me to be more assertive. She didn't say she was frustrated with me, but I could tell. I've got a radar for people getting annoyed with me.

A radar for disapproval, huh? So what happens if you try to say no?

I'm paralysed. I get sweaty and panicky. No words come out. I stopped therapy because it just got too hard. In the end that's all we talked about. I felt like such a failure. I laughed with a friend at the time that I failed therapy.

It sounds like lower brain activation, Mary. It may be that you get 'triggered' by a person's need, and that activates the freeze response. That can affect the language centres in your brain, and often means you can't find your words as your body drops into the frozen memory of how it was for you when you were a little girl, overwhelmed by trying to do an adult's task of taking care of your younger siblings.

Sounds complicated, but you're right. I honestly feel like I can't say no. Afterwards I might wish I'd said no, but I just can't. It makes me feel hopeless. I get annoyed with myself, and since I've been so tired the whole thing is worse.

It makes sense, Mary. When someone, especially family, needs something, an old pathway of survival is activated. I'll explain why this happens in the i-brainmap.

[*Mary sighs loudly.*] It's just easier to say yes, and then it's over and I don't feel that dreadful tension.

Sounds like you've developed some avoidance because staying in that dissonance is too uncomfortable. I want to show you what's going on in your brain and teach you some strategies you can use to develop more choices.

Sorry, but it's hard to imagine. Don't get me wrong – I love my kids and want to help them, just not every day. I'm so tired. Sorry, I shouldn't complain.

You can complain all you like here, Mary; but for the moment I'm more interested that when you said you're tired your whole body seemed to collapse. Were you aware of that?

Well, now that you mention it, yes, I feel collapsed.

Where do you feel that collapse most in your body, Mary?

In here. [*Mary points to diaphragm area.*] Like I don't have anything holding me up.

Anything else you're aware of?

It's hard to breathe.

Did you notice any thoughts or emotions, perhaps impulses, when you felt that?

Oh, yes. I wanted to curl up in a ball and crawl away. No, actually go get a coffee and a piece of cake. Yes, chocolate cake was definitely on my mind. There's a great deli with homemade cakes just around the corner.

So I wonder if when there's a lot going on internally your attention goes to chocolate cake, maybe for comfort, and it lets you escape the discomfort internally for a while?

Activation points

The body is constantly reacting to the environment, and many people have particular markers in the body that signal distress, overwhelm, dissonance or lower brain activation. Common activation points include the solar plexus, jaw, neck, shoulders and abdomen. Usually people experience a contraction, tightening, collapse, or sometimes a tremoring, like butterflies, in these activation points, or fidgeting in feet and hands.

The breath is a significant marker of activation or any agitation in the body. The breath is like a radar for what is happening in the body and mind, and you can also change it at will, which is why the breath is so important in working with body-memory maps.

I don't know, sorry. I just know that I'd rather eat cake than talk about my problems. Who wouldn't?

Yeah, fair enough. The trouble is that this pattern of avoidance, the way you use food to escape and comfort internal distress, may be part of the cycle tied to your reaction. Would it be okay to talk to the body about that before we talk more about cakes?

Well, I can tell you a lot more about cakes than I can about my body. [*Mary laughs.*]

I was interested that you went straight for the cake, in your mind, when you felt the discomfort in your body, and I wonder if that's your usual reaction.

Maybe. I guess so. Sorry, I'm not very clear, am I?

I notice you often say sorry, Mary. You don't need to apologise or censor anything here. I'm very curious about your thoughts and feelings and even the need to say sorry. And if you don't know something, that's also interesting to me.

Okay. I'll try not to say sorry again.

No, I'm not saying don't say sorry. I'm just curious that it seems to be a pattern when you don't have an answer or perhaps say things that you think might offend or upset.

Yes, I'm always apologising. Pathetic.

So you feel wrong or bad, say sorry, and then you feel bad about feeling bad? I don't want to get too side-tracked by it, but let's just notice when it comes up and what's going on for you when you say, or want to say, sorry. Okay?

Yeah, okay.

Back to the food thing. So what you do around food isn't very clear but seems to just happen? Is that how it feels?

Yep. Suddenly I've eaten a whole block of chocolate and I hardly even remember opening it. It's like some demon takes me over and I don't even know it. Then suddenly I wake up with an empty wrapper. Perhaps I have multiple personalities. What do you think? [*Mary laughs.*]

Sounds like there could be a dissociative quality in there.

A what?

Could be some kind of dissociation.

Meeting Mary

>
> **Dissociation**
>
> The extreme end of dissociation is Dissociative Identity Disorder or what was previously called Multiple Personalities and is often portrayed in dramas but is quite rare. On the other end of the spectrum, most of us experience some dissociation such as when we're driving the same route to work each day or doing a routine task. You could say we slip into a mindless state, which is quite helpful when we're bored, for instance.
>
> For those with a history of trauma or overwhelm, dissociation is a protective response that allows you to distance yourself from the experience of traumatic or overwhelming event(s). It's experienced as things seeming unreal or distant, or you feel unreal, almost as if you're in a dream. While this is protective during an overwhelming experience, if it continues you can have difficulty managing day-to-day situations, because you continually disappear into a kind of trance. But usually you don't recognise that it's happening. It is also problematic in therapy because dissociation can inhibit integration.

It sounds like the only way you had to nurture and comfort yourself as a child was through food, Mary, because your parents weren't available. It probably also gave you some control in an out-of-control world.

I felt happiest in the kitchen, especially when it was just me and Gran. Later, when Gran died, I was in charge of the kitchen. Alone in the kitchen, I could eat what I wanted, make what I wanted. If I wanted something, I learnt how to make it. I make a mean chocolate cake.

I bet you do. And it was the way you learned to comfort yourself. So food became associated with comfort and maybe control.

Can you fix me then?

If you were a car and I was a mechanic I might give it a shot. But you're a human being and I'm a human being, and I'm not in the business of fixing. Fixing implies there's something wrong with you, Mary.

Well, there is something wrong with me. I'm sure there is.

I don't think there's anything wrong with you, Mary. I think your brain has behaved exactly as it needed to. And then it got stuck on that set point, and that set point got wired in with more and more experience until it turned into a neural knot that's no longer helpful. In fact, it may even be detrimental to your health. It worked perfectly at the time, it was adaptive based on the resources available to you back then and helped you survive, but it's not working for you now. That's all, but it's not bad or wrong.

Can you change that?

I can't, but you can, or your brain can, once you have a new map and a few tools. In the beginning, I'll be like a compass to remind you in which direction to move, or like a line through and beyond whatever is happening that you can grab hold of when you get bogged or lost in a tunnel. But over time you'll know how to get yourself out of these brain knots.

You make it sound so easy, but I don't feel very confident.

Why would you? All your experience tells you that there is a problem and someone else has to fix it or fix you, which is the opposite of what I'm telling you. In fact, it's like a cultural anthem: 'Someone or something fix me, save me!' But we each have to do this for ourselves. Well, our brain does. You don't have to believe me, Mary. All you need do is experiment and test it for yourself and find your own evidence. That's what changes the brain, not me sitting here and babbling on about what you need to do to change. It's you discovering what works for you. I'm just giving you the pointers and a map and a few tools. Oh, and a compass, of course. But it's your journey. Who knows what you'll discover?

Uncover, more like it – all those old stinking bones down there. Not sure I want to dig them up.

We're not going to go through the garbage before we put it out. We don't need to dredge through all yesterday's muck. We let the brain do that. We just work with what's here now, especially how it's stored in the body.

You'll have to get through all the layers of fat to find it, Rita. [*Mary laughs.*]

Ouch. That seemed like you just gave yourself a good kick.

[*Mary looks out the window.*] I guess I do feel disgusted by this body. It's easier to make jokes about it before anyone else can. I try to tell myself it's okay and I don't really care. But I hate it. Hate myself this way.

Does hating yourself help or make you feel worse?

It's much worse. I'm likely to binge when I'm 'self-loathing' – I did a lot of work on that with my last therapist too. When I feel dreadful I just have to eat. I go into an eating trance. I can't get enough. Nothing fills me up. And then suddenly I feel awful, and I want to throw up.

Eating is the very first way we learn to soothe ourselves, Mary. And it sounds like it's the *only* way you know. So the worse you feel, the more you're going to eat.

Yep, that's true.

You're instinctively trying to soothe the lower brain because it's distressed in some way. We need to give you some other strategies to soothe the lower brain, so you can eat when you want to instead of using food as your only comfort and then having this battle with food and your body. I think the only place we can really rest and feel safe and at home is in the body.

Can't imagine why anyone would want to rest in the body. I can't get out of there fast enough.

Sounds like the body hasn't been safe for you, Mary. We want to see if we can find gentle ways into the body, so you can experience the body from inside your own skin.

No rush on that. Can we do some other stuff first? I'm interested in the map thing.

Part 2

The brain and the map

Chapter 6
Brain basics

In this chapter I give you 'The Brain 101', a very brief outline of the structures and some important principles of the brain function relevant to our discussion. This is a first sketch of the brain function, which I will add to as we go along.

Bottom up or top down?

To understand the general principles of brain functioning we need to go back to a time when humans lived in caves.

Our ancestor uncle and our ancestor father are sitting on a grassy knoll, the sun is shining – maybe they're fishing or inventing a kite. Then they get a whiff of wet lion close by. Our ancestor father, whose brain is wired bottom up, has a rapid-fire message arrive in his legs saying RUN! It's such a strong, immediate message that he leaps up and is back at the cave before he can say 'Robinson Crusoe', though of course that hasn't been written yet, so before he can say whatever is the latest saying, maybe 'Oh, woolly mammoth' in cave culture. He meets his future wife the following spring and they have several children, passing on his genetic material, with everyone leaping up and running away when they smell wet lion.

But let's imagine that the brain-body-mind of our ancestor uncle was wired differently. When he smelt the wet lion his brain sniffed and the message went via his big or thinking brain and he began to ruminate on lion welfare and whether the lion was getting sufficient feed because of the drought, or whether he should follow his brother back to the cave. No, wait, he was an artist and wanted to capture a lion in action to draw it over his bed in the cave. So he hesitated. And his genetic material wasn't sent down the line, but went down the lion!

Of course, we know that genetics and epigenetics are much more complex and fascinating than my story, but it's important to recognise that the way the brain responds to threat, *bottom up*, is effective for survival of the brain. Whether that is still an effective survival response, reacting to life as if you're being chased by a wet lion, in our modern day is another question.

Just to clarify what I mean by *bottom up*: it is that the lower brain is the one sending the messages, and that this happens outside awareness: it's implicit, involuntary and automatic. *Top down* refers to the big brain dominating and sending the message to the lower brain: it is voluntary, conscious, rational, and more, which will be discussed shortly.

In functional rather than structural terms, the brain is interconnected, and therefore any division we make is artificial.

The 'limbic system' is a misnomer

I don't use the term *limbic system* because it's confusing, and, as I said in chapter 1, it has a specific orientation, that of focusing on brain structure rather than interconnected function. Joseph LeDoux explains that the term is misleading. (www.youtube.com/watch?v=tjhCPhhzBqQ, 10:17–12:20).

Having the amygdala and the hippocampus in the same system ignores the fact that the brain operates very differently when the amygdala and hippocampus are connected than it does when they are disconnected, or when the hippocampus is offline. The impact of the hippocampus going offline during an overwhelming experience is central to i-brainmap and is discussed in detail in part 3 of the book. I use a brain model primarily based on function and experience, and only then on structure.

Dividing the brain into structures is somewhat artificial, but we need some way of ordering the functions so we can talk about it. Therefore I divide the brain roughly into three main functions: lower brain, big brain and *integration Zone* or *i-Zone*, which I'll introduce shortly.

The lower brain includes the amygdala and brain stem and is closely linked to body functions and reactions. It includes the most primitive functions of the brain, and is mainly responsible for survival, both in extreme situations of threat-alarm and also in maintenance of functions that keep the whole system ticking over.

Then there's the big brain, or neocortex, and all its complex functions, including higher-order thinking. The big brain, especially the left pre-frontal cortex, can make decisions to influence the rest of the brain – except when the brain is operating in a split-brain system or in survival mode, which brings us to the next cluster of structures and functions: the *integration Zone* or *i-Zone*.

The *i-Zone* is made up of functions and structures and, probably, types of cells – such as projection neurons, place cells and maybe even glial cells – anything in the brain involved in the interconnectivity and integration of the brain between all its different functions and structures. This interconnectivity is like a feedback loop constantly adapting and reflecting what is happening as the brain-body-mind interacts with the environment.

Visualise the brain as a communication network with a hub of structures involved in connecting all the different dots and dashes of the brain waves, chemicals, and electrical signals, and cells whispering to each other through walls; there is a lot of communication going on in the brain every nanosecond. But to do this effectively requires something to interpret and mediate all these dots and dashes and make sense of all the different languages and signals, maps and patterns criss-crossing the brain. The structures and functions responsible for all of this mediating and linking is what I call the *i-Zone,* which is headed up by the hippocampus. The hippocampus is like the master mapper: holding, ordering, orienting and reorienting, connecting and updating all the different maps or patterns of experience, language and learning of the different functions of brain-body-mind. I'm reluctant to name some of the other structures involved because these are still unclear in the nascent knowledge of neuroscience, but I associate any function or structure involved in attention, orientation and interconnectivity with the *i-Zone.*

Therefore the main reason I don't use the term *limbic system* is because putting the amygdala and hippocampus in the same system ignores the extreme difference between experience and brain function when the hippocampus and amygdala are in communication, and when they are not. A model of the brain that ignores the unique and weighty role of the hippocampus is like a model ship with no rudder. The main question for me during any experience is 'Is the brain interconnected or integrated?'; or I could also ask 'Is the hippocampus on?' Essentially the hippocampus is the captain of the ship, especially when the brain is operating in the wild, because it has to work out which map is needed for every experience.

It is likely that most brains in labs, during experiments, have a reasonably well-functioning hippocampus and are not operating in survival mode or experiencing high levels of activation, because they are, after all, volunteers. So in a lab the limbic system makes perfect sense, because the amygdala and hippocampus are probably operating in tandem, but this may not be a useful model for brains in the everyday.

Entering a lab is a particular orientation, and usually the researcher directs the brain's attention, so the hippocampus can hop out to lunch and no one will even notice. But having your hippocampus out to lunch when you're operating in the world is a very different matter, or mapper!

Chapter 7
Fight, flight, freeze and appease

In this and the following chapters, I show you how I do the i-brainmap in session. It's an actual map drawn on A3 cartridge in coloured pens. While it is a standard map, each brain will have a different response and therefore create their own personal version as I describe the common experiences of how overwhelming events can impact on brain function. Some common responses to i-brainmap can be observed in my dialogues with Jack and Mary.

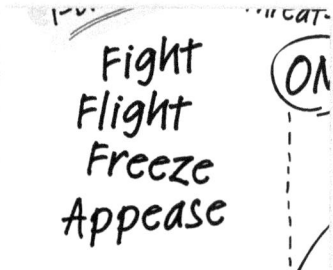

I will unpack the i-brainmap over seemingly several sessions (chapters) but typically I complete the map in one session with clients. Giving it to you in a more fragmented way and through a different medium means that you may not see the map as a whole or as directly as when I do the map face to face. So if you get confused, go back to the diagram of the whole i-brainmap on pages vi–vii. That's your reference point.

I begin this brain story by explaining the fight-flight-freeze or f-f-f response.

Fight, flight, freeze, but also please and appease

The fight-flight response is the body-brain's alarm system preparing you to deal with a threat. The body reacts rapidly – muscles contract, heart pounds, breath quickens and so on – getting ready to respond to the threat.

This 'on' switch of the Autonomic Nervous System (ANS) acts like an accelerator. It's referred to as the Sympathetic Nervous System (SNS) and involves chemicals such as cortisol and adrenalin. It's automatic, involuntary and instant, because trying to think and plan would be too slow. It's a physical reaction – *all systems go* – to help you survive the situation. Survival is the brain-body-mind's priority during threat, overriding all others.

When there's a hungry lion running towards you, your response has to be immediate. And when *survival brain* is triggered it grabs all your attention and resources, and the big brain that you can usually rely on for help in problem solving hardly gets a look in until the threat has passed and the survival brain has calmed down a bit. Then you can access your big-brain resources again.

As well as fight-flight there is also the freeze response. This is what people commonly experience during traumatic and overwhelming events. It's like a shock reaction when everything shuts down if you feel trapped and overwhelmed. And like the other responses it's protective during an extreme event.

You can observe the fight-flight-freeze, or survival, response throughout nature. Which survival response is triggered – fight, flight or freeze – depends on the animal and the situation. The more powerful the animal – for instance, a lion – the more likely it is to fight when threatened. A smaller and more vulnerable animal like a mouse will run away when it senses danger. But when an animal is trapped or overwhelmed and can't escape, it usually freezes or plays dead, like a mouse caught by a cat. This is a good survival tactic when no other resources are available because when the danger passes the animal can escape. The freeze response is the usual survival response for children whose immature brain–nervous systems are easily overwhelmed.

There's a late addition that I add to this list, referred to as 'please and appease'. So we'll call it the *fight-flight-freeze-and-appease* response to threat. You can see the *appease* response in animals when they're threatened. That's why I consider it more a biological than a conditioned, cultural or learned response. ('Tend and befriend' is different to 'please and appease' as I use it here, because 'tend and befriend' is more culturally conditioned and a learnt response; that is, there is some choice.)

Please and appease is automatic, like a flinch to duck and pull the head in. We see it in dogs when they're fighting. The weaker dog will usually cower or curl its tail and roll over or crawl on its belly. It's a signal of surrender and getting out of the way. The reason I've added this is that for some people, when there's been childhood trauma or early overwhelm, appeasing and pleasing can become a compulsive response, which they feel powerless to change cognitively or behaviourally.

BRAIN IN A BOX

A basic explanation of the body-brain's threat-alarm-defence response in a healthy nervous system

When there's a threat, a cascade of rapid-fire events is triggered in the brain-body-mind system. When you encounter a threat your amygdala does a crude appraisal – shape of snake on ground; big, black growling dog; truck veering towards you – setting off a series of reactions at lightning speed. The amygdala screams out to the hypothalamus. The hypothalamus sends a message to the SNS, which starts shooting off information to the body releasing adrenalin and noradrenaline (also called norepinephrine). And you bolt to avoid being bitten by the dog or snake, or swerve to avoid the truck.

That's the quick and dirty pathway, the crudest and most rapid survival circuit. But there are some other events taking place simultaneously but more slowly.

While your amygdala is doing the quick and dirty appraisal – like shape and outline, smell of wet fur: 'Aha, lion! Run!' – your big brain is doing its own, more refined appraisal, like a reality check – 'Hang on, the dog's behind a fence,' or 'Oh, that's just a long, bent stick' and that can slow things down a bit, except that the amygdala has already sent the signal and your body has reacted accordingly, heart pounding, breathless, muscles contracted, ready to run.

At the same time, the HPA-axis (hypothalamic-pituitary-adrenal axis) kicks in. Once the hypothalamus gets the message from the amygdala that there's a threat, a chemical chain reaction is set in motion releasing cortisol into the system.

Then the hippocampus is hit with the cortisol, and it sends negative feedback to the hypothalamus saying, 'Shows over. Down-regulate. Slow down'. And the system starts to slow and calm down, if all goes to plan.

This system is older than humanity. You can't change it or stop it, because the body-brain is wired for survival. What you *can* do is change some of what it's wired with and learn some other brain tactics to get off the loop if it gets stuck on alarm, even when there is no threat. But when it kicks in, your big brain doesn't get much say, especially if your hippocampus is out to lunch.

Mary eating, and fight-flight-freeze-appease

Rita: Essentially, anything that overwhelms the brain-body-mind can leave an imprint on the brain's threat-alarm or survival memory, which means your brain's alarm can become sensitive to any reminder or associations with that original event or situation, even if you're not aware of it. And probably one of *your* triggers is food.

Mary: Oh, great. So food for me is like a war veteran watching a war movie?

Kind of.

No wonder it's so hard to see the fridge as a friend. It does *feel* like the enemy, and I never know when it might attack. I have to be on guard around it all the time. Maybe I could learn refrigerator kung fu?

Sounds like you'd like to make light of it, Mary, but it also sounds like there's a lot of sadness around this battle with the fridge.

Yeah, I can make light of it when I'm here, but it can feel like an elephant in the room when I'm home alone. I can't relax if I know there's something sitting in the fridge waiting to be eaten. A piece of cake is like an enemy, just waiting to pounce if I relax for a moment.

It's interesting that you use the language of battle. Is that new or have you always talked that way about your relationship with food and your body?

It's always been there. It feels like I'm at war, and I'm losing.

Mary and post-traumatic stress

Mary: Sorry, Rita, but I have a question. Oops, there's 'sorry' again.

Rita: Just notice it, Mary. We don't want to make it wrong, because that flicks on the brain's alert response. When we make something wrong the brain starts screaming at everyone (in your brain, that is), 'We have a problem. Could be a threat. All systems on stand-by.' Instead, the message we want to give your brain is, 'Oh, look at that, I'm doing that 'sorry' thing again. Isn't that curious?' Because that gives your brain the message that everything is fine, we're just noticing this or that, no need for alarm. Does that make sense?

Yes, it does. Not as easy as it sounds, though.

No, because most of these patterns are linked to the lower brain's threat-alarm reactions, and as I've just said they are automatic and instant. Now, what did you want to ask?

Well, is it really trauma? Because I don't relate to that term. I don't feel like I had trauma in my childhood. I've got a friend who was abused as a kid. That's what I thought trauma was. But why is my brain like that? I didn't go to war – even if I'm in a war with the fridge.

The only 'why' we need to understand is why the brain is stuck, so you can change it and get it flowing again, and have more choice about how you respond rather than getting caught in old neural knots. We don't need to know *why* it happened in terms of what events or what 'dreadfuls' caused it originally.

Fight, flight, freeze and appease

Post-traumatic stress disorder and *the dreadfuls*

I don't use the word 'disorder' to describe post-traumatic stress (PTS), because it's a normal brain response to extreme or overwhelming events or conditions. For some people, it disorders their life because it impacts on every aspect. But the term 'disorder' is often taken on personally to mean 'there's something wrong with me and it's permanent'. When I use the term PTS or trauma I'm referring to the way an event or situation impacted on the brain-body-mind. The situation overwhelms the available resources, and, because a child has a lot fewer resources than an adult, the child brain is easily overwhelmed. Parents usually protect children from what is overwhelming, but if a parent is abusive or unavailable the child's brain is easily overwhelmed.

When a *dreadful* event or situation overwhelms the brain-body-mind, the system isn't able to integrate the event. What was protective during the traumatic or overwhelming event (dissociation, for instance) continues because the system has no other coping resources. Then the pattern can keep being triggered, and the system goes into that same alarm reaction again and again, creating a never-ending loop. It's this dynamic of ongoing threat-alarm-overwhelm and loss of integrity in the system that is the same whether you're a soldier who has been exposed to the violence and horror of war or a child whose mother wasn't available. The intensity and level of impact may differ, but the brain dynamic is the same.

Each brain is different, and we can never know what will or what has overwhelmed the brain-body-mind system. There is the usual list of *dreadfuls* that include war and violence, bullying, sudden death, and natural disasters. But there can also be invisible *dreadfuls* that leave an imprint for a lifetime, such as mental health problems in a family, infertility, a child with a disability, chronic illness, separation and loss, to name a few. Chronic stress, such as work pressure, or chronic illness can have the same impact on the brain-body-mind system. In short, any situation that overwhelms the system can result in this brain dynamic described in i-brainmap.

The brain and the map

Mary, freezing

Mary: Yes, sorry, I'm talking too much. Oh, sorry, sorry. Wow, I didn't realise how much I say 'sorry'.

Rita: Great that you're noticing. What if instead of calling it post-traumatic stress reaction we call it 'Stuck on di-Stress' – (drop the di) – 'Stuck on Stress' reaction – or SoS brain? How would that work for you, Mary?

Sure. SoS makes more sense. And it's how it feels when I try to say 'no', like something dreadful will happen. I guess I haven't put it into words before.

That feeling of *dreadful* tells us it's probably a lower brain threat-alarm reaction that's buried in the body from when you were a child. And when you're in survival brain it overrides your big brain's resources.

I go into a panic and get all tongue-tied.

That's why trying to think your way through it to change your behaviour may not work for you. As I've said, when the lower brain threat-alarm system is on, it overrides cognitive function.

Is that why that assertiveness course didn't work for me? I just got frustrated.

Possibly, Mary. But even good material or techniques taught in a 'cookie cutter' way can be ineffective. Integrated learning requires access to lower brain experience so you can make it your own, integrate it into experience, not just have lots of intellectual knowledge. Having lots of information about the brain or any technique won't necessarily change your experience or response.

It seemed to help when I was in the group. I felt confident, but I seemed to leave it behind each week. I'd usually forget to do the homework.

Well, there are a few things going on there, but you probably don't want a lecture on learning and brain change.

Well, maybe not ... unless it helps me say 'no', or helps with my fridge kung fu?

It probably wouldn't. That's why the i-brainmap explains things through experience, bottom up, rather than with information alone, top down. If I just gave you lots of information about the brain, or even practices that don't fit your experience, it might not help things change much, or only in the classroom – but then when the old trigger happens your sys-

Fight, flight, freeze and appease

tem reacts in the same old way. One of the most important principles i-brainmap shows you is that when there's lower brain activation it can be difficult to access your big-brain resources.

Like what I learnt in a group session, right?

Right. In fact, the big brain becomes the servant of the lower brain, and usually reacts to the distress with overthinking but without much rational thinking. Once the intensity has lessened, you can access big-brain resources, including rational thinking, but when it's full-on you're driven by the lower brain.

Is that why I get irrational when I'm upset but don't know I've been irrational until after it passes?

That's exactly it, Mary. The big brain is spinning its wheels in the mud of murky, lower brain distress. The whole system gets stuck on distress – SoS – and the brain tries to make sense of it. But it's usually based on wrong information, or unintegrated information, fear or overwhelm, or probably an old map from when you were six. 'Wrong map', I call it. Not wrong because it's bad, just the wrong map for this place and time.

Like I need to eat that piece of chocolate cake or die.

Yes, whatever is going on is usually experienced as life and death.

Can't we change that?

Trying to change it through thinking doesn't work. In survival mode, the wiser mind is cut off and is reacting to lower brain distress. We have to work from the bottom up. And until now you may not have had any way to understand or work with your brain. So, like any new skill, this will take time and practice and understanding of what works.

Okay. [*Big sigh.*]

Great. A parasympathetic sigh.

A what?

A genuine sigh can be a sign that the parasympathetic system has kicked in and the system is relaxing. That's a good link back to the i-brainmap.

The brain and the map

The 'on' and 'off' switches

Once the threat has passed – the truck has swerved back onto its own side of the road or you realise the bull is on the other side of an electric fence – then the 'off' switch of the ANS (the parasympathetic nervous system) comes on. This is like a brake that slows down the system. Another series of neurophysiological events kick in and you relax and breathe out. You get a 'phew' feeling, one of 'I survived, it missed me.' It's often experienced as jelly legs or feeling like a floppy rag-doll, or a sigh. The parasympathetic is like a recovery mode after a fast run.

In a healthy nervous system these two systems (the sympathetic 'on' and the parasympathetic 'off') interact seamlessly throughout the day, so you hardly notice the changes as your system adapts to the constantly changing demands of the environment.

Take driving through peak-hour traffic. If someone beeps the horn right behind you, you get a rush of adrenalin and go into high alert, ready to deal with a possible threat (the SNS, your internal accelerator, comes 'on'). You might curse or give someone the finger when you realise there's no danger and then switch on the radio and calm down (parasympathetic nervous system, your inner braking system, 'off' switch). Then you hear there's been a road accident on your route to work with delays of up to two hours and realise you'll be late for an important meeting, so your SNS cranks up again. This interaction between the 'on' and 'off' switches goes on throughout the day, like using the accelerator and brake in the car to adapt to the changing road conditions.

But when there's an overwhelming or traumatic event, it's like a power surge through an electrical system, which blows out the 'off' switch, resulting in faulty brakes, or the brain's brake becomes disconnected.

Chronic stress can have the same effect, and is like a gradual eroding of the 'off' switch. It's like constantly driving with a foot on the brake – you wear out the brakes, and then when you really need them they don't work properly.

What happens when the 'off' switch stops working?

This damage to the 'off' switch means the system is never off, and is like an electrical wire that's partially severed and keeps flickering – zzz … zzz … zzz – or like an accelerator that's stuck on, constantly revving the car.

In session, to illustrate this I hold up my two forefingers pointing at each other; each forefinger is one piece of the wire.

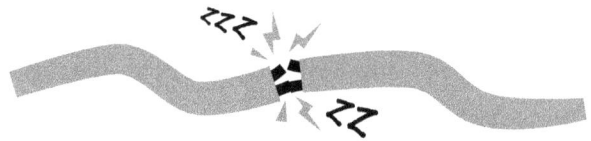

This means the system is acting as if there's constant threat. This is experienced as always being prepared or on alert for threat. This is called *hyper-arousal*, meaning the system is permanently wired in threat-alarm mode. You feel as if there's some threat or danger very close, because that's what your body is telling you, loudly, and you scan the environment looking for the threat. This scanning for danger is called *hyper-vigilance* or *watchfulness*. But in this case the danger doesn't exist in the environment, it exists inside you.

Something in the environment may remind you of something frightening and trigger a reaction in the brain-body-mind linked to a previous experience of overwhelm, and the brain whips out the old memory map. This map has a red flag saying threat-alarm, and the body-brain and the mind react accordingly. This triggering often happens outside your awareness, or perhaps you're aware of what triggers it, but your awareness is typically focused on either the trigger or the distress or the overwhelming feeling in your body and trying to stop it. Because the experience is so strong you believe that there really is a threat. You look around and see X or Y, so that gets confirmed as being the threat, when in fact it's just a trigger for an experience that might have happened twenty years ago.

Mary, first breath of AIR(s)

Mary: The thought of saying 'no' to my kids even though they're adults is just … I can't imagine it. It makes me breathless thinking about it.

Rita: Is that happening now, Mary? You sound a bit breathless.

Yes, it's happening. This feeling I get where I can't breathe.

Okay. We don't want to go into it right now, but we can work with that body response later. For the moment, Mary, can you tell me what jewellery I'm wearing?

What?

What jewellery am I wearing?

A watch and ... um, two rings. [*Mary looks closely at me.*]

Anything else?

[*She looks harder at me.*] I can't see anything else. Are glasses jewellery?

Not sure. But I wanted you to concentrate on here and now rather than get it right. How are you feeling now? How is your breathing?

A bit easier. It's still there a bit, but that panicky feeling has gone.

Good. So you're easily triggered, just talking about saying 'no'. That will make it easy to work with in session, but we need strategies that you can use outside session, which is when most of the lower brain activation happens.

[*Mary lets out a big breath.*]

Great, Mary. Your body is relaxing, no longer preparing for threat.

I do feel better now.

You just experienced an application of i-brainmap, what I call AIR(s), which I'll explain at the end of the i-brainmap. But for now I want to explain why the brain behaves the way it does and show you how you can do what I just did. Give yourself some AIR, you could say.

That'd be great. Some air when I'm locked down in that dungeon fighting the demons would be good.

The brain and survival

Imagine you're walking in the bush and almost step on a snake. The information is picked up visually, and there's a rapid-fire pathway through to the amygdala and lower brain. The brain-body-mind is constantly appraising the environment for threat. In evolutionary terms it's better to react (or overreact) too often than to get it wrong. Overlooking a potential threat could mean death. In other words, the brain is wired for threat or to find what's wrong because the brain is first and foremost a system for survival. If you don't survive, all the other clever things the brain does become useless, instantly obsolete.

Fight, flight, freeze and appease

The important point is that the message doesn't travel via the big brain but is relayed rapidly into the lower brain or what I often refer to as the body-brain. The alarm message goes directly down the brain stem and into the body; hormones are released, activating the fight-flight response, as described previously. Better to jump and ask questions later than to not jump and get eaten or bitten.

That's why we say it's automatic and involuntary. In an instant your heart is pounding, and you've jumped back from the snake, feeling a bit breathless before 'snake' has fully registered in your neocortex or big brain. This survival response evolved to be rapid. Your ancestor uncle sitting on the riverbank whose threat-alarm circuitry involved the big brain – 'Oh, is that a lion running my way or a hungry woolly mammal? Should I leap up and run for cover? Decisions, decisions.' – his genetic material didn't survive. He became the lion's lunch. Our ancestor father who leapt up automatically and sped off to his cave for safety got to share his genetic material.

The main thing to understand is that we can't think or talk (big brain) ourselves out of these threat-alarm reactions. You might tell yourself, 'I'm not scared of snakes. I'm not scared of snakes. I'm not scared of snakes.' But then when you're walking in the bush and nearly step on a snake, you leap back instantly, your heart starts pounding, and you feel breathless. Your body goes into a reflexive response of fight-flight outside your conscious control.

That experience of 'snake' becomes imprinted on the amygdala, so that next time you bump into a snake the same reaction will occur. Of course, it's easy to see why and how a snake gets imprinted in memory as a threat, but throughout your life much more complicated or obscure imprints occur that get wrapped up with threat-alarm. Many of these were laid down before you could talk or walk, through interaction with your parents' brains. (For a good explanation of this, see *Parenting from the Inside Out* by Dan Siegel.)

Your system reacts as if it's life and death because the imprint is in the amygdala and lower brain, tied with survival. Then, when you encounter that situation or thing in the environment next time, your amygdala will appraise it as threatening and the alarm is triggered.

If you try to change the pattern or habit, the brain can react with increased alarm because it has appraised the attempted change as threat and is trying to give you the message that you're in danger. So trying to stop or change the pattern can escalate the threat-alarm response, and you find yourself in a state of increasing internal distress, and the brain clings tighter to the loop, doing its job to protect you.

Mary, message in a brain

Rita: We want to give your brain the message that you're an adult now, Mary, and not the little girl who has to take care of everyone and everything or she might die, or they might die.

Mary: How do I do that? I've been trying, but it doesn't work.

Well, we need to use the language of the lower brain not the big brain, because the pattern is hooked up with lower brain survival stuff that was laid down when you were a kid.

Yeah, it kind of makes sense. But I don't speak 'survival'. I had enough trouble with Italian. Not good at languages.

Humour is a great way to shift the brain state out of alert/alarm.

My family don't think I'm funny.

I think you're very funny.

You do?

I think you're very witty and insightful. It's likely that your family see you only as the carer, and anything else is discombobulating for them.

Say what?! Yeah, that. They hated it when I went overseas with a girl-friend. They didn't leave me alone.

Yes, you stepped out of the paradigm they had for you. It is one of the hardest aspects of change that sometimes the people around us don't want us to change, but keep playing the same old songs, or games, trying to pull us into singing the old chorus line with them.

So how do I change that?

Well, we can't change anyone else, as you know. We all know it, but most of us keep wishing they'd change anyway. The other person may never change, but while you focus on them you are powerless and caught in wishing and hoping, which can be a way to avoid things or escape dealing with things differently. Like little-girl thinking.

Yeah, I do a lot of that wishing business. I wish my family wouldn't make so many demands.

Yes, but while your attention is on them and wishing, you don't notice what's going on for you and nothing changes. We want to change that orientation to what you *do* have some choice over.

Myself?

Yep. But with more of a focus on your body reactions than on your thinking, which makes it hard to change your behaviour because it's your body reactions that have become entangled in survival. That's why you don't have much freedom or choice.

Could be a long ride. New language, long rides, I'm wondering what I've got myself into here, Rita.

Yes, but you do have an amazing ally along the way.

You?

Well, I'll be with you. But no, I meant your brain.

Oh, that. Hmm. Hasn't been enormously helpful so far, Rita.

That's because it had the wrong map, Mary. Now we want to give it an updated and more relevant map.

Chapter 8

Triggers

In this chapter I discuss how the brain-body-mind is triggered by things that are associated with previous experience.

Triggers

- smells
- sounds
- images
- places, e.g. home
- people
- things
- time, seasons
- interpersonal – trust, intimacy
- pressures, stress
- specific, e.g. decisions, waiting
- internal states

AWAY / LOW

Jack, triggers and activation

[*Jack looks up from pacing as I arrive in the waiting room. His eyes swing wildly towards me but look through me.*]

Rita: Hi, Jack.

[*He nods once but says nothing. We walk to my room, and the moment I close the door he swears.*]

Jack: Some bastard nearly ran me off the road. Bloody idiot.

It looks like you're activated, Jack.

[*I take my seat, and after a moment Jack sits down too. He makes a fist at the air.*]

I'm activated alright. Bloody idiot drivers need to be locked up.

Hey, Jack, can you look at me? Can you see me? Do you know where you are right now? Jack, what colour are my eyes?

What? What are you talking about?

Jack, I want you to look around and tell me what you can see. Tell me what colour my eyes are.

I can't see them from here.

Look closer, Jack.

I don't know. Blue, a little bit grey, maybe. [*Jack leans forward.*]

And how many pomegranates can you see in the painting over my head?

Who cares?

How many, Jack?

Seven, I think. No, wait, there's one hidden behind the jug.

Thanks, Jack. Do you feel more present now?

I do. Yeah. [*Jack shakes his head.*]

You were highly activated just then. Do you know how high it was when I saw you in the waiting room? '0 to 10'?

I was about a '10'. No, maybe a '9'. I was '10' when I was going to punch that guy's lights out. He nearly drove me off the road!

Just notice if the activation increases again as you focus on the incident.

Yeah, it does.

So what is it now, '0 to 10'?

About a '6'. Maybe a '7' … '8' when I think about Mr Road Killer out there.

So just notice how quickly you become activated when you focus on the road incident and how your attention gets sucked into that memory and your lower brain becomes fully activated.

Sure does.

And yet you're just sitting here in my office and nothing dreadful is happening, it's just a memory.

[*Jack looks around the room.*]

Anything scary going on, Jack, right this moment?

No. But I think your paisley tights are a bit scary, Rita. [*We both laugh.*] What just happened when I walked into the room?

You were highly activated when you arrived because of the road incident. And I stepped you through a quick-hand version of the AIR(s) technique I use with the i-brainmap, which I'll teach you shortly. Essentially, I grabbed your attention because you were locked into the lower brain experience of terror and rage that had been triggered by the incident with the other driver. You couldn't even see me.

I don't even remember getting here.

Yes, it was hard to get your attention. Your eyes were glazed, and you couldn't focus on here and now.

Yeah, I was stuck somewhere else.

> Yes, stuck in the tunnel of distress. What I did was focus and reorient you through your senses to here and now. So by asking those questions I engaged some other parts of the brain, and the brain did the rest to work out that there was no current threat, once you could look around and see my paisley tights.
>
> The guy did nearly run me off the road. Lunatic.
>
> Just notice what happens in your body each time you focus on the incident. That can tell you if there is integration or not.
>
> My muscles tense every time I think of it.
>
> That's your body dealing with the threat as if it's still happening.
>
> But wouldn't you expect that? Considering the incident just happened on the way here and the threat was real because the guy was driving like a maniac? It's not like it happened forty years ago.
>
> That's true, and when there *is* a real threat you need your alarm on so you can deal with the threat and drive defensively. And with a recent event your brain and nervous system need some time to recover, to put all the pieces together and make sense of things.
>
> I've already made sense of it. He's an idiot.
>
> And then once it's passed, and the brain has integrated what happened, you can come back to now, spring back into recovery mode. 'Here and now' becomes the default position when the brain is integrated or integrating.

This rapid-fire reaction to a threatening event or situation trips the threat-alarm wiring in the brain, and a cascade of chemicals is released, sending messages throughout the system that cause the body to react, to fight or flee, to deal with the imminent danger. Because the brain is a memory system this experience of threat is imprinted in memory, especially in the amygdala if it is a frightening situation, with associated physiological reactions. Then if there is a reminder or trigger later, the whole quick and dirty activation occurs.

When there is real and current danger in the environment you need the threat-alarm to react quickly and effectively but also to recover quickly so you can access big-brain resources. The fight-flight-freeze response is only meant to get you out of harm's way, and then you move into recovery, decide what to do, and the brain integrates or learns from the experience.

In the above situation Jack was triggered by the incident on the road, and his alarm reaction needed to engage during that event. But then his interpretation kept it alive although the threat had passed. Interpretation and then anticipation of an event, especially an internal event of discomfort or anxiety, such as social anxiety, can perpetuate the activation once it is triggered and result in an activation cycle that becomes a never-ending loop.

Triggers

A trigger is anything in the current environment, either internal or external, that *triggers* the activation, because the brain, especially the amygdala, has made associations to some detail based on a previous experience of threat, distress or emotion. Anything can be a trigger because the brain so easily makes associations, especially during frightening or high-intensity events. That detail is then appraised and tagged with that emotional tone – such as, threatening, overwhelming, or disgusting.

Jack, trigger or activation?

Jack: I'm confused about the difference between triggers and activation. Do you use them interchangeably?

Rita: The trigger is the thing, place or sensory experience that triggers the activation process. Your boss's raised voice sounds like it's a trigger for you. When you say 'I'm triggered', yes, it's similar to saying 'I'm activated', but the focus in 'I'm triggered' is on the thing that triggered or the triggering process. Activation focuses attention on the internal experience and process and, as you will see, also links to the map. It's a different orientation, and orientation is a big part of integration, which I'll explain shortly.

Okay, so when I say 'I'm triggered' I'm powerless. It's happening *to* me. But when I say 'I'm activated' I'm tuning in to what's happening *inside* me. Is that it?

Yes, Jack. Focusing on what triggers orients outward to what is happening in the environment, which we have no control over except to avoid. Orienting to the internal experience of activation, on the other hand, opens up the possibility of choice, because the starting point of any brain change is awareness.

What triggers?

Each person has a unique set of triggers based on past experience. Below I list some of the common things that people report as triggers for re-experiencing or activation. Triggers are like tags on an experience that say to the brain, 'Remember this, remember this', so that when you experience that same tag in real time, the brain – because it's connected with an intense or extreme body memory – opens the whole map that has danger written all over it, written on the body. The alarm is 'on', activating the whole cycle. Then specific details or tags in the current environment can become imprinted on the brain and associated with this re-experiencing. Like the person who has a panic attack in the car and then associates driving and panic.

Some are conscious, but many are too subtle for us to be aware of – especially interpersonal or attachment triggers. Common triggers include:

- **Sensory triggers** such as particular smells, sights, sounds, tastes, touch or physical sensations. For instance, a war veteran may automatically duck for cover when he hears a loud bang from a car backfiring. Smell is one of the most powerful triggers because it has a direct pathway into areas in the lower brain.

- **Places, dates, times, people, seasons**. Often people are affected by anniversaries of when a trauma occurred. For instance, survivors of a bushfire can become quite anxious as summer approaches and during hot, windy days that remind the brain-body-mind of the dreadful event. A particular place, such as a car or a confined space, can be a trigger.

- **Interpersonal experience** such as intimacy, attachment, abandonment, being ignored, authority-bossiness, trust, betrayal, separation, disappointment, physical touching or closeness, someone's anger, conflict, specific kinds of relationships. Anything interpersonal can trigger lower brain activation. These are some of the most powerful triggers and yet often the most invisible, because we tend to assume it is about the other person rather than see the pattern of connection to the previous relationships tagged with trauma/overwhelm, pain or mistrust or some other intense emotion.

- **Emotional and psychological reminders** such as powerlessness, overwhelm, anxiety and any internal experience, such as hunger or heat, for instance.

- **Situations** such as making decisions, waiting, pressure, stress, conflict, being challenged or criticised.

- **Thoughts or remembering can be triggers.** Common thoughts that trigger are: 'No one loves/likes/wants me,' or 'They never ...,' 'They shouldn't ...,' 'I'm x, y, or z' (negative labels). Going over memories that are painful or defeating, such as times you made a mistake, can be a trigger. This going over things, if done to learn and change, can be a valuable part of remapping the brain, but if it's intrusive or done to punish yourself, like going back to pick a scab on a wound, it can be self-defeating.

In short, anything can trigger lower brain activation.

Triggers of early attachment

The imprint of our earliest relationships of attachment allowed our developing brain to acquire a vast knowledge that helped us adapt to our environment. Our brain was wired through mirror neurons between a parent brain and our infant brain. These pathways in the brain-body-mind are potent yet mostly inaccessible to the conscious mind.

Early attachment *is* a life-and-death situation for an infant. If the mother doesn't bond and love the infant, it could mean death (especially if you dwell in a cave and have no welfare system). These early attachment patterns are some of the most potent circuits in the brain and therefore easily triggered and activated in any relationship. Dan Siegel's book *Parenting from the Inside Out,* provides an excellent explanation of this.

Jack, home as trigger

Rita: So, tell me about the agitation at home, Jack.

Jack: As soon as I drive into the driveway I get a bit ... antsy ... I get that feeling of ants crawling in my guts. If I come inside and things are calm it seems to be okay, but if Ted's running riot and Katie is stressed it gets worse. I want to turn around and run out the door. That's when I really need a drink.

Sounds like you get triggered by home, Jack.

Home's a trigger; is that what you're saying?

Yes, I think so, Jack. You feel a sense of dread the moment you walk through the door, and you don't know what's happening except that you feel like drinking.

Yep, that's the one fact we all agree on. I need a drink.

That impulse or urge to drink could be your indicator that there is lower brain activation.

Home is the trigger, and needing a drink is the activation?

A sign of activation to avoid the internal discomfort that's arising. We'll talk about this shortly; primary and secondary activation. It's hardly surprising that home is a trigger, because your original trauma was in the home, and your childhood home was a noisy, screaming home that wasn't safe.

Yeah, but this is just Ted screaming because he doesn't want a bath, he wants to keep playing and knows it's nearly bedtime.

Yes, even though this is the normal, healthy noise of a young child, it could trigger your lower brain–body memories of home when you were a kid. In your parent's home, the yelling really did mean danger, and it sounds like your body re-experiences it when you walk through the door of this home.

That's exactly the feeling I get in my guts, a feeling that something dreadful is about to happen, especially if Ted's screaming. All I can think about is having a drink. It pisses Katie off. What a disaster. How do I stop it?

We can't stop the activation. In fact, we don't want to. That's like trying to stop a child having a nightmare. We can't control when and how it happens, but knowing what it is and recognising it when you're in it is what's important to begin with. That's why I give you the brain map. The thing is to recognise it and know that while it may be uncomfortable there's no current threat. When home is a trigger, it's particularly hard because there's no safe place, and often the body hasn't felt safe either. That's where our work is, Jack.

Let me get this straight. Are you saying that when I go home I'm remembering my home growing up?

Well, remembering implies that you're consciously remembering. This is like your body is remembering and re-experiencing the feelings of distress or an echo of those feelings from when you were a kid.

But I felt really frightened as a kid. This is a different feeling.

Yes, over time it can get wrapped up with other things, other pathways of reaction, including ways to dampen it – such as having a Scotch – and the way you interpret it. But the initial imprint may have happened fifty years ago.

Hang on, I'm not even forty.

Of course, it's quite normal to feel some agitation about lots of noise and screaming with small children around. It's just the intensity in your case and your reaction that means you probably don't know how to deal with it effectively. That's what suggests to me that it's activation. Something else that is often a symptom of early trauma is sensitivity to noise.

Oh, I've got that one all right. But my home now is nothing like the home I grew up in.

But your brain can still make the association with home. Home is a common trigger for people who've experienced early childhood trauma. Home is meant to be the safe place we 'come home to rest' each night. But when the first home wasn't safe, it can weave a thread of threat into every place you call home.

It makes me feel sick that my home is triggering something that happened almost thirty years ago.

The brain can change this, Jack. Although recognising it can make it seem worse initially. Until you're aware of it, you will automatically go into these old neural pathways. We want to help your brain update those old maps.

Invisible triggers, Helena's story

Some triggers are invisible, which makes it difficult to recognise the feelings as activation. Helena has an invisible trigger of time of day and year. She experiences some hard-to-name, vague feelings of restlessness and hopelessness in the evenings during late spring and summer.

When the body is a trigger

In some cases, such as chronic illness, pain or fatigue, the body can become a trigger. This makes integration more difficult because the person has often created sophisticated ways to disconnect from their body experience to manage the pain or illness, which is current and ongoing. So the body is cause and effect. Because of the limitations of this book I won't speak about chronic pain or illness directly, but I still use the same principles outlined in i-brainmap, although we tread much more gently. I also strongly encourage people with chronic pain and illness to develop a mindfulness practice.

Helena was sexually assaulted by a sixteen-year-old neighbour, throughout the summer she turned nine. She refers to the sexual assault as 'the games' and has never recognised it as sexual assault (because there was no penetration) or as having any major impact. 'The games' happened in the evening between about 5 and 6 o'clock when their mothers were inside cooking and before they were called inside for tea.

This time of the day and year became a trigger for Helena. Her body remembers the events from many years ago while her mind has long forgotten. As an adult Helena has developed a habit of reaching for a glass of wine at about 5 pm.

Awareness of our triggers

Often people focus on the trigger and see it as the cause of the activation. That's why it's easy to get caught in analysing or trying to recognise triggers with the intention of avoiding them. This can keep you hooked in anticipatory anxiety, vigilantly watching for potential triggers. Avoiding, controlling or even anticipating can perpetuate the loop, by giving the brain the message that the trigger is still a threat and must be avoided at all cost. This keeps the cycle active and often in the life-and-death or *dreadful* category. This fear of triggering the fear can perpetuate the cycle of anxiety; social anxiety is a good example of this, and over time the system becomes oriented to anxiety.

An analogy – leaving the baby in the department store

Imagine walking into a department store with a two-year-old in a stroller. An alarm goes off. Trying to discover why the alarm went off (is triggered), you leave the baby while you go to investigate. The child is distressed and screaming, and possibly even in danger, while you're off searching for the cause (the trigger).

Trying to find the trigger, or work out if it's a false alarm, or asking 'Why, why, why?' are like deserting the baby while you investigate. As you will see later in the i-brainmap, the thing to do is hold the baby, who is likely to be extremely distressed with all the loud noise. How you respond to the trigger is more important than what the trigger is, because how you respond is the message you give the brain, and that can either keep you in a spin or allow you to walk away from the screaming alarm.

 Awareness as it happens is the beginning of changing these patterns and taking the sting out of the trigger; but we are not trying to stop or avoid being triggered, because that tells the brain it is still dangerous.

Chapter 9
Stuck in old memory maps: hippocampus lost in action

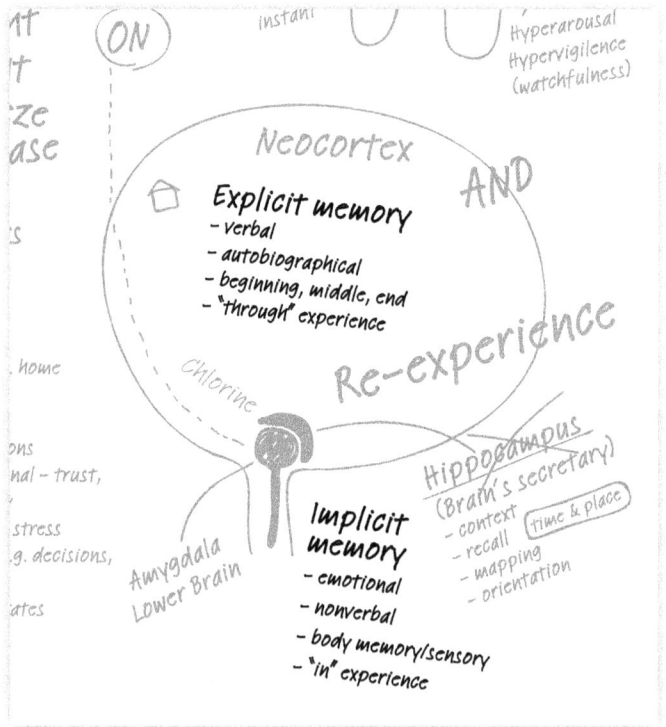

In this chapter I explain how traumatic and overwhelming events cause a glitch in memory and how this impacts on the brain. You'll get intimate with the main culprit in this glitch, the big guy of memory, the hippocampus. This material is quite dense so if you're not interested in the brain details you might want to skip to the dialogue with Jack and the *hippo* (campus) as I describe it to him in a more playful way.

Memory glitch

The brain is like a giant memory system. By 'memory' I mean the way experience shapes neural firing and connections. Each experience, especially when repeated, creates a unique network or map that then allows your system to respond to the current situation using that experience-network, or memory map. For instance, when I use the word 'tree' your brain-body-mind will open your memory map for tree, like a blueprint for tree. But if I say 'oak tree' it will be a more detailed representational and sensory map. And if I say 'oak tree in winter' or 'that oak tree in my neighbour's front yard', your system will be able to open even more precise sensory maps. If I'm a gardener I might have a different kind of map to an eight-year-old tree-climbing kid.

The brain can pluck out and open a particular memory map as required from a whole lot of maps of past experience, based on current experience, or triggers and associations. And most of the time you don't even notice all of this going on. For instance, when I pick up a pen to write I don't have to try to remember how to write and I don't think 'Is this a pen?' even though it's a blue pen and usually I use a black pen. This is an aspect of implicit memory referred to as 'procedural memory'. My brain makes the necessary associations based on previous experience so I can write with the pen, and I don't even know I'm remembering. I don't need to be consciously aware of it to do it, and I don't need to think about it or try to recall it. That's what I mean by the brain being a giant memory system: everything is a memory map, from your memory of spending summer at Grandma's farm to how to tie a shoelace or write.

Science is still uncovering exactly how memory works, but in this discussion we're interested in how memory can be affected by traumatic and overwhelming events.

Implicit and explicit memory

Memory is an extremely complex brain-body-mind function, but for our purposes we are interested in two types of memory experience and function: implicit and explicit memory.

>  There are two facets to explicit memory: semantic, which includes memory about facts and information, and episodic (sometimes referred to as declarative), which is autobiographical and about *my personal remembered story*. It is this latter aspect of explicit memory that I'll be referring to. Often I just call it 'explicit memory'.

Implicit memory is like body-experience memory. It's non-verbal and emotional; and it's sensory, through the senses. It is *in* experience: you drop into the immediate experience but usually don't have any recognition that it is memory, like the way you hold a pen or swing a golf club, or ride a bike, or the body memory of shame as you stood stuttering in front of your class; you just drop into it without thinking about it, your body knows how to do it.

If you drop into an implicit memory you can forget where you are because implicit memory is experienced as being fully in the experience. It can feel like it's forever because it's not connected to time and place but is direct experience with no context, which is why it feels like *fully and forever*. This is how a very young child experiences things. They are simply *in* the experience, without any story or naming of what is happening in that experience. It's direct experience, what I'll refer to as 'implicit memory', and it's associated with lower brain functioning.

Explicit memory involves verbal and autobiographical memories, *my story* or account of an event, and like all stories it has a beginning, a middle and an end. There is movement *through* experience as distinct from being *in* the experience with implicit memory. The important distinction here is that you can recognise explicit memory as *just a memory* because you have a sense of recalling it and know that it's not happening now and also know that it will fade or eventually end.

In an *integrated memory* of an experience, what we usually think of as memory or remembering, implicit memory and explicit memory are interconnected. You can give an account of events, tell your story, *and* feel the emotions and body or sensory memories associated with the memory, though they fade over time. Your story of the memory weaves your felt experience with words and meaning.

I will use an integrated memory of my own to explain what I mean. In my memory of my seventh birthday at my grandmother's farm I have a strong memory of Grandma's house; I can recall the sensory details of the house and garden, and all the smells; the peppercorn tree I climbed in is mapped in my body, particularly my scraped knees from the rough bark. As I recall this memory to tell it to my cousin all these sensory details spring up, although they are faded because it's quite a while ago. I might remember other details, such as the smell of lavender or the feeling of Grandma's big, cold, knobbly hands, still damp from washing up, on my cheeks as she kissed me on the forehead after I blew out the candles. I can describe it all using words and story to interweave all the bits and pieces of that experience: implicit and explicit memory are interwoven.

Memory can be fluid or fragmented

Memory is much more fluid than was once believed. Each time you remember something, it appears that the brain is reworking or reconstructing it and adding any relevant or more recent experiences. The brain pulls out that map of experience and makes a few adjustments based on current experience, continually updating the map. For instance, my memory of Grandma's farm is very different now than when I was a child. It has changed over the years as I've aged and had different experiences, and then when Grandma died it's remembered with that new piece of information wired in.

But with trauma memory or any memory that has overwhelmed the system, there is often a disconnection or *splitting between implicit and explicit memory*. This dis-integration or non-integration of memory means that the memory is not available to interact with the rest of the system in the usual way, but remains as a fragment of memory cut off from the whole. Because it is disconnected, it's experienced as a frozen, indelible memory and the brain can't recognise it as memory, and therefore no updating or integration occurs.

Bruce's fragment of memory

This is better explained through a story. Meet Bruce. He's forty. When he was five years old, his best friend drowned while they were together at the local swimming pool. In the years following the dreadful accident, Bruce has been able to tell the story (explicit memory) about the event. But then one day in the middle of summer he's driving past a swimming pool with his car window down and gets a whiff of chlorine, such a subtle whiff he hardly notices. In an instant his heart is pounding, he can't breathe, his muscles tighten and he sweats profusely. He panics and pulls off to the side of the road thinking he's having a heart attack.

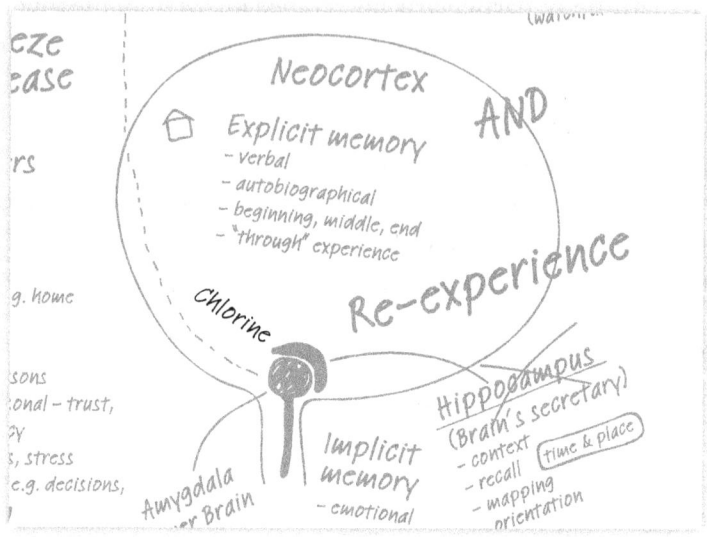

What has happened is that Bruce's lower brain or body memory has been triggered by the smell of chlorine. Bruce re-experiences the body-memory map of what happened when he was five years old. The rest of his brain doesn't recognise it as a memory but treats it as a current threat. Bruce has dropped into the experience (implicit memory) and can't access his other brain resources to help make sense of things. He also has no sense of time or place or that it will ever end. It feels like the experience is *fully and forever*.

The main problem in re-experiencing is that your brain doesn't know it's a memory but treats it as a current threat. Not knowing what is happening and having no tags that indicate that you're in a body memory is one of the main problems. It's the inability of the brain to recognise traumatic and overwhelming memory as past remembered events but re-experiences them as current that is the memory glitch in the brain that's at the heart of non-integration.

Many people re-experience an extreme, overwhelming or chronic event with no image or flash, as in a *flashback*, that indicates to them that they are re-experiencing. Instead it is a direct body experience without cues to suggest it is anything other than an immediate threat. For many people, the most challenging and disturbing part of post-traumatic stress is a lack of recognition or understanding that they have been triggered and are re-experiencing something from the past, and it's experienced as real and current because the physical symptoms are so immediate and there is no visual cue telling them it's a memory.

Sometimes a person can recognise it as past memory, but as they drop into the body-memory map the system is overwhelmed and they lose access to other resources and functions that could help the system integrate. The memory glitch I'll be referring to from here on is when the brain doesn't recognise this *re-experiencing* as memory but treats it as current.

In the story above, Bruce experiences the body sensations of shock and dread as if he's right back in the experience as a five-year-old at the swimming pool when his little friend drowned. His brain can't orient to here and now, and Bruce is lost in the experience but has no idea what is happening.

Added to this, Bruce is likely to look around to appraise what's causing his distress (the trigger), because that's what the brain does as part of its survival-protection system, and then his brain makes an association with what's going on during the experience. The brain learns what's safe and what's dangerous by making these associations and appraisals and then using that experience or memory-map to assess a situation or environment later. The only thing Bruce knows for sure is that he's in a car, driving. So it's possible that Bruce will think that driving or being in a car has something to do with his panic, and driving and panic become linked.

Perhaps Bruce will visit his GP and have some tests, only to be told it was a panic attack. If he's lucky, he'll be referred to a good psychologist or counsellor for some help. If he's unlucky, he may end up on Benzodiazapines and rapidly become addicted, so that now he has a new problem to deal with.

In short, Bruce's brain is unable to make the connection with the implicit memory of when he was five years old, but that memory is still very alive and active in his body and lower brain.

The hippocampus exposed

To explain why Bruce's brain can't make the connection between implicit and explicit memory, and why that memory was never integrated in the first place, I need to familiarise you with another part of the brain. This is one of the most extraordinary parts of the brain: the hippocampus. So before we proceed with Bruce's story I'd like to give you the dirt on our friend the hippocampus (and we certainly want the hippocampus to be our friend) because it's central to this whole brain story.

When in a healthy state and interconnected and linked with the hippocampus, our memory maps are dynamic and interactive networks of neural firing, continually being reoriented and reconnected within the current context or environment as it changes. Some maps involve cognitive representations, but there are many that don't, that are purely implicit, lower brain body-memory maps.

Interactive mapping as it occurs in a healthy, integrated brain is the hippocampus connecting the dots of maps with the current context.

Think of maps as dots and you could say the hippocampus joins the dots, or perhaps, more correctly, connects different parts of the brain so the whole system is interconnected. It's like the hippocampus is a kind of translator or mediator, an interconnector between lots of different parts or functions of the brain.

Each dot on the memory map is a neuron firing: it lights up and then hooks up with the next neuron, creating a *dotty picture,* the memory of interconnected dots. Of course it's much more complex than this, but essentially the brain is a binary system, and neurons are either on or off. Why some neurons fire and others don't is like a complex maths equation of probability that will probably keep scientists occupied for another couple of centuries.

One of the main functions of the hippocampus is to tell the brain which memory map to use in the current context. This gives the brain a way to orient, like having the coordinates of time and place, and therefore it's able to respond to the current context, or experience. Otherwise the world is just a jumble of stimuli coming at us, or from inside us.

You could say that the hippocampus holds open the map of the memory *and at the same time* is able to orient to here and now. This *contexting* and orienting is hardly understood because it happens in our interaction with the world and not in a lab, so it's very difficult to observe or measure.

Stuck in old memory maps: hippocampus lost in action

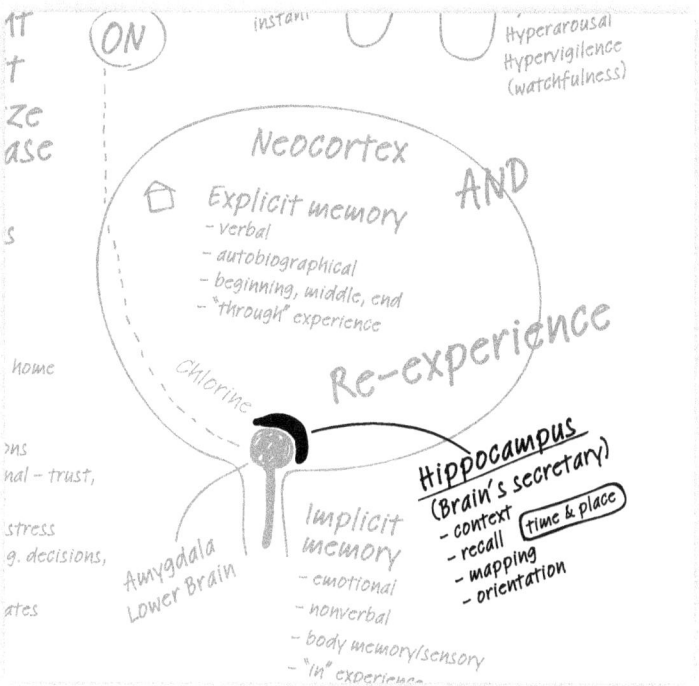

The hippocampus is sometimes referred to as the brain's secretary or what we'd probably call the admin system these days. It's responsible for, among other things, *context* (time and place), *recall*, interactive *mapping* and spatial navigation, or what I call *orientation*.

To explain the hippocampus in action lets go back to my seventh birthday at Grandma's farm. When I'm experiencing being seven at Grandma's farm, my hippocampus is recording the experience: sights, smells, emotions, thoughts and interpersonal experiences. These scraps of memory are dotted throughout different parts of the brain. Some sensory data will be lost rapidly because it's not appraised as important, but during extreme or significant events detailed sensory data becomes strongly imprinted, like the smell of chlorine, and can then act as a trigger for that body-memory map.

I don't use the term 'mental maps' or 'cognitive maps', which many writers do, because those terms imply that the maps are more conscious and visual than they are usually experienced. Often the memory maps associated with traumatic and overwhelming events are just a body-memory map, implicit memory, with no images or associated mental representations.

Storied memory

It's somewhat misleading to talk about memory as 'stored' because it implies that there's a little file of Grandma's farm somewhere in my brain. But I don't have a static file in brain storage called 'Grandma's farm' that my brain can open up. Instead I have lots of bits of information scattered throughout the brain, and then when I want to recall that day at Grandma's, my brain joins all the relevant dots of that memory map and I can access and remember the experience. The memory is changeable given the circumstances or context of remembering. A more accurate term for this process of memory is '*storied* memory' rather than 'stored memory'. Remembering that day when I was at my grandmother's funeral, for instance, will be very different to remembering it when I was a child or even now many years after her death.

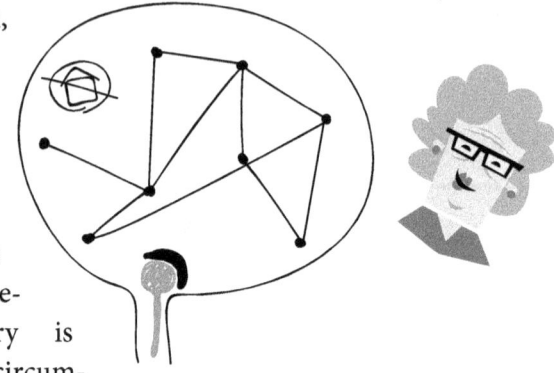

The hippocampus and the i-brainmap

Later, as I 're-member' that experience of Grandma's farm, the hippocampus pulls all the relevant bits of information together in the current context. That is, I'm sitting here in this room *AND* I'm remembering. I have a sense of recall; I know I'm sitting here (context) right now *AND* remembering Grandma's farm on the day of my seventh birthday. The memory has faded because the experience happened a long time ago, but it's as if I have a map of the memory *AND* I can move around it, examining or orienting to different parts as I choose, *AND* I know I'm here in this room describing it to you. I can put the memory down and pick it up again. I know where I am in relation to the memory (orientation). Here and now is the primary point of orientation. The *AND pathway*, as I call it, is a very important point because it's essential for integrating past traumatic and overwhelming experiences and involves the function of the hippocampus.

Of story and metaphor

The term *storied memory*, or *storied in the body* is a more accurate description of experience and function of memory than *stored memory,* which implies a static block of memory. *Storied* suggests interconnectivity and potential changeability. Story, although it may become frozen, as trauma memory does, has threads and strings like a delicate web interlacing and connecting thoughts and deep schemas, emotions, impulses and sensory experience throughout the brain-body-mind. Untangling this web to allow the brain to rewire is part of the process of integration.

Another term that suggests the same fluidity and connection with body is *embodied metaphor*. An effective metaphor is often surprising yet familiar; it makes sense yet keeps the memory alive, the same yet new, and connects or orients to the body through the senses, such as a surprising image.

Hippo offline

During traumatic or overwhelming experiences the *hippocampus goes offline,* and implicit and explicit memory become disconnected; you could say there is no AND pathway. So when some associated trigger occurs in the environment – like chlorine for our friend Bruce – we drop into re-experiencing the body memory, but our hippocampus can't recognise the body-memory map, or it's out to lunch and doesn't let the amygdala know that it's just a memory, so the system reads it as a current threat and acts accordingly to protect us, preparing the body to escape.

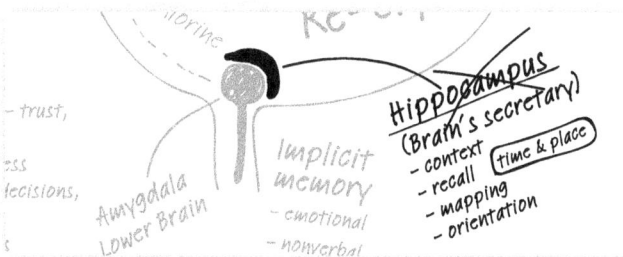

During trauma the hippocampus is flooded with cortisol; you could say that the secretary goes out to lunch or its attention is elsewhere. While it's out, or looking the other way, all those sensory details and feelings experienced during the event are laid down in memory, particularly in lower brain or body memory; in other words, it's embodied.

Jack, another perspective on the hippo

Jack: It all sounds very complicated, Rita. But I'm not sure how all this fits for me.

Rita: Okay. Let's take the experience of coming home. When you were a kid and your dad was cruel and violent your system was overwhelmed. Does that make sense, Jack?

Yep, and my fight-flight thing came on.

Yes exactly, like a little guard dog in your system trying to protect you from harm. But when this was happening the hippocampus, let's call it the slack controller, was out to lunch.

Why the slack controller? Is that like the fat controller in Thomas the Tank?

Yes and no. The fat controller, from memory, is pretty efficient. Is that right?

You bet. He keeps things running smoothly, ship-shape you might say. I guess that would be train-shape? Doesn't have quite the same ring.

Yes, the slack controller is very efficient when he's on the job. It's like he sits up in his little tower watching and directing all the sensory trains, spike trains and even trains of thought. He has the maps and knows where things need to go and which maps to use to keep the flow of traffic running smoothly.

That sounds like the fat controller.

Yes, but our slack controller is easily pulled off the job by this drug called cortisol, and sometimes divided attention, perhaps because it's just too much to take in. So he focuses on some small detail, like the smell of diesel, during an overwhelming event, and, as I said, he goes out to lunch, gets slack.

Then I guess there are trains going every which way with no one in the tower, or maybe some apprentice who doesn't know which maps to use with which train.

Yes, exactly, Jack.

Okay, so when I arrive home my slack controller aka hippocampus has deserted ship, and I have chaos on my hands with maps open all over the place, but no one knows which map to use.

Added to that, the map that's on top, that gets all your attention because it has danger written all over it, is the one that's driving things, and so the amygdala starts ringing the alarm –

And, let me guess ... there's no hippo home to tell them all it's a false alarm and get things moving and flowing again.

You got it, Jack.

No wonder Ted loves playing Thomas so much. He must be learning how to wire his little brain.

[*Laughing.*]

Growing the hippo

Hippocampal damage or shrinkage is indicated in most mental health problems, including post-traumatic stress, schizophrenia, bipolar disorder and conditions involving memory problems such as Alzheimer's.

So if you want to grow your hippocampus, and size does matter, put away your GPS, get the map out and give your brain a workout. In a well-known experiment with London cabbies, it was found that the cabbies' hippocampi increased in size when they learned 'the knowledge' to navigate the intricate web of streets of London. This is because the hippocampus is responsible for spatial navigation and orientation. Grow your hippocampus whenever you can, or better still leave your car at home and walk. Exercise, particularly walking, has been shown to increase hippocampal size and increase brain-derived neurotropic factor (BDNF), which is associated with neurogenesis.

Chapter 10
The gesture of integration

In this chapter I explain the dynamic between activation and integration in the language of the lower brain, an experiential story, embodied in a gesture, or embodied metaphor.

Explaining what happens in the language of the lower brain

Now I'll explain the process of moving through activation towards integration using a hand gesture that I call the *gesture of integration*. I want to give you an embodied metaphor, a more storied, experiential and gestural version of the brain dynamics in the i-brainmap using my hands, because it's closer to the language of the lower brain and easily remembered. Talking to the lower brain is the same as talking to a two-year-old. Stories, games, songs, pictures and movement are part of their language as well as anything repetitive, sequential and rhythmical.

Often when clients come back after I've shown them the hand gesture of integration they're using it themselves, sometimes not even consciously.

Gesture of integration: naming the parts

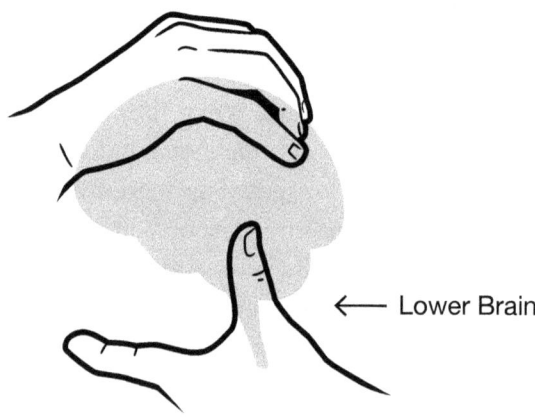

My thumb represents the lower brain and it includes the amygdala or threat-alarm system and other subcortical structures involved in implicit memory. Let's call it the 'child brain' because this function of the brain behaves like a two-year-old. It's emotional rather than rational, and impulsive or instinctive in that it's directed by body responses and needs, especially fear, and it is *in* experience without time or place. Another reason I call it child brain is that when it's distressed it's like a child having a tantrum or a nightmare, and most of you know you can't reason a child out of an intense emotional reaction while they're in the middle of it.

The brain functions associated with implicit memory develop up until the age of about two, so your earliest non-verbal experiences and memories, especially about fear and safety, which are mediated through attachment with caregivers, are embodied through implicit memory. Then, throughout your life, intense emotional, overwhelming or traumatic memories are stored like frozen berries in implicit memory, lower brain–body or child brain. The amygdala, your threat-alarm centre, is a key player in this function of the memory because it tags memories as dangerous or emotionally significant setting off an alert/alarm response.

And we could refer to the big brain or neocortex as the 'adult brain' or smart brain. It's rational and reasonable, like upper management or CEO; it plans and makes decisions just like an adult.

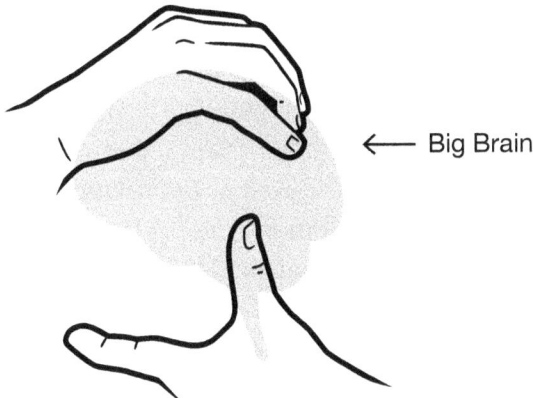

The nightmare

When the child brain is distressed and overwhelmed the brain is operating as a split-brain system and there is no connection between the child and adult because the mediator, the hippocampus, is offline.

When you re-experience a traumatic event, like when Bruce smelled the chlorine, it's experienced by the child brain as if it's having a nightmare. It is *in* the nightmare and experiences it as real and current. If the adult (brain) walks in and says, 'It's just a nightmare, go back to sleep,' then leaves the room, it won't make any difference to a two-year-old. The child brain is still distressed. Words alone, reasoning and intellectual understanding of what is happening, won't soothe a distressed two-year-old. To soothe the lower brain you need to use the *language* of the child brain. That language is detailed sensory awareness of here and now, and anything that soothes a two-year-old soothes the lower brain, such as rocking, sucking, touching and holding.

The helpful adult brain

The helpful adult brain recognises, or acknowledges, the child's distress and makes it explicit by naming it, 'Oh, you're scared because you've had a nightmare.' This helps the child learn the connection between nightmare and fear so the child begins to understand what's happening. This is different to getting into the story of it, or analysing the nightmare. By naming and making it explicit – 'This is a nightmare' – and giving it a cue word 'nightmare', it begins to establish a context or map for the experience of distress, something the child (brain) can orient to later when it happens again to make sense of the experience and not get so lost in it. (Our cue word is *activation*.)

And we need to switch on the light. Although this requires an adult-brain initiative, the light itself is more likely the hippocampus and friends – calling on the slack controller. The hippocampus needs to be able to orient the attention into the present to interrupt the loop of distress or activation cycle. This integration Zone is like a light of attention that can mediate between the child brain and the adult brain and has to be 'on' to make new connections and rewire the experience.

We switch on the light (the hippocampus) as the nightmare is happening, which switches on other functions and potential pathways in the brain. Before you can properly interrupt and soothe the child brain you need to get its attention or it continues to be hijacked by the distress of the nightmare. If you go straight to soothing without interrupting and getting the child brain's attention, the distress is alleviated for the moment but won't necessarily integrate the experience to change things in the future or in a way that the brain can generalise.

The gesture of integration

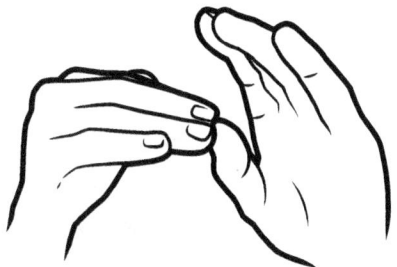

The adult brain, with the help of the hippocampus, gently, firmly and repeatedly interrupts the child's attention from the nightmare. This isn't grabbing the attention, as happens in distraction, because that can frighten the child brain, giving it the message that something is wrong. Quietly and persistently you interrupt the pathway of the nightmare or distress. At the same time you *reorient* the child brain's attention into the room, to what's familiar and safe and here and now, through focusing on detailed sensory awareness. 'Look at Teddy. Look at his funny button-eye. Remember when he lost his eye and we sewed it on?' 'Where's Jemima gone?' asks the adult, pointing to the shelf lined with toys, engaging the child, asking simple questions (not about the nightmare), and gently, firmly and repetitively bringing their attention into the room, interrupting the pathway or nightmare they're stuck in.

With repetition the attention gradually settles into here and now, letting go of the nightmare as the adult brain soothes the child, comforting, talking softly, rocking, giving them something to suck.

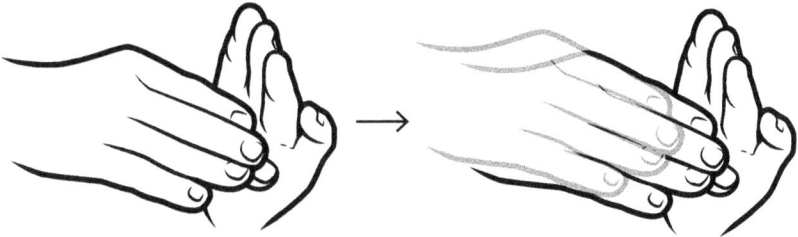

By acknowledging, interrupting and reorienting while soothing, the helpful adult brain brings the child brain's attention out of the nightmare and into the present, through detailed sensory awareness and engagement. It doesn't interrogate the child about what's in the nightmare or analyse the nightmare when the child is distressed. The priority is to soothe and comfort the child brain, showing the child that it's safe, and to do this the adult brain first has to get the child's attention, gently and firmly and often repeatedly.

Most adults will instinctively rock the child, give them a dummy or the 'blanky', or perhaps sing a favourite song or nursery rhyme. Rocking releases endorphins in the brain stem. Many people eat, suck or chew on something or rock themselves when they're distressed, because it's sensory soothing they need. These were the ways we were soothed by our parents, along with interpersonal contact and probably soft words like 'It's okay, there, there,' when we were babies. The message we want to give the small, frightened child brain is, 'You feel scared because you're having a nightmare *and* you're here now in your room *and* I'm here with you *and* you're safe.' This is the message that promotes integration.

 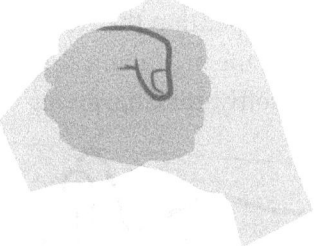

Beating up the child brain

Sometimes, because re-experiencing the nightmare has happened so often, the adult brain can get frustrated and start beating up on the child brain or trying to suppress it. It says something like, 'Stop it! Stop it!' or 'Get over it! What is wrong with you, you idiot?' and so on, which is like beating up the child brain.

The gesture of integration

This distresses the child brain even more. It's like yelling at a child for having a nightmare. Some people also try to use top-down strategies when they feel activated or overwhelmed, such as challenging their thinking as irrational or using self-talk. Sometimes these strategies work, but often people get extremely frustrated with themselves when these techniques don't work, or work initially then stop working, causing a rebound effect, which increases their sense of feeling powerless and defeated. This can be the equivalent of giving the child a flashcard when they're highly distressed or having a nightmare. It may distract momentarily, but it doesn't soothe or teach what a nightmare is. A momentary distraction doesn't teach you that you can get through this, so that when it happens again you can recognise it and soothe yourself or be more easily soothed. In short, it doesn't encourage brain integration.

Jack, interrupting vs. distracting

Jack: So I distract myself, right?

Rita: It may seem like distraction, but this has a different intention. The question you always want to ask is, what message am I giving my brain?

So, what message am I giving my brain with distraction? At least I'm not stuck in the nightmare.

Yes, true. Initially distracting or even stopping it may be effective and adaptive because it gets you out of the nightmare, but it can become an avoid-escape strategy. What you use to distract yourself can become an addiction; like technology such as computer games or Facebook for some people.

It helps with Ted, though, when he's having a tantrum. Usually you can distract him with Thomas the Tank Engine. It takes a while, but he can't resist Thomas.

The brain and the map

But I would say that what you're doing is getting Ted's attention, interrupting.

I still don't get how it's different.

When you're distracting Ted, how are you feeling? Calm or overwhelmed or maybe angry?

Fairly calm. I think it's kind of funny. I'm a lot calmer than Katie when he's having a tanty in the supermarket.

But when you're distracting your own brain when you're re-experiencing something, there's probably a bit of panic or perhaps even anger about it, do you think?

Oh yeah, I'm desperate to get myself out of that nightmare, and pissed off that it's happening and I can't stop it.

So there's a sort of grabbing onto anything that might get you out of that experience?

Damn right. Whatever works. Scotch is best.

So, that frustration and panic to escape the experience is the issue, not so much what you do. If you distract yourself calmly and repeatedly, as you do with Ted, you're still giving the brain the message that everything is okay. But if you're grabbing onto anything to pull your attention out of the experience, driven by panic and the need to escape, the brain reads the experience as still threatening – 'Keep it going, boys,' it's saying – and the alarm keeps ringing. It may subside eventually, but the experience of threat-alarm has been reinforced, and the only way you have to deal with it is escape. The loop is perpetuated.

I don't know if I can tell the difference. It's easy to stay calm with Ted because I know he's upset or tired or wants a lolly. I'm in charge, but when it's me going off it's like I'm Ted and I don't know how to help myself.

That's exactly what is happening, Jack. We could call your lower brain 'Ted' or 'Ted brain', because you're the two-year-old and have lost access to your adult-brain resources.

But don't you distract me in here sometimes? Isn't that distraction?

Good point. I suppose it looks like distraction, but I see it as getting your attention. I'm you when you're Ted, if that makes sense.

Yep. You do the parent thing when I'm in Ted brain.

Exactly. But, like you, I can see that you're distressed and caught in Ted brain, and I'm getting your attention, but I feel calm and I'm just quietly – and firmly and gently – bringing your attention back to the room again and again. I'm not going, 'Oh my God, he's activated! I have to get him out of the burning building.' I know you're safe, and I want to get that message through to you.

That's what you did when I arrived after the road thing, right?

Yep. It's as if I became your mediator, perhaps like the hippocampus, for your brain during activation. I recognised that you were distressed and acknowledged what was happening and got your attention so that you connected with me, and your brain got the message that it's safe and there's no current threat. I might have to repeat it till I can interrupt and get your attention and reorient you to the room, where it's safe – except for paisley tights, of course. The brain does the rest, which is to establish connection between child brain and adult brain. This is the essence of brain integration and involves the hippocampus being active and connecting and linking up with brain function involved in directing attention.

Well, I know it works. Yes, it was more like you were getting my attention, holding my attention, like you kept knocking on the door. More steady than distracting. No ... more both. I could still feel angry about what that guy did, but I could see you and hear what you were saying, after a while anyway. It was like a fog lifted as you did it. I think I'm getting it.

I think when you distract yourself with the intention to escape there is no AND. You're just leaping into another map and shutting down the scary map as fast as you can. Once the map is closed it can't be integrated. Or without the AND there's no chance for integration. And integration is what we're after. It's all about integration.

But I can't take you home with me to get my attention when I'm activated, can I?

No, but I don't think it would be helpful if I was there all the time.

Why's that? Apart from the obvious.

Because your brain would become dependent on me doing it. The brain is lazy or efficient, depending on how you look at it.

Or orient to it?

Yep, orient. Touché, Jack! The brain won't do anything more than it has to, because it has so many demands on its resources. So if we don't stretch and challenge it, it will just do the same old thing or let someone else if they're willing. Let me ask you this, do you want to be dealing with Ted's tantrums for the rest of his life?

No way. Imagine dragging a six-foot hunk – I'm sure he'll have my good looks – out of the supermarket. I don't think so.

So in some ways it's not just about helping Ted now. You want to teach him to soothe himself, so that when he gets upset he can regulate internal experience.

Well, that's not how I'd put it, but yes. I want him to be able to calm himself down.

And he's learning that through your response to him when he's upset. The brain is interpersonal, and in many ways his little brain is learning from your brain.

That's a scary thought.

He is getting thousands of years of human evolution through his interaction with your and Katie's brains – language, interpersonal skills, self-care; managing his emotions is just one of them.

It's amazing seeing him learn new words and put things together. Such a funny little kid. That's why I want to learn not to lose it, not get activated. I want to be a good dad for Ted.

Remember we're not trying to stop activation, Jack. How do you think it would be for Ted if you got furious at him when he has a tantrum or gets frightened?

Even scarier. He needs me to be firm and quiet. If I get mad he just gets more upset. It's happened when I've been really stressed. Ugly.

So coming back to your Ted brain, the same applies. Let me ask the same question of your own Ted brain. When you get mad at it for getting activated or distressed how do you think it responds?

Oh, I really get that. But it feels so real when it's happening.

It's real but not current. What I mean is that the intensity is over and above what is required given the current context.

So, to sum up, we want your brain to: learn to recognise activation; orient to the i-brainmap and say, 'Oh, just this again'; interrupt; reorient to here and now; and soothe the lower brain. You might distract it once you've interrupted the pattern but not as an avoid-escape pathway. Over time, the brain will integrate and change itself because you have a different experience when you're activated. It isn't just intellectual knowledge but an integrated understanding that develops from the bottom up through direct experience. It *belongs* to you, you know it directly. This allows you to respond differently or orient differently when you're activated.

Chapter 11
Primary activation

In this and the next chapter I describe some of the common experiences of primary and secondary activation. This isn't a tick list like an assessment but an invitation to become curious about your own experience of lower brain activation so you can begin to recognise when you might be activated as it happens. Awareness as it happens is the most important first point of integration, without which the brain can't make the necessary connections but will keep doing what it's always done. If that's working, great, keep doing what you're doing. But if you feel stuck in an old neural loop perhaps this description will help make sense of what is happening and provide a new way through.

An overview of activation

The biological reactions of threat-alarm are hardwired into the brain. But what triggers you and how you react is what I refer to as activation. How you interpret the activation is influenced by your earliest environment, your culture, gender and personality and, of course, your experience. I divide activation into two dimensions. This is somewhat artificial because when you experience activation it's usually a blur of reactions that I call the 'activation cycle'. Part of the work that follows the explanation of the i-brainmap is tracking and mapping your unique activation cycles.

Although an activation cycle can vary in response to different circumstances or triggers, often there are loops and patterns that repeat. The other noticeable thing about activation is that everyone seems to have a habitual orientation; that is, some people will focus more on the triggers, some on emotional or physical reactions, while others are more identified with their thoughts, or stories they have, about the experience.

The way you habitually orient to anything can become an over-identification, *this is me*, rather than *this is an experience I'm having*. Over-identification allows no room for curiosity or brain change. At the other end of the spectrum is avoidance, denial or ignorance of what is happening.

uring integration there is a different kind of
 crying, and brings relief. Often people
 as if it has permission to cry and express
safety grows.

 hard to concentrate or take in information
ng as if there's a rattlesnake under your
n that damn rattlesnake while trying to listen
 is saying. This is why kids who experience
 do well at school. They are the ones staring
le to sit still. They, and their teachers, often
 stupid or wicked, but it's usually that they
e information and are fighting demons that no
ead, they pick up other signals such as that the
 little Johnny in the seat in front is feeling upset
ey are often hypersensitive to emotions and
 unable to take in the facts and figures. Or some
ssive concentration on particular things while
 is under their nose.

you can't concentrate when you hear something
ember it. Added to this, the usual memory systems
ough trauma, which can affect encoding and retrieval
erything is laced with fear and suspicion.

nce – Either you can't get to sleep or you wake up
ht and can't get back to sleep. Because the lower brain
for housekeeping, when there is any disruption to it
disruption to basic functions such as sleeping and eating
As well, sleep is when the brain integrates, but if an
 triggered that releases cortisol it can agitate the system,
sleep.

ight sensitivity – It's as if the system is already overloaded,
with one more thing such as a neighbour using a power tool
y afternoon can feel catastrophic, like life and death.

en muscles are chronically contracted because you're
 relax, pain develops. Pain can be generalised, as in
lgia, or concentrated around activation points associated
t-flight physiology. Particular hot spots include the neck,
r and jaw, often resulting in headaches, or teeth problems
enching. The psoas is a powerful muscle that contracts to get
ing, but when it is chronically tight it can cause lower back

Awareness, on the other hand, is seeing what is really happening. It's like sitting on the edge of the activation cycle, seeing exactly what is happening as it arises but not getting caught in it. Awareness as it happens is the essence of what disentangles the mind from the activation cycle. Discussion after the fact or anticipating what will happen doesn't allow your brain to change or integrate the experience. In other words the only time the brain can change the map of that particular experience is when it's open, and experiencing it. Therefore, here I offer you some common expressions of activation to help you recognise when it's happening.

The difference between primary and secondary activations

Primary activations are unrefined and more immediate direct experience, and secondary activations are your reactions to the distressing internal experiences of primary activation. Primary activations or body experiences are tied to emotions, especially primary emotions such as fear and anger, and are at the heart of the activation. Secondary activations are like the covering: strengthening and protecting the cycle but stopping you getting to the cause.

There is no neat divide between primary and secondary activations. They tend to bleed into each other, which is why I use just one word, *activation*, for all of them. That's our cue word, like 'nightmare', to switch on the light in the brain during activation. Once you start working with the secondary activations, the primary activations often surface and you may experience them differently.

Primary activations

Primary activations include physical and emotional reactions, involving direct experiences of the body. Primary activations are closest to the language of the lower brain.

It's important to note that all of these reactions are a normal part of life. We all get anxious, and that's appropriate if, for instance, we're making a speech to several hundred people. The adrenalin rush gets our brain working in peak performance. But in the extreme or if they are chronic, these reactions can become debilitating.

Primary activations include (but are not limited to) the following:

Anxiety – can be experienced on a continuum from nervousness through to panic attacks. This is like the flight response.

Anger – from irritability through to rage. This is like the fight response. Another dimension of the fight response is *defending*, like the automatic defending of your territory or self or someone or something, such as a mother-dog defending her pups.

Dissociation – can be likened to the freeze response. Dissociative experiences range from vague fuzzy-headedness to experiences of depersonalisation, derealisation, numbing, shutting down, day-dreaming and so on. Dissociation is often experienced as disconnection from self or the world.

Passivity – is like appeasing and pleasing. It's fitting in and conforming to what others want or need. It's like giving in or giving up, surrendering and just going along with what others want rather than believing you have a choice to say 'no'; it's keeping your head down, feeling helpless. This also become a secondary activation of hopelessness or defeat as you feel unable to change anything, or like a victim of circumstance – 'life happens to me' – rather than finding the agency to influence your life. It can also be associated with compulsive caring or helping, as we notice with Mary.

Splitting – a feeling of being split. This can be experienced as a feeling of internal disconnection, such as a split between thinking (big brain) and emotion (associated with lower brain), or a split between certain qualities, such as inferiority and arrogance, creating a polarisation or all-or-nothing. Splitting can also be experienced externally, as feeling disconnected from others and/or self. It can be experienced as a push–pull between two polarities, such as feeling high then shut down or depressed. This jumping to extremes can be a sign of non-integration in the brain-body-mind.

Isolation, loneliness, withdrawal, being an outsider – feeling separate or disconnected from others or somehow outside, as if there is a thin film or a great divide between you and the world. It can happen whether you're in relationships, surrounded by friends and family, or sitting on a beach alone. It can be experienced as a blow from a cricket bat, usually in the stomach, or a feeling that can hang around your neck like a dead fish, making it hard to smell the sweetness of your relationships. It is perhaps the most avoided or denied form of activation, and often underlies a compulsion to find love at any cost. Many with this form of activation become writers!

pain. Chronic tension in your body can affect digestion and immune response – in fact, almost any system in the body.

Wired and tired – Your system is on high alert, ready to deal with the threat (wired or accelerating), but you're just sitting at the table eating dinner trying to act cool (brake), all the while watching for the snake. This is sometimes described as having the brake and the accelerator on at the same time.

Exhaustion – Being continually wired can lead to exhaustion, to chronic fatigue. Very powerful chemicals are released during fight-flight that are meant to come in short bursts to get you moving to survive the threat, and then switch off and recover. If they continue to flood the system, they burn it out.

Hopelessness – Often people describe a sense of hopelessness when this wired and tired feeling is going on because they don't know why it's happening or what to do about it.

Picture of depression – When we add these last three together, wired and tired, exhaustion and hopelessness, we get a picture of depression, but usually it is a long journey down the slippery slope of this whole stack of experiences that results in symptoms associated with depression.

Most of these reactions or primary activations are adaptive in the right situation. But when the brain-body becomes stuck in these responses they become problematic and have a ripple effect impacting on the whole system as you attempt to manage these difficult and painful internal states.

Jack, I'm always activated

Jack: But it happens to me all the time, Rita. I'm always activated.

Rita: Tell me what you've been noticing, Jack.

I was shell-shocked when I started to understand how my father's cruelty still affects me. I'd always known it, but I didn't understand it. I've spent my life trying to forget it. It's like a floodlight has been turned on in my head.

Yes, sometimes we can know something in an intellectual way but the knowing doesn't really belong to us. It sounds like you're starting to understand it through direct experience. And what else are you noticing, Jack?

I notice how irritable and on edge I am all the time, and I do mean all the time. I spoke to Katie about it. She cried when I told her what I was seeing. Since we talked about it something has changed between us – for the better. We've started planning a proper holiday, something we haven't done since we were married.

That's great, Jack.

Yeah, that side of things is great. But the problem is, now that I'm aware of it, it's driving me crazy that I'm like this. I want to stop it.

It's common to focus on activation once you understand what activation is and become aware that it's happening. Your brain has a new understanding now, a new map, but your brain has oriented to avoiding fear for years, so fear still runs it for a while. And it sounds like you've been trying to use the i-brainmap to stop the activation. That's like simply pasting the new map over the old maps, which are still strong, like roads you've taken a thousand times. Instead your brain needs to rework and integrate your maps.

Stop-stop-stop the activation

Jack: Okay, so to stop the activation I have to stop trying to stop it?

Rita: Just notice the emphasis on stopping, Jack.

I do want it to stop, it's dreadful. It's even worse now that I'm aware of it. I'm not so sure that Scotch therapy wasn't the best treatment for me.

In the short term Scotch therapy was great, but perhaps it had become not so adaptive?

Maybe. But drinking was sure better than this.

Okay, Jack. So when your intention is to stop – even if you're pretending it isn't, you can't trick your brain – the pathway is strengthened.

It's like I'm trying to trick my brain by pretending I'm not trying to stop it, but really I'm trying to stop it. Funny, huh?

We're all pretty funny that way. We try to avoid or hide what is difficult or uncomfortable, and in fact we're inadvertently wiring it in more tightly. In fact, what we're doing with the brain map approach is learning to get more comfortable with feeling uncomfortable.

Awareness, on the other hand, is seeing what is really happening. It's like sitting on the edge of the activation cycle, seeing exactly what is happening as it arises but not getting caught in it. Awareness as it happens is the essence of what disentangles the mind from the activation cycle. Discussion after the fact or anticipating what will happen doesn't allow your brain to change or integrate the experience. In other words the only time the brain can change the map of that particular experience is when it's open, and experiencing it. Therefore, here I offer you some common expressions of activation to help you recognise when it's happening.

The difference between primary and secondary activations

Primary activations are unrefined and more immediate direct experience, and secondary activations are your reactions to the distressing internal experiences of primary activation. Primary activations or body experiences are tied to emotions, especially primary emotions such as fear and anger, and are at the heart of the activation. Secondary activations are like the covering: strengthening and protecting the cycle but stopping you getting to the cause.

There is no neat divide between primary and secondary activations. They tend to bleed into each other, which is why I use just one word, *activation*, for all of them. That's our cue word, like 'nightmare', to switch on the light in the brain during activation. Once you start working with the secondary activations, the primary activations often surface and you may experience them differently.

Primary activations

Primary activations include physical and emotional reactions, involving direct experiences of the body. Primary activations are closest to the language of the lower brain.

It's important to note that all of these reactions are a normal part of life. We all get anxious, and that's appropriate if, for instance, we're making a speech to several hundred people. The adrenalin rush gets our brain working in peak performance. But in the extreme or if they are chronic, these reactions can become debilitating.

Primary activations include (but are not limited to) the following:

Anxiety – can be experienced on a continuum from nervousness through to panic attacks. This is like the flight response.

Anger – from irritability through to rage. This is like the fight response. Another dimension of the fight response is *defending*, like the automatic defending of your territory or self or someone or something, such as a mother-dog defending her pups.

Dissociation – can be likened to the freeze response. Dissociative experiences range from vague fuzzy-headedness to experiences of depersonalisation, derealisation, numbing, shutting down, day-dreaming and so on. Dissociation is often experienced as disconnection from self or the world.

Passivity – is like appeasing and pleasing. It's fitting in and conforming to what others want or need. It's like giving in or giving up, surrendering and just going along with what others want rather than believing you have a choice to say 'no'; it's keeping your head down, feeling helpless. This also become a secondary activation of hopelessness or defeat as you feel unable to change anything, or like a victim of circumstance – 'life happens to me' – rather than finding the agency to influence your life. It can also be associated with compulsive caring or helping, as we notice with Mary.

Splitting – a feeling of being split. This can be experienced as a feeling of internal disconnection, such as a split between thinking (big brain) and emotion (associated with lower brain), or a split between certain qualities, such as inferiority and arrogance, creating a polarisation or all-or-nothing. Splitting can also be experienced externally, as feeling disconnected from others and/or self. It can be experienced as a push–pull between two polarities, such as feeling high then shut down or depressed. This jumping to extremes can be a sign of non-integration in the brain-body-mind.

Isolation, loneliness, withdrawal, being an outsider – feeling separate or disconnected from others or somehow outside, as if there is a thin film or a great divide between you and the world. It can happen whether you're in relationships, surrounded by friends and family, or sitting on a beach alone. It can be experienced as a blow from a cricket bat, usually in the stomach, or a feeling that can hang around your neck like a dead fish, making it hard to smell the sweetness of your relationships. It is perhaps the most avoided or denied form of activation, and often underlies a compulsion to find love at any cost. Many with this form of activation become writers!

Decision-making – can become difficult as a result of the experience of splitting, as you jump between each possibility but can't find the middle ground. (There can be added pressure if this primary activation is tied to secondary activation, where there is a fear of getting it wrong or making mistakes. This combination can immobilise you.)

Shame – a feeling that there is something wrong with you. 'I'm not okay,' 'I'm different' or 'I'm not normal,' 'I'm damaged': these are common residual experiences following trauma, especially if the trauma is interpersonal in nature. Feelings of shame can be magnified by 'splitting' and disconnection from others. Most people experience the physiology of shame as distinct from a cognitive reaction, which is more associated with guilt. It's likely that shame is tied to survival, probably because in tribal times to be shamed meant possible exclusion from the tribe, which meant death. For most people guilt is experienced as a more cognitive, behavioural and psychological phenomenon, more about others and external events, whereas shame is deeply buried and usually tied to your sense of self as not being okay, as being flawed in some way. See the work of Brené Brown for more on shame.

Trust and safety confusion – this is an inability to read safety and danger. You can ignore danger when there is a real threat, or feel unsafe when you're just sitting at home at the dinner table or in your therapist's office. The body may be experienced as dangerous, as it constantly signals danger, because the alarm system is always on. When the body becomes dangerous it can't be trusted as an internal reference, so you orient to externals to make sense of the world and determine an appropriate response. This perpetuates hyper-vigilance and externalising, typically focusing on the trigger or blaming someone or something for your feelings and reactions. This inability to orient to self impacts on identity and relationships and can impact on confidence in decision making.

Overwhelm – feeling easily or frequently overwhelmed by small things.

Powerlessness – when you are overwhelmed and unable to do anything about the situation, feeling defeated. It is central to traumatic or overwhelming events and can be deeply buried so that it becomes an invisible perpetual state.

Stuck sadness – is like being stuck in sorrow but crying doesn't help or bring relief. There are several variations on stuck sadness: can't stop crying, or crying at everything (but sometimes unable to cry about personal sadness), or unable to cry even though there is a feeling of buried sadness. During integration there is a different kind of crying; it is gentler than stuck crying, and brings relief. Often people cry as the brain integrates, as if it has permission to cry and express old sorrow as its sense of safety grows.

Poor concentration – It's hard to concentrate or take in information when your body is behaving as if there's a rattlesnake under your chair. You have one eye on that damn rattlesnake while trying to listen to what the other person is saying. This is why kids who experience early trauma often don't do well at school. They are the ones staring out the window or unable to sit still. They, and their teachers, often conclude that they are stupid or wicked, but it's usually that they can't concentrate on the information and are fighting demons that no one else can see. Instead, they pick up other signals such as that the teacher is stressed or little Johnny in the seat in front is feeling upset about something. They are often hypersensitive to emotions and potential danger but unable to take in the facts and figures. Or some have extreme, obsessive concentration on particular things while unable to see what is under their nose.

Poor memory – If you can't concentrate when you hear something then you can't remember it. Added to this, the usual memory systems are disrupted through trauma, which can affect encoding and retrieval of memory, as everything is laced with fear and suspicion.

Sleep disturbance – Either you can't get to sleep or you wake up through the night and can't get back to sleep. Because the lower brain is responsible for housekeeping, when there is any disruption to it there can be disruption to basic functions such as sleeping and eating or digestion. As well, sleep is when the brain integrates, but if an experience is triggered that releases cortisol it can agitate the system, interrupting sleep.

Noise and light sensitivity – It's as if the system is already overloaded, so dealing with one more thing such as a neighbour using a power tool on Saturday afternoon can feel catastrophic, like life and death.

Pain – When muscles are chronically contracted because you're unable to relax, pain develops. Pain can be generalised, as in fibromyalgia, or concentrated around activation points associated with fight-flight physiology. Particular hot spots include the neck, shoulder and jaw, often resulting in headaches, or teeth problems from clenching. The psoas is a powerful muscle that contracts to get us moving, but when it is chronically tight it can cause lower back pain. Chronic tension in your body can affect digestion and immune response – in fact, almost any system in the body.

Wired and tired – Your system is on high alert, ready to deal with the threat (wired or accelerating), but you're just sitting at the table eating dinner trying to act cool (brake), all the while watching for the snake. This is sometimes described as having the brake and the accelerator on at the same time.

Exhaustion – Being continually wired can lead to exhaustion, to chronic fatigue. Very powerful chemicals are released during fight-flight that are meant to come in short bursts to get you moving to survive the threat, and then switch off and recover. If they continue to flood the system, they burn it out.

Hopelessness – Often people describe a sense of hopelessness when this wired and tired feeling is going on because they don't know why it's happening or what to do about it.

Picture of depression – When we add these last three together, wired and tired, exhaustion and hopelessness, we get a picture of depression, but usually it is a long journey down the slippery slope of this whole stack of experiences that results in symptoms associated with depression.

Most of these reactions or primary activations are adaptive in the right situation. But when the brain-body becomes stuck in these responses they become problematic and have a ripple effect impacting on the whole system as you attempt to manage these difficult and painful internal states.

Jack, I'm always activated

Jack: But it happens to me all the time, Rita. I'm always activated.

Rita: Tell me what you've been noticing, Jack.

I was shell-shocked when I started to understand how my father's cruelty still affects me. I'd always known it, but I didn't understand it. I've spent my life trying to forget it. It's like a floodlight has been turned on in my head.

Yes, sometimes we can know something in an intellectual way but the knowing doesn't really belong to us. It sounds like you're starting to understand it through direct experience. And what else are you noticing, Jack?

The brain and the map

I notice how irritable and on edge I am all the time, and I do mean all the time. I spoke to Katie about it. She cried when I told her what I was seeing. Since we talked about it something has changed between us – for the better. We've started planning a proper holiday, something we haven't done since we were married.

That's great, Jack.

Yeah, that side of things is great. But the problem is, now that I'm aware of it, it's driving me crazy that I'm like this. I want to stop it.

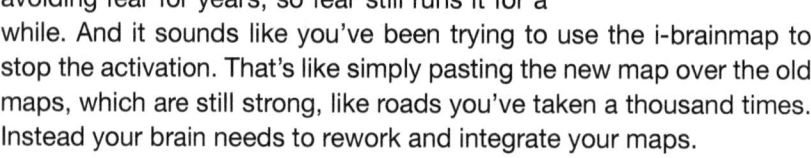

It's common to focus on activation once you understand what activation is and become aware that it's happening. Your brain has a new understanding now, a new map, but your brain has oriented to avoiding fear for years, so fear still runs it for a while. And it sounds like you've been trying to use the i-brainmap to stop the activation. That's like simply pasting the new map over the old maps, which are still strong, like roads you've taken a thousand times. Instead your brain needs to rework and integrate your maps.

Stop-stop-stop the activation

Jack: Okay, so to stop the activation I have to stop trying to stop it?

Rita: Just notice the emphasis on stopping, Jack.

I do want it to stop, it's dreadful. It's even worse now that I'm aware of it. I'm not so sure that Scotch therapy wasn't the best treatment for me.

In the short term Scotch therapy was great, but perhaps it had become not so adaptive?

Maybe. But drinking was sure better than this.

Okay, Jack. So when your intention is to stop – even if you're pretending it isn't, you can't trick your brain – the pathway is strengthened.

It's like I'm trying to trick my brain by pretending I'm not trying to stop it, but really I'm trying to stop it. Funny, huh?

We're all pretty funny that way. We try to avoid or hide what is difficult or uncomfortable, and in fact we're inadvertently wiring it in more tightly. In fact, what we're doing with the brain map approach is learning to get more comfortable with feeling uncomfortable.

I get it. But I'm not sure that I 'get' it, if you know what I mean.

You get it intellectually, but it's not necessarily embodied yet or integrated so that you can access that knowledge during activation. You don't own this new map yet.

Something like that.

Stop it!

The more we struggle to stop something the more the brain gets the message that it's dangerous, that *something's wrong*, which consolidates and perpetuates the pathways of emergency in the lower brain's alarm system. By struggling, avoiding, or trying to stop or escape activation, we actually make it stronger. Instead, we need to approach the activation gently and observe mindfully using techniques that encourage integration, and keep moving through it.

Trying to stop it is like:

- Being caught in a spider web. The more you thrash about the more entrapped you become.
- Trying not to think of a pink elephant. Go on, try.
- Slamming on the brake in the middle of a skid. You're likely to spin out of control.

Although it may seem helpful in the short term because it alleviates the distress momentarily, trying to stop it is like treating the symptom and not the cause. Trying to stop or escape activation can quickly become a secondary activation.

A story to avoid

There was once a monastery on the edge of a jungle. One day an old monk and a young monk were out in the garden, and the old monk asked the young one to fetch him a shovel from the garden shed. The young monk ran to the garden shed and rushed through the rickety door and into the darkness. In the dim light he froze in terror when he saw the longest snake he had ever seen curled up on the floor. He rushed from the shed and ran back to the old monk.

'There's a huge snake in the shed,' he said breathlessly.

Together they went back to the shed, and the old monk locked the door and hung a sign on the door saying 'Beware of snake'.

At first, no one dared enter the garden shed because the story of the huge serpent spread like wildfire through the monastery. Everyone avoided the small shed at the edge of the garden until it was forgotten, overgrown with thick jungle vines.

Then one day, many years later, a great master who was visiting the monastery was walking in the garden. When he came to the little shed, overgrown with vines, he asked his companion what was inside. He was told the story of the great serpent locked in the shed and how the monks could hear it whispering in the wind some nights and they all shook with terror and were glad that the shed was locked.

The old master asked his companion to find the key and bring him a torch. Eventually the monk returned with the rusty key and a torch, and with a lot of grunting and shoving the door was opened.

The master entered the small shed taking the light with him. From inside the shed, the companion heard his master laughing and inched closer to discover what the old master had found. He stretched his neck so that one eye peeked around the door and looked down to where the master was shining the torch, and there on the floor was a long, fat coil of rope. The old master looked up and said, 'There's your giant snake, my friend,' and they both laughed till their bellies shook.

We don't change the brain, but the brain can change itself

We can't change the way the brain works; we can only work with it so it can change itself. That means not trying to stop or avoid the automatic reactions because then we only get into struggle, creating another, secondary activation that keeps the brain on alert/alarm.

Over hundreds of thousands of years, the brain evolved first and foremost to survive. We don't want or need to change that. What we may need to change is what has gotten entangled in that survival reaction, though it may be outside our awareness. When we get activated, often all we're aware of is the distress, and that is where we start, with awareness – not with struggle, which will only perpetuate the pattern. This is the thing that I have to keep repeating for everyone, including myself.

Nor is it a matter of just sitting in the distress, because that can also overwhelm and perpetuate the distress. Somewhere in between, on the middle path, there is change and freedom from these old habits of reaction that no longer serve us.

Chapter 12
Secondary activation

In this chapter I describe common patterns of specific secondary activation.

Secondary activations are your reactions to the experience of primary activation and include cognitive and behavioural reactions, or impulses, and relational orientations. They usually develop to avoid, control or somehow manage the distressing internal states of primary activations. Many people are more aware of secondary activations than primary activations because when the activation cycle has occurred for many years these habits of reaction or secondary activation become entrenched, and the original feelings and reactions that they were intended to avoid become invisible and less accessible. Secondary activation can cover up the primary activation.

Adaptive or mis-adaptive?

Secondary activations are typically adaptive responses relevant to the age you were and the resources you had at the time traumatic or overwhelming events occurred. But over time they can become maladaptive or what I call *mis-adaptive*. In other words, they miss the point or become a bigger problem, like Jack's drinking, than the primary activation they were intended to fix. The reason I use the term *mis-adaptive* instead of maladaptive is because maladaptive assumes it's bad or wrong ignoring the original purpose, which was to adapt to overwhelming experiences with limited resources.

The difference between whether something is adaptive or *mis-adaptive* is how much choice you have.

Social anxiety is a good example of how an adaptive secondary activation over time becomes *mis-adaptive*. It makes sense to avoid something that is distressing, such as a snake. But what works in the external environment is often not effective when it comes to the internal environment, because you can't escape yourself or your internal experiences.

For example, in the beginning you may avoid parties (external) because they 'make' you feel anxious (internal). Parties trigger your anxiety. Avoiding parties helps reduce your anxiety in the short term, so in the beginning it's adaptive. But over time you may use avoidance of places and situations more and more to manage your internal distress – because it works. Next you avoid supermarkets and driving because they make you feel anxious. It works because you don't have to face your anxiety. Then you stop leaving the house, and finally you won't leave your bedroom. The fear is driving your choices. In this way, avoidance becomes increasingly *mis-adaptive* because you have less and less choice.

Your intention, or how you choose to respond, gives the brain the message about experience for future reference. So even though a particular behaviour may appear the same from the outside, such as leaving the room, it might be done with the intention to avoid or the intention to find a different way through an entrenched pattern in a relationship, which each give the brain a very different message.

Common types of secondary activation

Note that these reactions aren't all behaviours. Some secondary activations are internal reactions, such as a suppressing or controlling uncomfortable emotions.

Some secondary activations are called Tension Reducing Behaviours (TRBs). I only use the term TRB for specific behaviours of self-harm a person uses to reduce their distress, such as cutting.

There is no neat divide between different secondary activations. Many overlap and are a combination of avoid and control, and are unique for each person. Common secondary activations include the following reactions.

Avoid-escape reactions

Avoid-escape reactions can be internal (such as suppression of intense emotions) or external (such as behaviour that avoids situations) or a combination of both (as in social anxiety):

- alcohol and drugs, which are our most socially accepted strategy to avoid-escape (often referred to as self-medicating, though)
- technology as an escape, which can fast become an even bigger addiction than substances

Secondary activation

- any compulsive behaviour, such as shopping or overeating
- denial, suppression, repression
- minimising or denying the impact of a problem, such as ignoring a significant symptom or health issue
- 'No. I won't/don't want to' resistance to trying anything helpful

Many thinking patterns are based on avoidance, such as:

- wishing and hoping
- wishful thinking
- living in fantasy.

This avoid-escape thinking becomes problematic when it inhibits your capacity to accept and deal with current situations. Wishing and hoping means that, instead of dealing with events as they are, you wish they were different. This seems innocent enough, and it may be, but it can become *mis-adaptive* if it means you avoid dealing with a current situation that's uncomfortable or difficult but instead cling to an idea of how you think things should be, leaving you perpetually frustrated and disappointed. It may be associated with a whole fantasy life or just a thinking style, which might be adaptive if you write fantasy but not if it stops you taking steps to getting a job or taking a course because you'd rather dream about your amazing career in design or as a musician.

Mary, when wishing and hoping are part of the problem

Mary: I feel overwhelmed and just wish it would go away.

Rita: So you feel overwhelmed and start wishing but don't do anything about it?

Yep.

Wishing keeps you in a passive state, Mary. It's a child-like response that was all you could do as a kid. Instead of taking action you drop into that habitual reaction. Do you know what you're telling yourself when it happens?

This shouldn't be happening to me. It's not fair. I don't deserve this. I wish it'd stop.

There's something interesting here that I think sounds like some belief that, if you're good and do the right thing, then good things should happen.

Yes, and if they don't it's not fair.

So we have something about fairness and justice here, that the world should be fair and just. Do you think the world is fair and just, Mary?

No, I know it's not. I've lived too long to think that.

So you don't believe it rationally, but it's a default position, laced with wishing and hoping, like little-girl thinking, that if you're good the tooth fairy will come and Santa too.

Yes, I feel like one of those little girls. I feel like I can't do anything. I just want something like magic to happen. I don't like feeling like that kid that's always overwhelmed and can't change anything. But I still wish it would stop.

Just notice that wishing, Mary.

Oh no, now I'm not allowed to say 'sorry' or wish for anything either!

Again, Mary, this isn't about stopping what you're doing or making it wrong, which doesn't help. It's about getting curious, because that changes the message you're giving your brain, remember?

Hard to get that one. Mmm. Not sure I'll ever get this.

Awareness is the first thing, Mary, that's all. Just noticing this. 'Just this', whatever is happening right now. We don't want to make it wrong. That's all. And sometimes the seemingly harmless things are the tip of an iceberg, so let's just keep an eye on wishful thinking because I think it's a sign of activation.

Control reactions

When your inner world feels scary or out of control, you're likely to put energy into trying to control the environment, especially to eradicate anything that triggers a reaction in you. It may also take the form of internal control through ignoring, denying, defending or suppressing emotions that are uncomfortable. As you can see, there is no clear divide between avoid and control reactions.

Some specific manifestations of control reactions include:

- **perfectionism or perfectionistic thinking**. For instance, 'I can't be happy or okay unless everything is just right or perfect.' Or 'There's no point even trying if I can't do it perfectly.' Often perfectionism is driven by anxiety.
- **'fix it', 'gotta get it right', 'gotta work it out', 'gotta *get* it'**. This can become know-it-all thinking. Many of us have an inner Mr or Ms Fix it.
- **being driven**, in any way, from working excessively or being driven to meet some particular standard, either your own or someone else's.

Control reactions can inhibit integration by keeping you constantly looking for what is wrong, with a view to fixing or making it perfect. This pattern says that while there is any activation at all you must have failed, or this approach is failing, because all attention is on *what's wrong*. You could call this the 'What's wrong with this picture?' approach, where you have to examine everything to find the mistake, the gap or lack, the speck of dust or lint, the something missing, and usually you can find something. It seems harmless enough, but it may be one of the biggest blocks to effective change and integration because focusing on the problem gives the brain the message that there is something wrong, and keeps it on high alert, which maintains the physiology of anxiety and thereby creates a self-fulfilling prophecy.

Mary, trying to work it all out

> Rita: What I notice, Mary, is how hard you work at trying to work it all out in your mind – like you have to know and get it right.

> Mary: Yep. I just want to know. Is that so strange?

> Not strange, Mary, quite normal. The trouble is that it may not be helping to manage the internal distress you experience. It may even be get-

ting in the way of what is helpful, because when you get anxious you seem to get hooked on trying to find what is wrong and wonder 'Why, why, why?' Does it help, do you think?

Not really. I usually end up in a spin. Sometimes when I've re-read my journals I can see that I just go round and round in circles. And then I end up exhausted and usually go to the fridge for help.

Refrigerator therapy. So you know overthinking or ruminating doesn't really help, but the impulse to work it out continues? And maybe a bit of wishful thinking to boot.

Yep. I go over and over things. I want to fix things, especially with the children, and now the grandchildren.

It sounds like one way you coped as a kid was to become Little Miss Fix It. Work it all out and fix things, especially for everyone else. But the emotions connected to the survival–child brain, or to people, need soothing not fixing.

Yeah, the kids get mad at me sometimes when they tell me their problems and I try to sort it out for them. I just want to help. And feeding everyone always helps, of course.

Yes, eating something is usually soothing and distracting and seems to be tagged with fixing for you, Mary. Would you be willing to notice the impulse to analyse and work things out and call it activation?

If I can see it happening I can, but usually I just get into it automatically.

Yes, that's the thing about activation. It can be hard to notice it as it happens. I'd like to encourage more curiosity, and less of the 'gotta work it all out, get it right'.

I'll try.

The other thing is that as soon as the brain thinks it's worked it out or got an answer it gets lazy on us and just pulls out an old map and says 'Oh, she's just doing that old map, and I've already got one of those'. It's curiosity and attention that are key elements in brain change, so let's keep them active.

Okay, I'll try just to stay open to what you're telling me.

And just notice if you get hijacked into trying to work it out or get it right.

Struggle

Struggling against what is happening is often a combination of 'avoid and control'. This is a big inhibitor to integration and can take many forms. What struggle does is keep the lower brain in high alert, vigilant. The struggle can be internal or struggling against circumstances in the environment. Learning to accept is the ground of change and the antithesis of struggle. Acceptance isn't passively tolerating things but an active response that includes how you orient to an event or situation. We'll discuss this later.

> *... the curious paradox is that when I accept myself as I am, then I change.*
>
> *Carl Rogers*, On Becoming a Person[2]

Either–or

Technically 'either–or' belongs in 'thinking', but I've put it in a special category of its own, to highlight how you can get caught in such polarities as struggle and surrender. Acceptance and even mindfulness techniques are sometimes misinterpreted as giving up, giving in, doing nothing or just grinning and bearing the distress, and are seen as the opposite of only one other option: struggling against the situation that's causing the distress. Neither giving up nor struggling is effective in brain change. If you struggle, as I said, the brain goes into alert or alarm, but if you just give up and do nothing the cycle is perpetuated, because nothing changes. The brain will keep doing what it's always done unless it's interrupted during the activation, like interrupting a live broadcast. Between these two, surrender and struggle, is an active acceptance that recognises things as they are and moves with them and through them, like riding a wave.

Defences and defensiveness

Defence is a primary activation, a protective reaction like fighting to defend ourself, our territory or our family, just like a mother lion protecting her cubs. Defences also develop as secondary reactions in an attempt to protect us from feeling vulnerable, which is how we usually experi-

---

2   Carl Rogers, *On Becoming a Person: A Therapist's View of Psychotherapy*, Houghton Mifflin, New York, [1961] 1995, p. 17.

ence primary activations. While this is adaptive it can become *mis-adaptive* if it becomes extreme or gets attached to something that perhaps doesn't require protecting – like protecting your pride in the same way you might protect a small child, as if it's life and death. If you feel like you want to die when your pride is hurt, your ego is probably entangled with your survival brain.

A common form of defence is the critic – an inner or an outer critic. Being critical of yourself or others is usually a type of defensive protective reaction. Often the inner critic starts out (usually through a parent or adult) protecting you by helping you learn to avoid making mistakes or making a fool of yourself. Over a lifetime it can become so crippling that you never take a risk and try something new or allow yourself to play and be creative, because the critic cuts you down at the knees before you can step forward. Or you may be unwilling to take on healthy criticism or feedback, or even learn new ways of doing things, because your defensive reaction works so automatically. Being able to discriminate between feedback, or constructive criticism that is valuable, and criticism – another's or your own – that is undermining or diminishing is difficult if not impossible when the inner critic becomes overly powerful, because it's entangled with survival.

The 'overs'

Anything that begins with 'over', meaning extreme or disproportionate reaction given to the current situation, belongs in this category. The *overs* are driven by lower brain activation and we respond to a situation as if it is life and death or keep going over and over something because the brain is in split-brain mode and no messages are getting through.

- **Over-thinking** – This is the big brain spinning its wheels. Thoughts are usually repetitive and frequently irrational, or not helpful but stuck in an old story.

- **Over-reacting** – when reactions are disproportionate to an event. For instance, you may feel murderous rage when someone takes your parking space.

- **Oversensitive** – This is associated with hyper-arousal and hyper-vigilance. It's like having no skin. Everything seems to affect you deeply and can easily overwhelm you because your system is already switched on, so it doesn't take much to create an intense reaction, like the neighbour's dog barking on Sunday morning.

- **Over-talking** – Compulsive talking or an inability to be quiet and still is usually an indicator of internal discomfort or distress as you try to release or avoid the internal distress through talking incessantly.

- **Over-identification** – You may identify with certain emotions, thoughts, beliefs or a story of 'what happened to me' or 'I'm always xxx' or 'I'm never yyy'. It may be excessive identification with work or a role: 'I am a mother' or 'I am a teacher'. You can become over-identified with your story, so that you live out of that story and allow it to define you and shape your life. For instance, the story of the victim or rescuer may dominate life.

Mary is a good example of over-identification with her role as carer or 'little mother'. She sees this as who she is and therefore has little choice about how she responds. For her, the role has been bound up in threat-alarm, making it impossible for her to say 'no' without invoking a sense of impending doom.

Stuck or sticky thinking

Sticky thinking is like a sticky web the mind gets caught in. Any repetitive thinking, when you go over and over the same thought or become entrapped in a cycle perpetuated by your thinking, is sticky thinking. There are numerous sticky thinking patterns (more commonly known as 'thinking styles'):

- 'black–white' or 'right–wrong' thinking, which reflect a split-brain system
- all-or-nothing thinking
- personalising, taking everything personally
- catastrophic thinking, which matches internal experience rather than a current event
- either–or thinking, which was discussed above.

One of the reasons I don't use top-down techniques (such as cognitive therapy or self-talk) with people (initially) to manage these thinking patterns when the system is stuck on overwhelm is that these sticky thinking patterns usually reflect the internal state. You could say that sticky thinking is the effect or symptom that perpetuates what is happening rather than the cause.

Take the person who has had a car accident, for instance. After they recover, when they get in the car and attempt to drive, they might have a panic attack or imagine a catastrophic event. In reality it's unlikely they will have a car accident, but each time they get in the car their body remembers that they can have an accident. In this case, I use a bottom-up approach, working with their body states or direct experience to reduce current distress, because it's their body remembering the catastrophic feeling associated with driving a car that is generating the catastrophic thoughts. Reducing the overwhelming distress in the body often changes the thinking brain, which adapts as it integrates the traumatic memories.

On the other hand, if we approach their catastrophic thinking by challenging the thinking or looking for evidence it's likely that they will focus on the fact that they can and have had a motor vehicle accident. Even if they cognitively tell themselves it probably won't happen again, their body is likely to continue to experience overwhelm as if something catastrophic is about to happen. To ignore this or try to override it can create an internal struggle or conflict, which perpetuates the activation cycle.

Storied mind

Storied mind refers to the stories we get stuck in. Although making stories about what happens is the usual process of the mind-brain and part of integrating experience, using the term *storied mind* describes how the stories can get stuck. Common stuck-stories are: *the victim myth*–that is, 'I'm a victim (always a victim)'; *blaming*, or making someone else wrong. Many classic fairy tales and myths could fall into this category, such as frog kissing, or believing that if you love someone enough they will change, good versus evil, heroes and heroines or villains, happy ever after, waiting to be rescued-loved-freed-healed-saved-enlightened, to name a few.

Wishing and hoping stories (including *if only*, or *if/when … then*), reinforce the non-acceptance of whatever is happening, watching and waiting for some perfect moment or experience 'out there' somewhere if only you could find it. Wishing and hoping or grabbing onto a story that doesn't fit with current circumstances can keep you feeling powerless because your orientation is towards the wished for story and not on dealing with the reality of how things are. The *entitlement story* is a fierce kind of wishing and hoping that can keep you stuck in expectations that the world *should* behave in a way that suits you and give you what you want, expect or demand. And when that doesn't happen, rage is often the result, because *how dare they...*

A give-away sign that you are operating from storied mind is when you use words like 'always', 'never' and 'can't'.

Secondary activation in relationship

All of the above patterns of reaction can have expression in relationship. Not just your relationship with others but also your relationship to self, to body, to food. You can have avoidance or control reactions, high expectations of another or of yourself, or get caught in an either–or struggle between giving up or controlling. I don't want to define every pattern of reaction, but instead invite you to become more curious about your reactions as they arise. How you try to control or avoid situations, where you get into struggle against what is happening, or where your critic operates. This isn't a tick box but a journey of discovery into yourself.

There is one issue that needs a special note, and that is your relationship with self and especially *identity*. Sense of identity can become entangled with past trauma or over-identification with being a victim-survivor. This can make integrating past trauma and all the protective layers of secondary activation particularly difficult to integrate because you have come to think it is who you are. And if that dissolves, what is there, who are you? If the answer seems like it might be nothing or nobody, there can be a terror of the abyss of nothingness that you may face as the brain integrates. This is like a space that can feel interminable when you are in it, when the old patterns start to fall away but the new insight or pathway hasn't yet emerged. It can be very frightening and discombobulating.

Identity issues are complex for many who experienced early trauma because orientation is outward. There are two reasons for this orientation: hyper-vigilance (or watchfulness), and because the body feels dangerous and feelings seem overwhelming so you learnt to avoid contact with the internal environment and to mistrust its messages. This creates an external orientation or focus of attention with minimal or no self-referencing. How do you know who you are if you're outside looking in? That's how many people experience themselves when there has been early trauma/overwhelm. The movement of integration takes you into self, through direct body experience, but this can feel alien in the beginning, which is why it's important to have support.

The brain and the map

Mary, how do I tell when I'm activated?

Mary: So when I notice a secondary activation, like being an extreme helper, I'm activated by fear or some discomfort, but I go into the helping and controlling thing. Is that what happens?

Rita: Let's look at a specific example, Mary. That might make it more concrete for you. Can you think of an example?

Well, Don and I took our grandchildren, Toby and Will, to this theme park on the weekend. Don is really rough with the kids sometimes, and I hate it. He had Will on this swing thing and was making it go really high. Will loved it, and Toby was laughing at them. I could just see an accident happening. I was getting lunch ready, but I went over and started yelling at Don but trying to keep my voice down because there were people everywhere, other nice, quiet people sitting serenely under trees. I wanted the ground to swallow me up. It ruined our whole day.

It's tricky, isn't it, because there was a possible danger that someone could have been hurt. There are a jumble of complex emotions and activations that are all tied up in the actual events when you felt you needed to protect your grandchildren. There's the helper and also the defender of your pups, and out pops the critic to join in, and then your controller comes out as well because you feel scared. What a party. And then shame and guilt arrive to throw a bit of fuel on the flames. So much going on, Mary!

Don's so careless. I hate the feeling of wanting to disappear. I felt so powerless.

So you want to find a way to deal with the current situation without all the old maps, but the brain needs *some* maps to orient to, to make sense of things. It always uses past experience to deal with current events. We just want to make sure it's using the best map for the current situation and that the map is flexible and continually being updated.

So how do I tell if I'm activated or if my concern is real?

Well there's no neat divide or right answer to this. I would say you could initially assume you're activated, especially if it's an extreme response. We don't want to stop these reactions. We just want you to be able to manage them and reduce your distress – your activation – enough so that you can access your big-brain resources and make the best choice in any situation. A tell-tale sign of activation is a compulsion – you feel like you don't have a choice. But of course if there is immediate danger you need to act.

Secondary activation

No, I didn't have a choice. I was over at the swing yelling at Don before my feet even touched the ground. I hardly remember the rest of the day. I just stuffed down lunch.

A story might help you make sense of this, Mary. This is my story. I call it the 'dog story', and it's something that happened to me.

My dog story

It's a foggy midwinter morning and I'm walking alone. As I get further along the track away from any houses, a picture starts flashing through my mind of being attacked by a dog. I try to shrug it off and talk myself out of it, but I start to feel a bit anxious. I tell myself it's silly, but at the same time I start looking around through the mist and shadows to make sure no dogs are lurking there. As I keep walking, I have flashes of being attacked by the dog. The images get more vivid and more frequent, but I can't work out where they're coming from. 'What the hell is the matter with you, Rita? You're being ridiculous. Calm down, there's nothing going on,' I tell myself.

But now it's turned into a pit-bull terrier. I can see its pink eyes watching me, and its powerful jaws, and it's in Technicolor. Now the dog is jumping at me. My heart's pounding and it's hard to breathe, and I want to scream. Then I realise that I'm a long way from any houses, and no one will hear me if I scream. Now I see the pit-bull attacking me on the ground.

The whole time this is going on, I'm telling myself not to be so ridiculous because I know I'm imagining it but I keep looking around. It feels intensely real because my body is behaving as if I'm actually being attacked by a pit-bull.

Although I keep trying to challenge my thinking as irrational, I don't believe myself, or at least my body and emotions don't believe me. I know it *can* happen that dogs attack, because I was bitten by a dog while I was walking in the bush years ago. I know it's real (just like you know kids *can* have accidents). It doesn't help when I tell myself it isn't real because my body feels it as real. (It's like telling an infant not to be scared because they're having a nightmare.)

Then suddenly I recognise that it's activation and I feel my anxiety start to go down. But I continue to scan the trees for wild dogs, just in case. Each time I do this my anxiety increases. Again I remind myself that it's activation. Now that I know what it is I can access some strategies I have. I give it a number, it's a '7' now, and I watch the ground, stones on the path as I walk, noticing the details. I put my hand on my solar plexus and gently rub that area of my body where I feel most distressed. I still feel a bit scared and at the same time I know where I am and that I'm okay and that nothing dangerous is happening right now.

Now it's a '5'. I'm walking and watching and listening. I hear a bird and feel my feet touching and leaving the ground. As my body calms I suddenly remember that last week a large, black German Shepherd came running up behind me. Scared the 'bidgeebuzz' out of me. I heard this heavy breathing coming up behind me, turned and came face to face with the dog running towards me, and not an owner in sight. I'd never seen the dog before and had no idea if it was friendly.

'Flash-forward' is like a flashback, only it's in the future. Your body experiences some internal state of distress associated with the past and then projects it into the future, and you imagine the details to make sense of the internal experience, usually imagining the worst or some catastrophe but often not recognising the link with the past experience. This is what I call a 'flash-forward'; it's not a smart car.

It seemed weird that I didn't remember that incident during activation. It was as if my brain couldn't make the connection to what had triggered my flash-forward until I had calmed down. That's because the alarm part of my brain had taken control, and everything else was less available or not available while my brain was screaming, 'Danger, danger! Run for cover!' But once I could flick on the light and my brain started making connections I remembered the big, black dog running towards me.

Mary, looking for something bad to happen

Mary: Oh, yes. That's exactly what happens. It's so real I can almost see bad things happening. My imagination goes wild. That's why I got so mad at Don.

Rita: Not only that. It's probable that you do remember the times when something bad does happens because it confirms your belief or expectations, but if nothing bad happens you soon forget it. It's as if you're watching and waiting for bad things to happen – as if you're oriented to accidents. The brain evolved to have a negativity bias, to find the problem or danger.

That sounds dreadful – like I'm looking for something bad to happen.

It's not that you want it. It's just that your body is remembering or playing the same old track, and you're re-experiencing it as future, based on the internal experience of now, which is based on yesterday or memory. Let's just say you're playing the dog story.

I'm still not sure if the thing at the park was real or activation.

Well, the experience was very real. Your body was in a highly anxious state, and that's about as real as it gets. The question is whether your reaction was appropriate or helpful for the situation.

Okay, that makes sense. I'm glad you're not trying to tell me I'm imagining things, because it feels real.

The i-brain map isn't about not acting or responding to deal with what is real. It's about taking the sting or intensity out of the bite of lower brain reactions enough that you can bring your attention into the present and access your big brain to assess and deal with things more effectively.

Mary, important not to make activation wrong

Rita: The important thing is not to make activation wrong. It's just the way your brain wired itself in response to experiences in your childhood that were overwhelming for you.

Mary: It does help to think about it like that instead of the other.

The other?

That I'm damaged, crazy … you know … the mad grandma at the park.

Okay, so now we're getting deeper into story and meaning making; how your brain made the connections to patterns that repeated; how you made sense of things. Story is like a connective web that links up all the separate bits and pieces of experience and makes them into something coherent, like a map. The trouble is that when the system is fragmented your stories can become fragmented too and stuck. So where a healthy system will keep upgrading a story or narrative as more information and experience comes in, when the system is fragmented you can get stuck in old, calcified stories. Then those stories drive you and dictate your response to the world.

Like my story about being a carer?

Exactly, Mary. So now let's talk about story and meaning making.

Chapter 13
Making meaning

In this chapter I explain meaning making and how it can perpetuate an activation cycle. I also explain how repeated stories and interpretations of experience orient us in specific and often invisible ways that influence how we see the world.

'Meaning-making' as I use it here is the overarching term for our stories, thinking and beliefs.

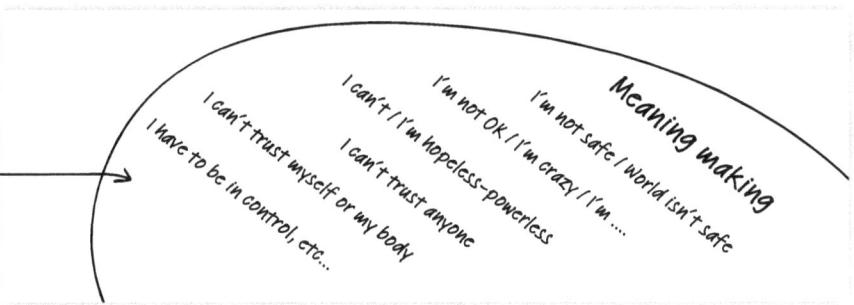

Meaning-making

The brain is a meaning-making system. If I draw two dots and a curved line underneath – a smiley face image – your brain will make a face. The brain joins the dots to make sense of things, making meaning out of all the stimuli coming at it every moment. And the brain makes meaning based on experience.

This automatic meaning response to experience is part of the brain's efficiency, but it can also inhibit brain change. When the brain uses an old map to decipher new experiences through making associations it says, 'Oh, this is the *All politicians are out for number one* map', or 'This is the *See, you can't trust anyone* map or the *See, no one cares about me*, map', for instance. These maps become your lens, your limited filters through which you understand the world. They also allow for an efficient brain that can rapidly put something through a known filter then spend its attention elsewhere.

The brain especially needs to determine whether something is safe or dangerous. So, if your internal alarm system is going off continually the brain creates meaning based on that experience, which tells you the world's not safe or you're not safe. Then you interpret the world through a filter of fear and lack of safety, and this belief is perpetuated as you constantly check for danger, and your body responds accordingly.

Jack, the boss and his colleague

Jack: You know, my boss's stupid behaviour doesn't have anything to do with me. He treats us all like idiots.

Rita: And does anyone in your office have a different response to his behaviour?

Yes. Fiona does.

How does she respond?

She doesn't get wired about it like the rest of us.

So do you think she has a different interpretation of his behaviour?

I guess so.

If you could read her mind, Jack, what do you imagine she might be thinking about your boss's behaviour?

Well ... in meetings when he's having a go at her she stays calm. She answers his questions and gives him more than he asks for. She's the only woman in the team, and if anything he's tougher on her than anyone. I don't know what she's thinking, but I guess she doesn't take him personally or see his bullying as a reflection on her work. One time the boss balled her out because she hadn't done something in a project she'd been working on for weeks. She responded by saying that he had never discussed that as part of the original proposal, she had a copy in front of her, and would he like her to include it now. You should have seen the look on his face.

So she put it back on him rather than taking it on as her mistake or problem and getting defensive?

Yeah. It's as if she really trusts herself and isn't trying to prove anything.

Is that way of thinking different to the way you think, Jack?

Hell, yeah. I'm trying to prove things all the time. I take it personally when he gets on my case. I always think I should've got it right, but sometimes he expects the impossible, or he hasn't even said he wants something done and then in a meeting asks why it wasn't done, like what happened to Fiona.

Do you trust yourself, Jack?

Nope.

It can be very hard to trust yourself and your responses when the body has felt dangerous because the alarm is on all the time. Until you can discriminate between activation and which body reactions you can trust to guide you to respond to the world, I think it is very hard to trust your responses and decisions. So your brain makes meaning based on mistrust.

Hmm? Need more time to think about that one, but sounds right.

Stories and beliefs orient you to the world

Stories can be seen as a way you orient to the world. If you have a story of lack, for instance, then you are likely to orient to what is missing or not available – glass half-empty. On the other hand, if you have a story of optimism or plenty you are likely to orient to what you have and experience a sense of appreciation and gratitude.

It's not just your stories that create a problem but your orientation to them, such as whether you're *in* the story, like a character that just follows the script, or you're the narrator or author of the story. As a character in a stuck story you're powerless and caught in a *Groundhog Day,* but as the author or narrator you can direct the action and change the story.

There can be a great divide between embodied story that you live inside, often without knowing it, and the stories that you tell consciously. It's a mistake to assume that by telling your story you can access the deeper stories or embodied metaphors. While this may be true at times, it is often not the case with intense emotional memories or trauma, because, as we've discussed, what is embodied can split off from the told or conscious memory or story.

Earliest stories

Your earliest stories, related to attachment, are the most deeply embodied and usually invisible and difficult to access, and therefore hard to change. It isn't within the scope of this book to discuss attachment except as it relates to traumatic and overwhelming experiences and as part of orientation, which will be discussed in chapter 15.

Core beliefs: the pea under the mattresses

If we drill down into Jack's stories until we get to his core beliefs it's likely we'll find that he doesn't feel 'good enough'. Perhaps he believes that there's something wrong with him. Some of our earliest beliefs operate like the pea in the story of the princess and the pea. Those hard little peas were bedded down early in life, often before you could talk. Then throughout life you lay down so many mattresses or layers of defensive padding (secondary activation) that you've forgotten what the original *pea* was, such as self-doubt, shame, loneliness or feelings of unworthiness.

Like the princess or prince in the story, you toss and turn and squirm constantly because you always feel the discomfort, something digging in hard beneath the softness and comfort you've tried to create to stop feeling that pea. Then something or someone comes along that helps the pea grow, perhaps into a bean stalk! This is what happens to Jack's beliefs about himself when the boss talks down to him. Fiona, on the other hand, has a different belief about herself.

Shifting your orientation away from the other person's behaviour to notice what you're telling yourself or how you've interpreted the situation can give you a new perspective. Orienting to your own reactions rather than the trigger is like looking for the pea or, to really mix up our fairy tale metaphors, climb the beanstalk and deal with those nasty giants that have been rumbling around up there in the clouds and keeping you awake each night. This approach, uncovering the pea or core belief under the mattress, is an essential part of Cognitive Behaviour Therapy.

Jack, hiding failure

Jack: I've never said this to anyone, but inside I feel like I'm a failure, and I have to keep working to show someone ... [*Long silence. Jack looks out the window.*]

Rita: Just notice that, Jack ... be curious about whatever's happening right now.

... show my father I'm not a failure.

Often in childhood abuse the child blames himself for his parent's behaviour – and is ashamed.

Making meaning

I know it's not my fault that my father was abusive.

You know it intellectually. But your lower brain may still experience or interpret it as somehow your fault, even though rationally you know it's not true. Shame is one of the slipperiest of experiences, yet it drives people much more than we realise. It's so deeply buried in the psyche that we're hardly aware of it.

Another pea under the mattress?

Exactly. Shame can be difficult to access, especially through the big brain, through thinking. Added to that, we have a whole culture that's shame-intolerant, so we don't want to see our shame, let alone claim it so that we can deal with it.

One way in which trauma-overwhelm in childhood can impact on stories and meaning making (depending on the developmental stage when it happened), is that children will blame themselves or think events are their fault. One reason this happens is that until a certain age (when Theory of Mind develops) a child doesn't have a full understanding that others are separate. Young children believe they are at the centre of the universe, so anything bad that happens can be seen as their fault. They also have magical thinking that goes something like this: 'Because I did X or am Y this bad thing happened, and if I could be different, better, perfect, invisible, or hadn't wished my sister would disappear, Z would never have happened. Therefore, I won't step on cracks in pavements anymore.' This can result in a fat pea of shame and self-blame that can persist for a lifetime hidden under the mattress.

Shame on society

We tend to avoid shame collectively as well as individually. In terms of the brain's evolution, shaming was probably the original way of creating compliance in the tribe. If you did something wrong and were shamed or rejected by the tribe it meant death. You couldn't survive outside the tribe alone in the early evolution of the human brain. That's why I see it as a primary activation involving a body-brain reaction to threat, especially interpersonal threat: it's tied to a deep survival response. We pad the feeling in all kinds of ways to avoid or control it; in short, we avoid experiencing shame directly. And, as you know, that gives the brain the message that you're currently in danger, so the reaction is perpetuated.

As I said above, guilt and shame are sometimes confused and can get psychologically entangled so that it's hard to distinguish between them. The main difference is that guilt is more cognitive and about behaviour: 'what I *did* wrong'. Shame is more about oneself: '*I'm* not okay, *I'm* wrong'. Shame runs much deeper. It is a primary emotion and has a physiological component.

Until about forty years ago in most western societies, shame was a common way of parenting. Many family cultures were saturated with shame, and children learned that there was something wrong with them and they had to work hard to fit in and please and appease others, do good or find God – then they would be saved from the shame and the sin inside them. It's a great basis for religion because it gives the church a lot of power to tweak the shame button and then offer to save people.

Nowadays, we don't want kids to feel any shame. We work hard trying to keep kids happy. We overcompensate and, as a society, have become intolerant of shame, or shame-denying. We avoid and deny shame, but it hasn't gone away. In fact, it drives us more than ever as we try to sidestep it or pad the pea of shame hiding under the mattress. Anything we avoid results in the brain creating a brain knot around it that gets thicker and thicker and tighter and tighter. But like the pea and the prince or princess we still feel the lump digging into our hip at night.

People often say to me, 'I know I shouldn't care what people think.' But we do care what people think. The brain is tribal, interpersonal, and wired to care what others in our tribe think. The challenge is to know your tribe and who is worth caring about what they think, and make sure you are at the centre of your tribe. In other words the best way to avoid shame, or living to please-appease others, in a sustainable way is to know your own values, listen to yourself first, and choose what is important to you each day, each moment. Much easier when you find others who live by similar values, find your tribe, even if it's one other person. It may be better to walk alone than to be in the wrong tribe and live in shame. Perhaps that depends on how strongly you get activated by loneliness!

Core beliefs from trauma

Some common core beliefs/schemas or ways of meaning making for those who've experienced traumatic or overwhelming events include:

- The world's not safe.
- I'm not safe.
- I can't trust anyone/I can't trust myself.
- People leave me.
- I can't cope.
- I have to be in control.
- I'm special, different, entitled.
- I'm damaged, weird, crazy, not okay, will never be okay.
- No one understands me. No one can understand me.
- I'm alone. I'll always be alone.
- I have to make it right.
- I don't deserve X or Y, love, money, peace, good things ...
- I have to work hard for X or Y.
- It's all my fault. Everything is my fault. I'm responsible.

These beliefs are based on an internal experience, not on current events. Because, no matter how safe you might be, if you experience constant fear or hyper-arousal, you still feel unsafe and will develop core beliefs based on your experience.

If you have any of these core beliefs we could work with you in a top-down way, challenging your beliefs or getting you to try talking yourself out of the feeling that something dreadful is going to happen. But the feeling is real, so that is your experience, and the brain makes meaning based on experience (even if that experience happened twenty years ago) if it's still alive in the body now. But once you learn to down-regulate lower brain activation it's much easier to challenge your thinking or talk to yourself to find a different response.

It's often difficult to talk yourself out of these feelings or body memories, as we've discussed previously. It's also why I don't work too much on a person's thinking until they can manage their internal distress and soothe the lower brain. Just talking doesn't usually change the body-memory map of experience. It can help if the relationship with the person you're talking to is supportive and provides what you didn't get when you were unsafe, overwhelmed and alone. But often the body memory remains, and therefore we need to work from bottom up.

Mary, when talking helps and when it doesn't

Mary: Sometimes I can talk myself out of it. I tell myself it's okay, not to worry, and I can calm myself down.

Rita: I would say that works because of your intention and the way you're saying it, not so much the words. Those same words may have no impact at all or even escalate the distress if they're said harshly.

So, are you saying it's the way I'm talking to myself, not what I'm saying?

That's what I think. Because the language of the lower brain, where the distress is, isn't verbal, it picks up on emotion or the feeling quality of what you're saying.

Like when you croon to a baby and make cooing noises that are just babble?

Yeah. Like you're making soothing sounds and holding and rocking. The infant hears the tone of voice rather than understands the words. Let me put it another way: what if you said those same words, 'It's okay, don't worry about it', in an angry voice? How do you think you'd react?

I guess I'd get more distressed. Hmm. Even the way you said it then made me feel a bit uneasy, but I knew you were just giving me an example, so it makes sense.

That is one of the reasons I call it the child brain – to remind you that the way to soothe the lower brain is the way you soothe a child. Once it's less distressed we can talk to the whole brain using thinking and language, but not while it is being run by a frightened kid.

Chapter 14
The integration Zone or i-Zone

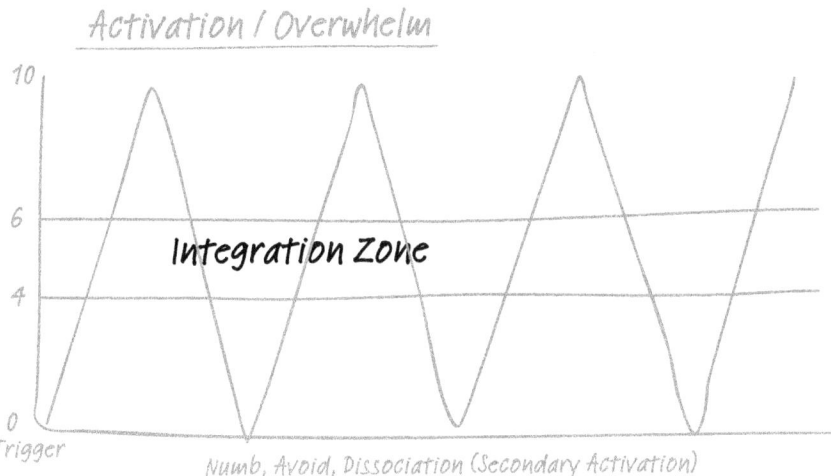

In this chapter I explain integration in more detail: the theory, the experience and the significance for the brain. I explain the importance of moving gently and consistently towards the *integration Zone* or *i-Zone* during activation. As the brain develops more capacity for integration you can enter the *i-Zone* more easily.

When you can begin to recognise activation as a signal that the brain is trying to integrate something, rather than as something dreadful to be avoided or stopped, you are more readily able to enter the *i-Zone*, and the brain begins to change.

The brain and the map

Initially I used the term integration Zone as a metaphor to understand how the brain integrates traumatic experience, but in the past few years I've come to consider it as an important area of functioning in the brain that includes certain brain structures and possibly certain cells associated with the interconnectedness of the brain. What I refer to as the *integration Zone* appears to be similar to what neuroscientists are calling the *Default Mode Network*.

I haven't named particular structures that may be involved because I believe it is more complex than what has been discovered by brain science. It's likely that the function of brain integration includes not only functions and structures of interconnectivity but perhaps cells and brain capabilities we don't yet understand.

The integration Zone is the brain functioning as an interconnected system, brain-body-mind responding moment to moment to changes in the (internal and external) environment.

Jack, bad activation?

Jack: I thought activation was the bad one that I'm in all the time – that I need to stop.

Rita: Just notice how you orient to activation, Jack. What you tell yourself about it.

What? That I hate it? Hate the way it makes me feel, and I want to stop it?

Yes, all of the above.

Yeah, I know that experience like I know my hands. I've been living with it my whole life, trying to avoid it, and I came to you because I want it to stop, and some days it seems worse, not better.

Sounds like you're frustrated, Jack, and feel that things aren't changing fast enough for you.

You bet.

So just notice what's happening in your body when you say that, and feel the frustration about the process.

Do we have to do this again? Can't you just give me some quick strategies so I can get back to the table?

Hmmm.

Yeah, okay, okay, I know. That's the old way and won't help this integration thing. I get it, some days anyway, but I just wish all this would stop.

So notice what's happening in your body as you say that, Jack, because it's the body-brain driving this, and your interpretation and thinking keeping you in the loop of frustration.

[Jack closes his eyes and then opens them instantly.] I can hardly breathe. It's like there's something heavy on my chest and something stuck in my throat, like a pressure there.

So, if it feels okay, Jack, just close or lower your eyes and maintain contact with the internal experience to let the brain know this isn't dangerous anymore. We want to give the brain different feedback.

But what is it? Why do I feel like this?

Let's call it *activation*, Jack. That's all we need to know. I've got a hunch, but let's not make any assumptions about it. We can talk about it later if we need to. How strong is it '0 to 10'?

It's a '9'.

Jack, if it feels too intense just open your eyes a little and look down at your feet. I can direct you through it if you need me to help you regulate with opening the eyes, or we can access the skills you've been developing ... Let me know ...

[Jack opens his eyes a little, bending forward slightly to look at his feet.]

What's happening now, Jack? What are you noticing?

[Jack closes his eyes and sits back in the chair.] Yeah, it's gone down a bit, maybe a '7', perhaps a '6'. I'm okay.

And what's happening in your chest?

The pressure has lessened. My throat is still clamped, like there's something in there.

So notice that, Jack. What else are you aware of in your throat? Maybe see if you can move in closer.

It's interesting, it's different. There are different tones, maybe textures, in there ... Interesting ...

Hmmm.

I can get right inside it ...

Aha. Notice how it is to come in close ... and if it changes as you come in closer still.

Inside ... it's not what I expected ... It's not all dark ... there's light in here ...

So notice that, Jack, and how it is when you're curious towards it.

It's kind of throbbing, like it's alive ... cool ...

And what's happening in your chest, Jack, where you felt the pressure?

Hmm ... can't find it ... Maybe a little bit, but that feeling has gone. Wow. [*Jack opens his eyes.*] How amazing is that!

So just notice your attitude and orientation to the internal experience of the body right at this moment, Jack. How would you describe it?

Well, like I'm an explorer. No, maybe Sherlock Holmes. Yeah, I'm Sherlock Holmes, and I'm investigating something dreadful and finding the hidden clues. It's quite exciting really.

So you're curious and open to what you might find?

Yep, and I'm focused. I'm really tuned in.

And how does it feel in your body to approach activation this way?

I guess this is activation, isn't it? Funny, I hadn't made that link. Not so bad. Well, interesting, to be honest.

So quite different to how you were feeling about activation when we started?

For the moment. I'm not saying I'll feel like this at home.

And of course activation presents differently, and different things trip us up.

Is that why I get caught up in my thinking?

I think that's what you're usually most aware of, Jack. You've been oriented to your thinking about the trigger or other person or situation, and you've been unable to access these internal reactions because they pull you back into your earliest experiences of being overwhelmed and powerless. But yes, you habitually orient to your thoughts or the other person.

Yeah, and I feel powerless.

And I think rage is often an indicator of powerlessness and the fear that goes with it. What's interesting is that your attention is on the thing that you are least able to change – the other person, usually your boss.

Ha! That's a good one, isn't it? So instead of getting out of the trap of that cycle, I keep myself stuck in it, because I'm stuck on what I can't change. How wild is that? Not very smart, right?

Well, Jack, we want to be gentle, as we would towards a small child, when we begin to uncover how we've survived and protected ourselves when life overwhelmed us. You were once a little boy, living in terror, doing the best you could. Your brain-body-mind constructed a protective pattern the best way it knew how at the time. Then it kept doing it for all the reasons we've discussed. In fact, trying to change it can feel threatening to the system. I wondered if that is why you get so activated about activation.

That would make sense. I've done this to lock it all down and forget all the pain, and now I'm turning to look it in the eye. I'm even giving it a name – activation. It's like poking a big dog that's been locked up in the shed for months, or years.

And that has driven your attitude and orientation to activation and to change. Change can feel threatening because your system has built up layers of protection so you don't have to feel the fear. So responding differently, like not trying to avoid-escape or approaching with curiosity, can create a panic or frustration and intense ambivalence of wanting to change and not wanting to change. Or only wanting to change in the way that you associate with stopping the feelings, not by moving towards and through uncomfortable feelings into integration and so giving the brain different feedback.

So I'm frustrated but maybe it's because I don't want to change. Is that what you're saying?

I'm saying that any change in the stability of the system can feel threatening.

Okay. Like I want to change but I don't want to change?

Exactly.

Yep, I've got that one. I want to change but only so I feel good or don't feel bad.

That's why we need to come in close, gently, and not try to change anything, because we can trigger a whole alarm reaction. But if instead we move towards the experience with curiosity, the brain can change. This is the paradox of change. We don't want to freak the kid out. We want to treat it as you would treat your son. This little guy, your Ted brain, is working hard and has worked hard all your life to keep you safe. It just needs to know it can put down the gun.

The brain and the map

A baby with a gun is always a worry. I think that's been me. I can see him with his grubby face – he's howling, his filthy nappy is dragging on the ground, he's got a bottle in one hand and a gun in the other. That would be me.

And how do you want it to be, Jack?

I'd like to grab the gun from the little fella and throw it away. Then pick him up, change his nappy and give him a bath and something warm to eat. Poor little guy, he looks like no one loves him.

Nice, Jack. Much kinder than how you sometimes approach little Ted brain.

At the top of this graph is a '10'. Ten is code for when your system is in full alarm mode, what we're calling *activation*. This is the cue word that helps your brain recognise what's happening, like the little kid having a nightmare.

Down at the bottom is a '0'. This zero includes avoid, numb, dissociation and most secondary reactions and the urge to avoid-escape overwhelming distress. For Jack, this means reaching for a Scotch.

Some people are mostly in a state of activation and overwhelm (8–10), what we call 'hyper-arousal', and ready for threat. And some people are constantly down at zero in shutdown: numb, avoidant or controlled, controlling. But often people experience both, like 'wired and tired'.

The brain is a self-organising system

The brain is an incredible self-organising system. It takes every experience and organises it into a map or network of pathways, and sometimes highways, for easy access so the map can be used later to respond to similar events. Then, when you have any experience or encounter in the

The integration Zone or i-Zone

environment, the brain pulls up the relevant map or network to make sense of what is happening and responds accordingly.

The brain is like a massive memory system with files and blueprints for everything. Not actual files but interconnected networks of information-experience, what we call 'memory' or 'learning', scattered throughout the brain, and this process of integrating and sorting is happening all the time. You could say that the brain is a constant gardener or is always doing the housework. This is down to what I call the *i-Zone*, the *integration Zone*, or like what's referred to as the Default Mode Network. The brain sifts and sorts through new experiences, working out what goes with what, creating new maps and linking to existing memory maps or adapting and upgrading old maps based on new experience.

This system usually works effectively with memory that isn't linked to traumatic or overwhelming events. The brain simply processes the experience or information into the correct connection or association and makes any adjustments so that maps and networks are continually updated (what we refer to as learning), though as your brain ages it is less likely to update and more likely to rely on existing maps, possibly coffee-stained or moth-eaten.

But what if the brain is using the wrong map to make sense of the current situation? What if the brain is using an old map or a fragment of a map that doesn't fit this experience here and now? What if the brain's filing system doesn't know what is relevant or irrelevant in the constant stream of stimuli coming at it from the environment, and is therefore overwhelmed or treats everything as a threat? To explain what happens with traumatic or overwhelming memories, let's go back to our friend Bruce and the chlorine.

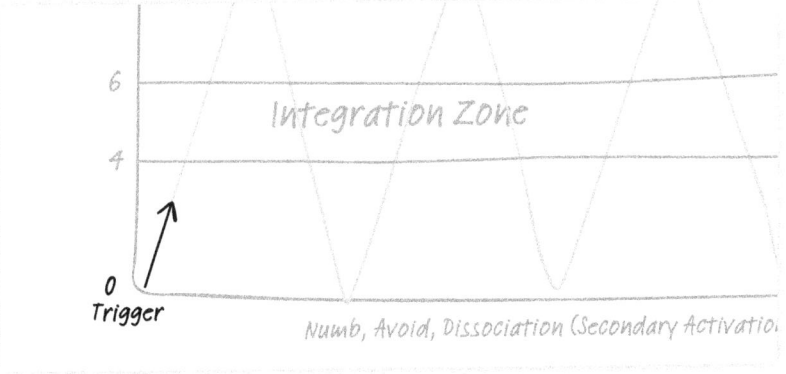

Bruce smells the chlorine (trigger), and his brain tries to recognise and find the right map or network so it knows how to respond to this chlorine smell. The brain starts to connect the smell of chlorine with previous experience. 'Sniff, sniff, hmm, what's that smell?' asks the brain, as it checks the system for associations with past chlorine experiences – of course this it happening at lightning speed without any words.

The brain tries to make the relevant connections but the smell of chlorine is tied to an old memory map of trauma in the body-brain that is fragmented or frozen rather than integrated, and suddenly the body drops into re-experiencing the original body memory associated with chlorine. Bruce's system drops into alarm-survival mode and overwhelm, (leaps to a '10' on our scale), and his brain is unable to integrate the memory because everything is focused on dealing with danger-threat-alarm, which he's experiencing as current through the body.

Remember that when the brain is in survival mode it overrides the other functions in the brain, and therefore it can't make the necessary connections to recognise the activation; it's just *in* the experience, lost in a dark tunnel. There is no interconnectivity in the brain, the hippocampus doesn't recognise the experience because it was out to lunch when this experience was imprinted, and there is nothing to mediate between lower brain and big brain.

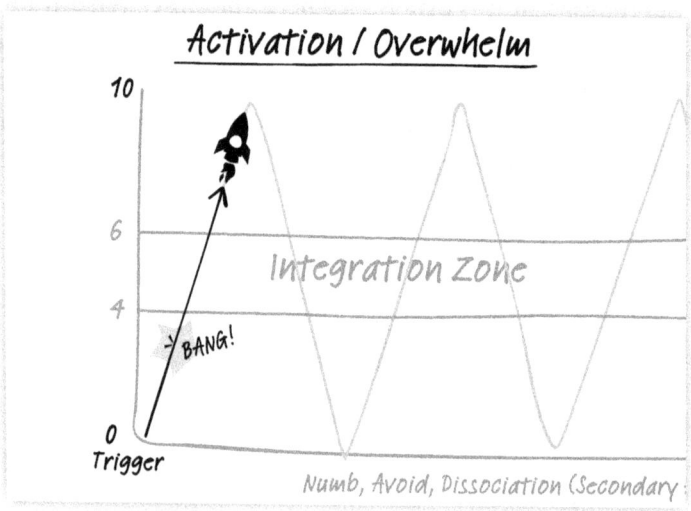

The lower brain is fully activated, and Bruce feels overwhelmed and extremely distressed. The brain doesn't recognise what he's experiencing as a memory, something that happened thirty-five years ago in Bruce's case, but treats it as a current threat.

The instinct of escape: 'Get out of there!'

When the lower brain is highly activated (8–10) and overwhelmed, in threat-alarm mode, the whole system screams, 'Danger, danger! Get the hell out of there! Do something!' The brain drops into survival mode, grabbing all your attention. A cocktail of chemicals and hormones flush through the body so you have the biological resources to escape the danger.

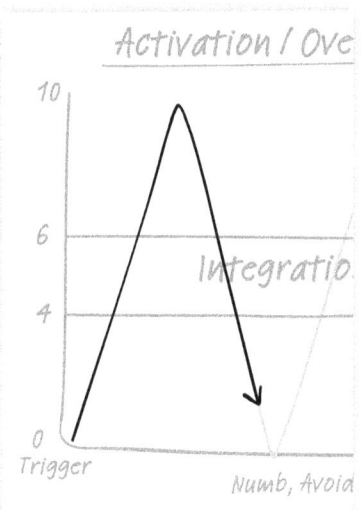

This alarm response is the perfect survival system when a lion is running towards you. It mobilises you to escape to safety. But if the danger is in your body, based on something that happened thirty years ago, then it's like running away from yourself, and you can't escape that feeling of terror or dread because it's inside you. So instead you go numb, shut down or do something else to escape or reduce the distress. You reach for a drink or a cigarette, storm out, try to suppress feelings of vulnerability, yell, scream, talk a lot, and so on.

The roller coaster

This escape gives you momentary relief because you've avoided or escaped the distress for the time being, which reinforces the avoid-escape response. But then something else gets triggered – say, for Bruce, his young son wants to have swimming lessons – something reminds you of or triggers the overwhelming events that the brain hasn't been able to integrate, and you're activated again, and again, and again.

The brain and the map

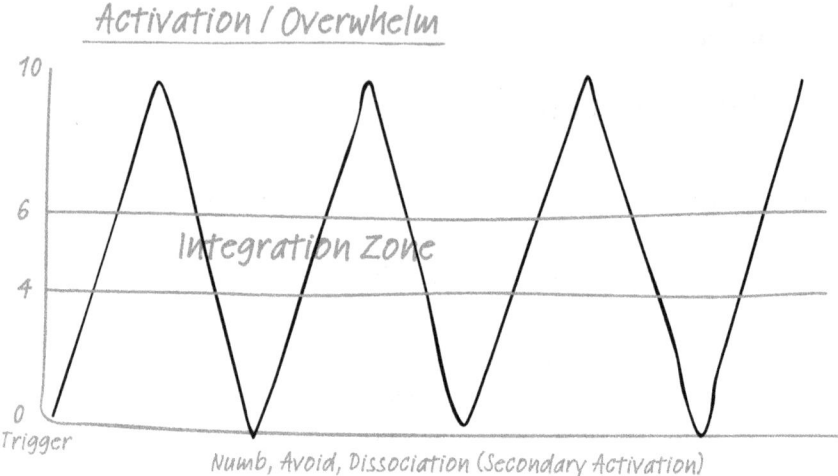

In short

To explain it simply, the brain is continually making associations and trying to integrate or connect all the dots, including traumatic or overwhelming events. But when trauma memories are triggered, it re-activates the material, which the brain doesn't recognise as memory for all the reasons we've discussed, so the brain treats the situation as a current danger, and re-experiences it as overwhelming. The brain can't integrate when it's overwhelmed/activated because it's in survival-defence mode and completely focused on responding to the perceived threat. The lower brain overrides other brain functioning that would normally allow the experience to be integrated to become just a memory, rather than re-experienced as real and current. In short, no integration occurs.

Remembering versus re-experiencing

Remembering means you know you're remembering, but re-experiencing is like dropping into the memory as if it is real and current. Integrating a traumatic memory doesn't mean forgetting it; it means learning to remember so that it isn't re-experienced but remembered, like watching the movie rather than being in the movie.

A further complication

To complicate matters, the brain needs *some* activation (the map needs to be open) to be able to process and integrate the material. If you are right down in your comfort zone of avoid-escape or numb (at 0 on the axis), it's like locking the door and never revisiting that material or staying on the beach rather than going into the water. That would be fine if the tactic worked, except that you continue to get triggered by events or situations. In other words, avoidance doesn't work. In fact, it perpetuates the problem, as we've discussed previously, because the brain continues to get the message that the experience or memory is still threatening, which activates the alarm response, and so on.

But if you are fully activated, at an '8', '9' or '10', and the system is in overwhelm, operating in survival mode, the brain is unable to integrate the material because it's busy dealing with the threat as immediate danger. This is like trying to put your washing away with an armed burglar in the bedroom. You don't care about neatly folding and putting away your clean underwear because all you can focus on is the armed burglar.

Enter the integration Zone, the i-Zone

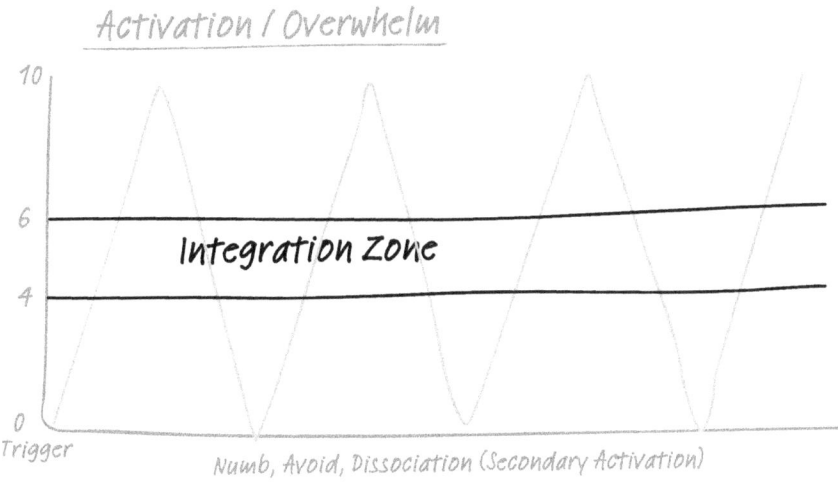

In here is the *i-Zone*, what John Briere calls the *window of tolerance* or *therapeutic window*. It's a bit different for everyone and will change as your brain integrates. When your brain can access the *i-Zone* it's able to integrate the material or the body-memory map. The *i-Zone* is like *the*

edge for a sports person, who challenges herself but doesn't go beyond her capabilities; or in yoga, stretching to your limit but not causing injury.

We can't *do* integration, the brain does that – but we can create the conditions that encourage the brain to integrate. Just like we can't heal the body but we can give the body what it needs to heal itself. Gardening is another metaphor for this organic process: we can shape and encourage when we understand the principles, but we don't actually grow things, Nature does that. We can, however, create optimum conditions for growth.

I want to teach you some techniques to use when you drop into activation, to help you move towards the *i-Zone* to provide the right conditions for brain integration. The main technique, AIR(s), is based on mindfulness, and is a structured sequence to assist you to move through the activation and give the brain different feedback to the old pathways and responses that have kept you stuck in the loop, or activation cycle.

This technique can help you to reduce your distress or activation, bring your attention into the present and help your brain become interconnected again. It can help you enter the *i-Zone*. When you can do this you have a different experience of what's going on, and, especially important, you start to believe you can manage it. Your brain reads the situation as no longer threatening. Change the experience, and you change the brain.

Although it may seem that the aim of the technique is to reduce the level of distress or activation, this is only partly true: we are not focused on reducing the distress because that can easily become another avoid-escape reaction. The main reason for reducing the activation is to bring you into the *i-Zone* to give the brain a different message. Once you enter the *i-Zone*, the brain can begin to integrate the memory map of overwhelming events and change the way you make meaning of the experience.

Powerlessness

One of the most debilitating things about post-traumatic stress is feeling powerless, so beginning to understand what is happening (having a map) begins to change the experience of activation. Next, developing strategies you can use when you feel overwhelmed is essential to changing the experience. Your job is to reduce the level of distress sufficiently to move towards the *i-Zone*.

Once you learn the techniques to move into the *i-Zone* you'll probably refine them over time and develop your own strategies, as you understand what works best for you. But the other thing that usually happens is that the brain starts working with you and does a lot of the integration effortlessly and outside your awareness, like the Default Mode Network does, because that's the brain's job – to makes associations and integrate experience, to learn and change.

Jack, activation to integration

Rita: In the beginning the main thing is simply to recognise what's going on as activation. If you can flick on awareness during activation, the brain can start to make new connections.

Jack: Okay, so you'll show me how to do it? Because at the moment I have no idea how to get into this zone you keep talking about.

You don't have to work it out. You don't have to ask, 'Oh, am I integrating or overwhelming? Am I in the zone yet?' Your job is firstly to recognise that it's happening and name it as activation. Just naming it begins to interrupt the old pathway and create the possibility of a new pathway, as your brain builds an association with this new map.

So I'm not trying to stop it when I see it happening?

No, Jack. This is the hardest thing to 'get'. We are so used to trying to stop or avoid feeling bad that we respond automatically that way. But, remember, we are working with the brain here, the most sophisticated system in the universe. We are simply creating the conditions for the brain to do the integrating.

So my job is to be aware and call it activation? Like if the kid is having a nightmare?

Yes, through awareness you're flicking on the light or switching on parts of the brain. The brain does the integrating. Doing something comes last, because if we do something without the other steps we're not allowing the brain to switch into integration mode. And usually the doing is to escape the activation.

Not doing? Hmm, that's novel. Sounds Buddhist to me.

Well, the Buddha did teach what we now realise is perhaps the most practical and accessible technique for brain change that we know of. Once you switch on the light in your brain you're more likely to be able to get your attention and bring it into the present. Trying to work out if you're getting it right, asking 'Is this overwhelming me or am I integrating? Am I there yet?' is like going back into the 'fix it–work it out–get it right' mode, and likely to keep the big brain in a spin but unable to make the necessary connections. What I'm describing is more like moving with and holding on at the same time.

Like surfing. You have to give in to the wave but stay focused and sort of in control, directing all at the same time.

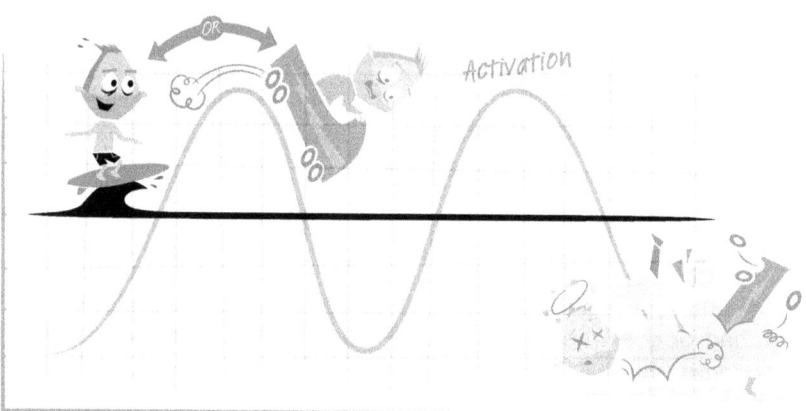

Perfect metaphor, Jack, for moving between activation and integration. It's the difference between riding a wave and being tumbled by a wave. The wave still happens – that's the activation, but how you respond can be very different. If you go out too far into deep water before you have the capacity to ride large waves, you're likely to get dumped and overwhelmed. Like the feeling of overwhelm you describe at work.

Yep, that's like being dumped by a big, fat rogue wave.

But if you start in the shallows and build your skills on smaller waves, you gradually become more proficient and can tackle the larger waves until you can ride any wave, even those tricky rogue waves. In clinical terms, it's similar to what we call titration of the trauma material, learning to deal with the waves coming at you in manageable bites.

I think I like the surfing analogy better than ti – titration. It sounds like a disease. But I can see myself out in the ocean riding those giant waves with the wind in my hair, salty skin …

You could think about the mindfulness technique AIR(s) I'll show you shortly as the surfboard that supports you to ride the waves. But there are other techniques you could use. You might use a variety of surfboards or change or stylise it to suit your needs.

Sounds like I'm getting the beginner's surfboard.

In the beginning, I suggest you just assume that any distress is activation. If it's not, you'll be more present to what's going on anyway and can respond appropriately using all your resources.

Just ride the waves, huh?

Yep. Remember you need some activation, a wave, for the brain to integrate. We're not making activation wrong or trying to stop it, nor are we trying to make it happen. We're just giving you more choice about how you respond when it's happening.

I can't learn to surf by sitting on the beach or reading a book, right?

Right, you have to get wet. Your job is to do manually what the hippocampus couldn't do during the traumatic or overwhelming experience, which is to give the brain context – place and time, recall and a map, and something to orient to when it's lost. The mindfulness-based technique I call AIR(s) encourages this process.

Jack, looking for integration

Jack: Argh! I just wish I could get a clear answer about what integration looks like, what the signs are that I'm integrating. I'm so used to setting goals and deadlines and measuring how I'm doing, it's driving me crazy not even knowing what the end result looks like.

Rita: If you think you know what integration looks like, you're likely to go looking for those signs. You'll have an expectation, an orientation that will prime the brain. Instead of allowing and being with the wave, you'll start to direct your attention, probably to how the wave *should* be and how you *should* respond. With this perfect wave or expectation in your head, aka 'the signs of integration' that don't match current reality, your brain will read your situation as wrong, or at least not quite right. You'll have to get it right, and your brain will switch to alert, because something is not quite right. Then it might start to worry that you're not integrating and lose faith in what you're doing. Alternatively, you'll try to make something happen, what you expect to happen. This is all secondary activation.

Oh no!

Do I detect a hint of cynicism there, Jack?

Rita, please can we just get on with it. Give me the dirt on integration, measuring integration. Please!

There is none, Jack.

This is very frustrating.

Okay, let me ask you this. How do you measure a wave? What is the goal or outcome of a wave?

I don't know. It doesn't have one. It's just a wave.

That's integration, Jack. Sure, we might measure the impact of the wave, its velocity, or say the surf's up, but each wave is just a wave.

But how will I know what to look for in integration? How will I know if I'm on track?

Your integration process, your wave, will be unique. Your brain will integrate whatever it needs to, and we can't predict that. We can see signs – perhaps it's that your anxiety is less or you enjoy things more and sleep better, but these are like the froth on a wave. What is actually going on is beyond what we can understand.

Brain magic?

Yes, Jack, brain magic. And watching for signs only orients you in a particular way that's likely to reduce integration. As I've said, your job is simply to move towards the i-Zone during activation, and the brain will do the rest; that's its job.

[*Jack shrugs.*] So I'm not taking a photo of the wave. I'm just riding it in the moment without trying to measure how well I'm doing. That's integration.

Sounds like a good definition of the process of integration, Jack.

Small spontaneous difference

The best indicators of brain integration that I've observed are small spontaneous changes, like doing something fun that you haven't done for years, or improved sleep, less of an impulse to engage in addictive behaviours. When your usual focus is on what isn't right, you can easily overlook these small subtle spontaneous changes, and it's useful to keep an eye out for any slight difference. Especially notice if you're getting more pleasure and enjoyment out of things.

A metaphor or story for integration

There was once a sea zoo, an aquarium, and the owner-trainer acquired several dolphins from the wild and began to train them to do tricks so they could perform for the public. When he noticed them doing something he wanted them to repeat, he gave them a fish. We call this *operant conditioning*. Over several weeks, the dolphin trainer 'taught' the slippery, splashing troupe numerous tricks, all for a few fish.

Then one morning the dolphins came out and performed a whole new series of tricks the trainer had never seen before. They 'got it' and invented their own tricks. They didn't need him to teach them; they just needed to understand what he wanted them to do.

For me this is the same process that occurs in integration. It is how the brain integrates when it 'gets it'. In this case, the tricks we're giving it are in the i-brainmap and application of AIR(s) but these have been developed in an attempt to replicate what occurs spontaneously in the brain as it integrates.

The brain is a genius at integration when it has the right information that communicates to all parts of the brain, not just the intellect, and when we reduce the inhibitors to integration. It 'gets it' and develops its own tricks. At first it's a bit cumbersome, and we need to feed it fish (fish oil is good too). In the beginning it takes time and effort to change old pathways, but over time the brain does its magic just like the dolphins and comes up with some tricks of its own. I call this the 'dolphin connection' or 'integration'.

Integration is the brain's default

Integration is a spontaneous process in the brain, like the default when everything is working as intended. As I've said, we don't *do* integration, the brain does; we create the conditions for integration to occur, especially regulating activation and orienting to here and now and reducing what inhibits integration. AIR(s), the technique I'll unpack in the following chapters, articulates some steps in moving through activation towards integration, like learner wheels on a surfboard. Yeah, I know that analogy doesn't work, but I made you look!

Before we move into AIR(s) I'll discuss the importance of orientation and what I call the 'AND pathway' in the next chapter. I see this as central to brain integration.

Chapter 15
Orientation and the AND pathway

In this chapter I discuss orientation and the AND pathway in detail because they are at the heart of integration and underpin i-brainmap. I explain relevant theories and hypotheses about the brain that I've developed in working with clients (especially in the context of i-brainmap), the techniques I've developed (AIR(s) and i-AM), and through studying available research. But because of the scope of this book I have simplified my theories and hypotheses into threads of ideas in order to invite your curiosity, so you can take the ideas and run with them to investigate for yourself.

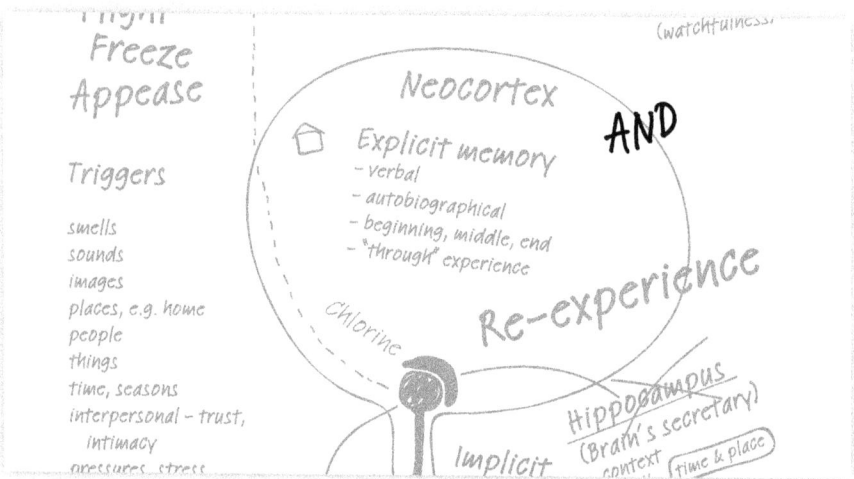

Orientation

By *orienting* or *orientation* I'm referring to how you meet an experience, how you are in relation to an object, situation, experience, person or anything else. This includes which senses you use to detect something, where you are in relation to it, what context or environment you are in, and even how you hold your head in relation to your shoulders; these are all factors of orientation. Whether you habitually orient to your internal or the external environment, to either–or, or to both internal *and* external is part of orientation. And which body-memory maps are associated with an experience or stimuli, and what your mental representations of that experience are, because after repeated exposure to a situation the brain tends to orient towards your memory map of experience rather than orient to the moment-to-moment emerging experience. We call this 'learning' or 'lazy/efficient' brain.

Orientation includes all levels of experience, and I'm proposing that it underpins all brain functioning. Before we can respond to anything we have to attend to it, and that involves our orientation to it. What we attend to, how we attend, which memory maps the brain uses in response, are all the invisible threads of orienting that define how we appraise, interpret and then respond to any given stimuli.

Common maps of orientation

Through repeated experience the brain develops recognisable maps that orient us, such as: *glass half-full/glass half-empty, turning towards – approach, turning away – withdraw, looking forward* to something, *getting on top, getting on with things, blaming* or *finding the problem, solving the problem.*

How we orient to another person will influence how we see them; do I focus on how I am *different* to you or how we are the *same*? If I focus on what you *do,* or your family of origin, I may have a different experience of you than if I ask you how you feel about X or Y or which footy team you barrack for or who you vote for.

How you orient in the morning can affect your mental state and the tone of the day. Do you focus on the fight you had with your partner the night before, the fact that the neighbour's dog woke you at 4 am again, the big meeting at work that you haven't done enough prep for, who will take little Tommy to his dentist appointment? Or on the holiday to Europe you're planning? Or, feeling overwhelmed and exhausted, all of the above? Most of us don't notice how we orient our attention; it happens habitually or in response to the demands of the environment.

Orientation is mostly invisible and layered (as water is to the fish), like the intention behind an action that gives the brain a specific message. These invisible layers of orientation, such as the difference between an orientation that is accepting or avoiding, can affect everything. We

The brain and the map

develop habits of orientation like a series of maps based on repeated experiences and responses that the brain uses to orient to the world.

Changing your orientation from the inside can be difficult. It's like the eye trying to see itself. You need a mirror. Relationships are that mirror. Psychotherapy can be a mirror, a way to reflect on your way of seeing things. Most therapeutic approaches are inherently reorienting. CBT, for instance, orients attention away from the event or trigger and orients you towards your thinking or interpretation of the event and your behavior. Mindfulness is one of the most effective techniques because it teaches you to become aware of your orientation and also how to reorient attention.

Orientation includes intention and attention

Orientation is a specific neurological function that involves the hippocampus but is often referred to in the literature as navigation. The term 'navigation' (or 'spatial navigation') is too limited for describing what I call 'orientation' but is likely the same function. The term 'navigation' doesn't recognise how essential orientation is in brain function, because most of the focus (or orientation) in brain science has been on spatial navigation in a physical environment (usually of rats) and on memory function when the hippocampus is studied. But orientation is most important for brains in the wild, because it directs what the brain orients to, or doesn't orient to, and therefore how we know the world. It's also likely that orientation underpins learning and memory.

But to understand orientation we need to go right back to the beginning.

 **The orienting reflex/response and i**

I don't use the term 'orienting respor term is used to refer to a more specific referring to as orientation, although function. In the orienting response stimulus that is novel, significant, predictab aspect to this is habituation, which refers stimulus that is repeated will lose its sal a time.

The orienting response is orientati in response to external stimuli. I'm curring continually as the brain orie and stimuli. I'm proposing that th directs attention and therefore pret and respond to the world.

I also think the 'imprinting' lings as they 'attached' to t' usually mother (though ir also the same function a

I'm suggesting that the orienting function

In the beginr

When you were
This is so fun(
The body is '
   At birt'
smells, s
bawl. F
you'd
else
y

provi
to mother ,
kickstarted by a n

As I was saying, in the beginning the baby brain's primary orientations are around food and comfort, pleasure and pain, and safety. These are the foundation for all other maps about the world.

So what about my brain? If Mum was scared because of the way my father treated her, my brain got that message?

Yes, Jack. So your body-brain wired in fear-danger along with safety of closeness to your mum. But the good news is that your brain is plastic. You can change these early maps. And I think the fastest way to do that is change your orientation, which I think is more fundamental than attachment.

Yeah, but isn't it all wired in?

Yes it's wired in, Jack, but with awareness and curiosity you can give the brain-body different feedback and create new maps of experience that let the brain know that everything is safe now.

But what about all the fear stuff I got from Mum's brain?

Well, along with that fear, your mum was a 'good enough mother' and gave your brain sufficient nourishment and safety and responded to your needs. That's how you love Katie and Ted, because you've got a love map.

A love map, Rita!

Is that a bit too fluffy?

Well, it could be a ... movie ... or maybe a book. But it wouldn't be something I'd read.

The point I want to make is that those early body-memory maps of experience have a particular orientation. Threat-danger is a primal orientation, but when that was mediated by your mother your brain was able to develop some maps of safety: *I'm scared and I'm safe because Mum's here* maps. If you're alive you probably got this much. Then later came the attachment maps, which are more complex brain-body maps of experience.

But I don't get why it's so important whether you call it 'orientation' or 'attachment'.

Because I think it's much harder to change patterns of attachment and easier to change orientation. And orientation is much more primal than attachment.

And?

The brain and the map

Well, when you drop into survival mode I need to orient or reorient your attention rather than engage interpersonal brain function or attachment, because you will probably push me away. Or you might grab onto me, attach, rather than creating the conditions for the brain to integrate. This happens because while you're in survival mode your interpersonal brain function is disconnected and drops into more basic brain function.

So when I'm activated I still have the capacity to orient but not to attach or connect with someone?

Yes, often that's what people experience. It's like the brain reverts to basic functioning, like baby brain, which includes the capacity to orient but not the more sophisticated functions of attachment and interpersonal functioning, when it's in survival mode. So it's unlikely I'll be able to help you reconnect through interpersonal contact. First I focus on orienting or reorienting, otherwise you can stay stuck in survival brain.

Is that why I stonewall Katie when I feel crap, stressed out ... activated?

Yeah, that could be one reason. And it's very hard to override that wiring of wanting to withdraw when it's associated with survival and feelings of threat-alarm.

So instead of trying to talk to Katie, I what ... how do I orient, or reorient?

Well I'm going to teach you a technique that is based on orienting or re-orienting, called AIR(s). You reorient through the senses, usually to here and now so your brain gets the message that there's no current threat: count pomegranates, or listen for birds. Engaging the orienting function brings the hippocampus online, so you've entered the integration zone – that brain functioning which also hooks up to the left prefrontal cortex; everyone (in the brain family) is online, you could say.

So when I drop into activation all my interpersonal equipment isn't available. And I can't make contact until I can orient or de-activate, because I'm oriented to threat. Is that it?

That's it, Jack. That's why orientation is fundamental to this process of integration. Orientation is the missing link between activation and integration. And it's a more accessible brain function to mediate distress than interpersonal, or cognitive, functioning, which are unavailable when the brain drops into survival mode.

 The i-brainmap, AIR(s) and inter-Active Mindfulness are all different ways to help the brain orient or reorient. The map gives you something to orient towards when you're lost in activation, and the techniques help the brain reorient. Mindfulness teaches how to orient and reorient the brain.

Attention is to orientation what emotion is to mood

Attention is how you focus awareness in any moment, what you focus on. As you repeatedly attend in a certain way, your brain builds memory maps based on repeated experience, especially about what is significant: a sense of place or placement, the context for experience, is all part of the map. These are your *habits of attention* and are central to orientation, creating a loop. Some of your most basic orientations, often invisible because they are assumed, were developed through your earliest contact with your mother and how she responded to you and your different experiences. These are your earliest body-memory maps.

Meet AND

AND is a particular orientation. Your first AND pathway was between your body and your mother. As I said, your primary orientation was and is through the body. Having mother to orient towards when you felt scared, overwhelmed or hungry gave your little brain the message, 'I feel scared, starving, in pain ... AND there's that big soft warm, smelly thing called 'mother', suck, suck, burp, pat pat. Now I'm warm, clean, fed, Phew! Everything's okay,' and some delicious chemicals flooded your bloodstream, 'Ooh, this is good', and you grinned up at Mum with your big, wet, toothless grin and wriggled your fat legs.

In the beginning, before your 'mother map' was established, your mother needed to be holding you for your brain to get the message that it was safe, that everything was okay. But as your experience of mother was repeated consistently, *mother equals safe*, Mum only needed to come into the room and speak in that ridiculous way 'goo, goo' and your body-brain opened up that memory map of *everything's okay, Mum's here*, and your body relaxed and you stopped screaming. This was the beginning of the AND pathway, your brain was able to move through a distressing experience because it had a larger map that told you everything would be okay.

If your distress was too high, a nightmare say, then your mother might have needed to revert to the more basic model and hold and rock you, because you had disconnected from your higher-order maps and dropped into baby brain. Until Mum could soothe and comfort you to down-regulate, your brain couldn't make contact through visually seeing her or hearing her voice. Your mother had to revert to the primal language system, touch and contact with your distressed little body, because higher-order functioning wasn't available, not until you were more settled.

The AND pathway as a unique state of orientation

The AND pathway is a specific orientation and at the centre of brain integration; it's what the brain does when it is integrating, interconnected, interacting, in flow. When it is stuck on stress or overwhelm it is split; there is no AND. The i-brainmap and the AIR(s) and inter-Active Mindfulness techniques imitate this brain state of interconnectivity.

The i-brainmap provides the brain with a map that offers a different orientation to the experience of activation and integration: a whole-brain, inclusive (AND), interconnected and interactive orientation. AIR(s) and inter-Active Mindfulness replicate the AND orientation, which is the healthy state of the brain when it's not stuck on stress, and encourage integration and interconnectedness.

Jack, AND or yes but ...

Rita: 'I feel scared, but I'm still here,' is different to saying, 'I feel scared, and I'm still here.'

Jack: Isn't that just semantics?

Language reflects subtle differences in our relationship to things. You say it, Jack.

Okay, 'I'm here ... but ...' No. 'I feel scared, but I'm still here.' 'I'm scared, and I'm still here.'

or the external environment, to either–or, or to both internal *and* external is part of orientation. And which body-memory maps are associated with an experience or stimuli, and what your mental representations of that experience are, because after repeated exposure to a situation the brain tends to orient towards your memory map of experience rather than orient to the moment-to-moment emerging experience. We call this 'learning' or 'lazy/efficient' brain.

Orientation includes all levels of experience, and I'm proposing that it underpins all brain functioning. Before we can respond to anything we have to attend to it, and that involves our orientation to it. What we attend to, how we attend, which memory maps the brain uses in response, are all the invisible threads of orienting that define how we appraise, interpret and then respond to any given stimuli.

Common maps of orientation

Through repeated experience the brain develops recognisable maps that orient us, such as: *glass half-full/glass half-empty, turning towards – approach, turning away – withdraw, looking forward* to something, *getting on top, getting on with things, blaming* or *finding the problem, solving the problem.*

How we orient to another person will influence how we see them; do I focus on how I am *different* to you or how we are the *same*? If I focus on what you *do,* or your family of origin, I may have a different experience of you than if I ask you how you feel about X or Y or which footy team you barrack for or who you vote for.

How you orient in the morning can affect your mental state and the tone of the day. Do you focus on the fight you had with your partner the night before, the fact that the neighbour's dog woke you at 4 am again, the big meeting at work that you haven't done enough prep for, who will take little Tommy to his dentist appointment? Or on the holiday to Europe you're planning? Or, feeling overwhelmed and exhausted, all of the above? Most of us don't notice how we orient our attention; it happens habitually or in response to the demands of the environment.

Orientation is mostly invisible and layered (as water is to the fish), like the intention behind an action that gives the brain a specific message. These invisible layers of orientation, such as the difference between an orientation that is accepting or avoiding, can affect everything. We develop habits of orientation like a series of maps based on repeated experiences and responses that the brain uses to orient to the world.

Changing your orientation from the inside can be difficult. It's like the eye trying to see itself. You need a mirror. Relationships are that mirror. Psychotherapy can be a mirror, a way to reflect on your way of seeing things. Most therapeutic approaches are inherently reorienting. CBT, for instance, orients attention away from the event or trigger and orients you towards your thinking or interpretation of the event and your behavior. Mindfulness is one of the most effective techniques because it teaches you to become aware of your orientation and also how to reorient attention.

Orientation includes intention and attention

Orientation is a specific neurological function that involves the hippocampus but is often referred to in the literature as navigation. The term 'navigation' (or 'spatial navigation') is too limited for describing what I call 'orientation' but is likely the same function. The term 'navigation' doesn't recognise how essential orientation is in brain function, because most of the focus (or orientation) in brain science has been on spatial navigation in a physical environment (usually of rats) and on memory function when the hippocampus is studied. But orientation is most important for brains in the wild, because it directs what the brain orients to, or doesn't orient to, and therefore how we know the world. It's also likely that orientation underpins learning and memory.

But to understand orientation we need to go right back to the beginning.

>
> ### The orienting reflex/response and imprinting
>
> I don't use the term 'orienting response' because that term is used to refer to a more specific aspect of what I'm referring to as orientation, although it may be the same function. In the orienting response, attention is drawn to stimulus that is novel, significant, predictable or intense. The other aspect to this is habituation, which refers to the process whereby a stimulus that is repeated will lose its salience and be ignored after a time.
>
> The orienting response is orientation observed from the outside, in response to external stimuli. I'm suggesting that orienting is occurring continually as the brain orients to internal and external cues and stimuli. I'm proposing that the way the brain orients habitually directs attention and therefore how we experience, perceive, interpret and respond to the world.
>
> I also think the 'imprinting' that Konrad Lorenz observed in hatchlings as they 'attached' to the first moving object they encountered, usually mother (though in Lorenz's work they attached to him), is also the same function as what I refer to as 'orienting'.
>
> I'm suggesting that imprinting and even attachment are built on the orienting function of the brain.

In the beginning

When you were born your primary orientation was through the body. This is so fundamental to human experience that it is often overlooked. The body is to the brain what water is to the fish.

At birth the world was sensory overload for your delicate system: smells, sounds and cold air assaulted your senses and you started to bawl. But then you smelt something familiar. A big, soft, warm thing you'd later call *mother*. You *oriented* to her and could forget everything else. Your mother was a one-stop-shop for all your survival needs: *ahh* – your brain-body could relax.

At birth you didn't have the brain equipment for anything much more than very basic survival, and some interpersonal blueprints or instincts; if you had all the equipment your brain would have been too large to be birthed. But the hippocampus was already 40 per cent mature at birth, providing enough equipment to orient to mother. This capacity to orient to mother was all you needed to survive, and mother could do the rest, kickstarted by a flood of oxytocin so she'd feel all gooey at the sight and smell of you and want to protect you. In that critical period after birth your brain was imprinted with 'mother' through your senses, particularly smell, taste and touch, because your other senses were still underdeveloped. Very rapidly your baby brain would develop the mechanisms for other sensory recognition, learning and attachment built on this capacity to orient.

Jack, and orientation

Rita: When Ted was tiny and he was hungry or in pain, how did you know?

Jack: He screamed, and his little body would sort of curl up in distress. Yeah, I get what you mean. It's like his body expressed exactly whatever he was feeling, like his body was his brain. No divide.

Yep, that's exactly what I mean. Before his mind developed and he had any understanding of what he was feeling, he just felt, and his whole body responded.

He let us know loud and clear when something was wrong. He had a great set of lungs on him from day one.

Then through orienting to his mother's brain, his baby brain started wiring itself, mapping patterns of experience of the world (especially safety and fear to begin), which was initially about food. His brain started learning patterns of response to the environment based on repeated experience and pruning away neurons that weren't used.

Pruning?

Yes, 'pruning' is the term used to describe the loss of neurons in the first few months after birth; capacities that aren't needed. At birth the brain is like a blueprint of possibility, but then what gets repeated is wired in and what isn't experienced or needed falls away.

A bit like muscles? Use it or lose it?

Yep, same principle. And Ted's little brain was orientated to Katie and you to get all this experience, like growing a brain, and your house is the garden. His little brain couldn't cope with everything in the environment at once. He needed to develop this after birth or his brain would have been too big to be birthed through the usual canal. His brain could ignore most of the stimuli in the environment and just orient to Mum. As his brain developed he could take in more and more of the environment.

Like Thomas!

Well, when you drop into survival mode I need to orient or reorient your attention rather than engage interpersonal brain function or attachment, because you will probably push me away. Or you might grab onto me, attach, rather than creating the conditions for the brain to integrate. This happens because while you're in survival mode your interpersonal brain function is disconnected and drops into more basic brain function.

So when I'm activated I still have the capacity to orient but not to attach or connect with someone?

Yes, often that's what people experience. It's like the brain reverts to basic functioning, like baby brain, which includes the capacity to orient but not the more sophisticated functions of attachment and interpersonal functioning, when it's in survival mode. So it's unlikely I'll be able to help you reconnect through interpersonal contact. First I focus on orienting or reorienting, otherwise you can stay stuck in survival brain.

Is that why I stonewall Katie when I feel crap, stressed out ... activated?

Yeah, that could be one reason. And it's very hard to override that wiring of wanting to withdraw when it's associated with survival and feelings of threat-alarm.

So instead of trying to talk to Katie, I what ... how do I orient, or reorient?

Well I'm going to teach you a technique that is based on orienting or reorienting, called AIR(s). You reorient through the senses, usually to here and now so your brain gets the message that there's no current threat: count pomegranates, or listen for birds. Engaging the orienting function brings the hippocampus online, so you've entered the integration zone – that brain functioning which also hooks up to the left prefrontal cortex; everyone (in the brain family) is online, you could say.

So when I drop into activation all my interpersonal equipment isn't available. And I can't make contact until I can orient or de-activate, because I'm oriented to threat. Is that it?

That's it, Jack. That's why orientation is fundamental to this process of integration. Orientation is the missing link between activation and integration. And it's a more accessible brain function to mediate distress than interpersonal, or cognitive, functioning, which are unavailable when the brain drops into survival mode.

As I was saying, in the beginning the baby brain's primary orientations are around food and comfort, pleasure and pain, and safety. These are the foundation for all other maps about the world.

So what about my brain? If Mum was scared because of the way my father treated her, my brain got that message?

Yes, Jack. So your body-brain wired in fear-danger along with safety of closeness to your mum. But the good news is that your brain is plastic. You can change these early maps. And I think the fastest way to do that is change your orientation, which I think is more fundamental than attachment.

Yeah, but isn't it all wired in?

Yes it's wired in, Jack, but with awareness and curiosity you can give the brain-body different feedback and create new maps of experience that let the brain know that everything is safe now.

But what about all the fear stuff I got from Mum's brain?

Well, along with that fear, your mum was a 'good enough mother' and gave your brain sufficient nourishment and safety and responded to your needs. That's how you love Katie and Ted, because you've got a love map.

A love map, Rita!

Is that a bit too fluffy?

Well, it could be a ... movie ... or maybe a book. But it wouldn't be something I'd read.

The point I want to make is that those early body-memory maps of experience have a particular orientation. Threat-danger is a primal orientation, but when that was mediated by your mother your brain was able to develop some maps of safety: *I'm scared and I'm safe because Mum's here* maps. If you're alive you probably got this much. Then later came the attachment maps, which are more complex brain-body maps of experience.

But I don't get why it's so important whether you call it 'orientation' or 'attachment'.

Because I think it's much harder to change patterns of attachment and easier to change orientation. And orientation is much more primal than attachment.

And?

Notice you just dropped the 'I feel' in the second one. Even that is a shift in orientation. In the 'I feel' statement, you're *with* the feeling of being scared, but in the 'I'm scared' statement, you're more *in* the feeling. The difference between 'with' and 'in' is orientation. That's orientation; it's almost invisible. In fact, a give-away sign of how you are orienting is the language you use. It's not the language itself but what it points to.

I sort of get it, but ... something's missing.

Let's take that as our 'how'.

Take what?

The way you just questioned me then, or invited some curiosity.

Oh, okay.

That's your 'how'. You're curious about what I'm saying, right? You don't quite get it yet, and you want to know more. We could call that an orientation. Your interest or curiosity is an orientation.

I'm with you so far.

Probably the easiest way to understand it is to compare it to other orientations. So if another guy, let's call him Joe, was here he might not like vague ideas, and instead of staying curious and working through his confusion by asking questions he might just shut off and tell himself, 'I don't know what she's on about, she's crazy' or something like that. Another person, say Josh, might orient to 'I have to know, I have to get it right.'

Sometimes that's what I do, right?

Yes, sometimes. And then a guy called Jake might have to tell me that I'm wrong. Each would come at it differently, and their orientation would dictate their reaction, even their perspective and how they attend.

Okay, that makes sense. So it's kind of the personality and kind of what's happening now, and some other stuff and all that goes into the pot and you get orientation. Something like that?

Yes, something like that.

Hey, like the blind men and the elephant.

Yeah, the blind men and the elephant is a good metaphor, except that I'm saying not all blind men are the same. Each of us already carries maps of orientation that direct us in how we focus attention, not just what we focus attention on, but whether we approach with curiosity or defensively or perhaps withdraw in fear or from boredom and disconnection.

The brain and the map

It's complicated. You need a 3D version of the blind men and the elephant – and it would need to be interactive, of course.

Of course, Jack. You have a curious brain that likes to play given a chance, which is why we can discuss these things. But my brain can shut down and not want to come out to play when I'm with a brain that says 'Prove it' – a critical brain or a know-it-all brain.

That's what happens to me with short Pete. It's like everything shuts down, and I go into stupid mode.

Good insight, Jack. So let's work with that to see if we can create a different orientation to your boss, so you don't drop into dumbo brain.

The blind men and the elephant

There was once a group of three blind men travelling together in India when they came upon an elephant standing in the road. Each of the blind men grabbed hold of a different part of the elephant and exclaimed that their experience was the truth. 'It's like a leathery snake,' said the first, who had a hold of the elephant's tail. 'No, it is a great column,' called another, who had hold of the elephant's leg. 'It is like a giant serpent coiling,' said another, who had hold of the trunk. All day the blind men argued about who held the truth of the beast they could not see. Finally the elephant strolled off to eat some straw, and the blind men sat on the dusty road arguing about who was right.

Jack, how orientation changes

Jack: Can you give me an example of orientation or how it changes?

Rita: Okay, let's say you have an orientation of being 'less than' or not as good as other people. Perhaps you go into a please-and-appease response. Or what if you have a 'blaming: who did this?' or 'victim: who did this to me?' orientation. When something goes wrong in your life you automatically look around for someone or something to blame.

Hmmm, that might be getting a bit close to the bone, Rita.

So something goes wrong, and you automatically orient externally, scanning to find what is wrong and what or who to blame.

Isn't that helpful? If there's a problem like a flat tyre I can fix it, right?

Yes, good point. This orientation of finding the problem and fixing it works very well when it comes to the mechanical world, but not when it comes to relationships or your internal experience. We could call it orienting to 'what's wrong' or perhaps 'fix-it' or blaming. All similar but slightly different. But the orientation is to *other*.

So my orientation is outside myself?

Yes, and it's a common orientation if there's been trauma because your system is often vigilant, scanning for threat, and when something goes wrong this scanning is ramped up until you find the problem.

It works for me.

But does it, Jack? It's helpful if you can fix that other, like a flat tyre, but we can't fix or change other people.

We should be able to.

Can you change your boss?

Nope. God knows I've tried.

The only thing you have any choice about is how you respond to his behaviour, but that means first shifting your orientation.

But that feels like I'm just letting him get away with his bad behaviour.

I didn't say anything about what you do. The first and most important shift is shifting orientation or shifting attention. From what I've seen this is the fastest way to change the brain. Intentionally shifting your orientation engages the hippocampus, so you have the potential for integration and brain change. While you habitually orient the same way, the brain is just on auto-pilot and no change is likely to occur.

But can't I think my way out of it? Is that a change in orientation?

Great question, Jack. Possibly. If your brain is interconnected – that is, if the hippocampus is online, and you're in the i-Zone – then you can probably use your thinking brain. But often your orientation is already focused in your thinking brain, while ignoring the lower brain activation. But it's the lower brain that's driving the distress or activation, and the overthinking.

Of course, and if my lower brain is on alarm I'm doing that splitting thing and those two aren't communicating. The little guy, Ted brain, is running the show. Right?

Right. So changing your orientation probably means something other than focusing on big-brain thinking, which is likely to be in a spin if there is lower brain activation. First, you need some new way to orient, something different to orient to, another point of orientation. I propose you orient to the i-brainmap, but there are other things you can orient to, and these might change over time.

And I'm giving the brain a message to wake up because something new is going on here, because I'm reacting differently instead of in the same old Ted-brain way.

You got it. That's why the first step to brain change involves changing the orientation. Otherwise the brain will operate on auto-pilot, and nothing much will change. Mindfulness is the best tool for this. It's like a muscle in changing orientation, whereas trying to think your way out of things may not help if that is your usual orientation, which it is for most people in our culture. We just get hooked into a rationalisation of lower brain distress but nothing changes.

Like I keep blaming the boss instead of considering what options I have. I go over and over the same old arguments in my head but nothing changes.

Exactly, Jack.

The AND pathway, the i-brainmap and the i-Zone

By establishing an AND pathway during activation you change your orientation to activation and therefore the experience of activation, interweaving the old map with new understanding and experience. As we say, change the experience, and you change the brain.

Because we want to encourage brain integration, not just take away the symptoms of distress, it's essential to cultivate an AND orientation.

In other words, what you do is less important than your intention or how you do it, like the way you approach the wave. When you invite curiosity and attention, with an intention of moving through rather than fixing or stopping, you give the brain different feedback, which encourages integration.

Creating an AND pathway changes your orientation by maintaining contact with the experience of distress rather than pulling away or trying to stop it, which as you know is likely to alarm the brain and perpetuate the pattern.

AND creates connection replicating the brain function of integration.

Turning towards – i-AM

Turning towards the internal experience of distress, or activation, tells the brain it is no longer threatening. When you feel threatened you turn away, run away, shut down, if it's overwhelming, cover your face; or you might stare fixedly at the threatening experience if you're dissociative. That's how your system is wired to respond during the threat, and if you continue to pull away, cover your face, or fixate attention the brain reads it as a current threat because nothing has changed.

Gently turning towards, softening attention to be curious, bending in close as a child bends in to a flower to see the beetle on the petal, gives the brain (including the lower brain) the message that the threat has passed. This is possible in session because I can continually reorient attention when it gets stuck. And when a person feels overwhelmed I consistently make contact as they experience the internal distress, creating an AND pathway – they feel overwhelmed AND they can hear my voice and respond to my questions.

Turning towards and bending in close *reorient*, creating an AND pathway. This is the principle underpinning the process of inter-Active Mindfulness (i-AM) that I use in session with clients.

One reason we may not yet fully understand the orienting function in the brain is because observing a brain in a specific context, such as a research lab, establishes a particular orientation. But the brain's capacity to orient in the everyday is what allows us to have such rich and complex lives, because we can shift attention, orient and reorient to the internal and external environment. The brain needs to make instant moment-to-moment decisions about how to orient, based on maps of experience. Until we can observe a brain in the wild it's unlikely we are even close to understanding how the brain orients and reorients when left to its own devices or how we choose to reorient. A key player in all of this is the hippocampus, and probably other brain functions involved in interactive brain mapping.

Most problems with mental wellbeing stem from some interruption in the brain's capacity to orient. One obvious one is Alzheimer's disease. The person can perform perfunctory tasks if they are directed to do so, oriented in a particular way. But their brain is unable to orient to the environment and then to the relevant body-memory map to make a cup of tea, for instance. But put a cup of tea in their hand and they will drink it, because the brain can orient to the *drink a cup of tea* map based on specific cues, cup in hand. It's as if the brain is working from fragments or disconnected scraps of memory. The hippocampus is affected in Alzheimer's and almost all disruptions to mental and emotional wellness.

Other ANDs in treatment models

Although known by other names, the AND pathway is central to several other therapeutic techniques used for treating post-traumatic stress. Babette Rothschild and others call it 'dual awareness', and Peter Levine uses a term called *pendulation,* which involves moving attention back and forward between two experiences. The AND pathway is central to EMDR*, as the clinician invites the client to hold the trauma memory in their awareness AND at the same time watch the pattern of finger movements with their eyes.

Mindfulness is the ultimate AND. When you observe without reacting, attending to something with curiosity, seeing your experience as it is, not based on what you think it is or what you wish it was, but seeing it like a child looking at a caterpillar crawling along a vine, the brain gets the message that there is no threat. Then it doesn't need to fire up that old pathway to keep you safe. Of course with very established pathways you need to repeat the new response to change the old pattern.

*EMDR is Eye Movement Desensitization Reprogramming, a psychotherapy technique developed by Francine Shapiro – usually to assist clients to process past trauma.

Part 3

AIR(s) flow

AIR(s)

Awareness as it happens AH!
    This is activation   0-10

Acknowledge – naming
    I'm feeling – body, emotion
  or I'm thinking / remembering – e.g. overthinking
  or I'm doing / impulse – e.g. drinking, eating

(AND)

Interrupt – gentle & repetitive

(AND)

Re-orient – here & now
    Date............ Place............ Time............ Age now.....
    Looking, I can see.................... – sensory detail
    Listening, I can hear................ – sensory detail
    Touching, I can feel................ – sensory detail

(AND)

Soothing – gentle
    And what do I need right now?

Chapter 16
Introducing AIR(s): Applying the i-brainmap

Applying AIR(s): Moving through activation to integration

In this chapter I explain the AIR(s) technique, which is a sequence used to assist the brain to move through activation towards integration, and is based on the principles outlined in the i-brainmap. I write the AIR(s) sequence on the back of the copy of the i-brainmap that I give to clients. The i-brainmap and AIR(s) technique belong together. Using mindfulness-based techniques without the map doesn't catalyse brain-body-mind integration as effectively as the combination of using the i-brainmap with AIR(s).

I developed AIR(s) over many years by observing and tracking the spontaneous process of integration that occurs in the brain when there is no interference or disruption to the integration process. Identifying the essential principles for AIR(s) has meant experimenting with what works, continually adjusting and adapting.

While the AIR(s) technique was built primarily on direct observation of the experience of brain integration, I also read widely and have drawn on the work of Babette Rothschild, Bessel van der Kolk, Peter Levine, Pierre Janet, Dan Siegel, Bruce Perry, and more recently, Moshe Feldenkrais, Gregory Kramer, Francine Shapiro, Ron Kurtz, Gene Gendlin, and many others.

The principles outlined below also apply to inter-Active Mindfulness.

The following list contains the main principles I've identified in the process of integration and sustainable brain-body-mind change.

- **Give the brain-body-mind different feedback**
  An essential element in creating momentum through activation to integration is shifting orientation, or responding differently, which gives the brain new feedback. The message that this activation loop is no longer a threat needs to be embedded in the feedback.

- **Create a map to use when lost in activation**
  The i-brainmap is just such a map. It needs to be a whole-brain map based on experience, not just a theoretical map. Without a whole-brain map, integration is less likely to be generalised, and therefore each trauma remains a fragmented body-memory map that must be worked with separately.

- **Be aware of what is happening as it happens**
  The only time you can integrate an old body-memory map is when it is open and activated, and brain change begins with awareness as it's happening – with mindfulness. It includes awareness of subtle changes arising and passing away, and other dimensions of the experience – that is, different orientations to the experience.

- **Interrupt and reorient**
  Interrupting the existing pathway or activation cycle and then reorienting gives the brain-body-mind new feedback. Interruption has to occur before reorientation, otherwise integration is inhibited or limited.

- **Orient towards something that is different from the usual orientation and experience of activation**
  A map is good, but it may be something else, such as orienting to here and now, or a different experience. This changes the experience.

- **Follow a sequential process that keeps you moving through the experience, not stuck in it**
  The main thing is not to get stuck during activation to integration. Having a sequence of steps to focus on allows the brain to keep moving and attending to the present, rather than being fixated or frozen, but also allows the brain to keep the maps of experience open and engaged. The hippocampus is also indicated in recognising and sequencing events.

- **Access sensory detail**
  Using the language of the lower brain is essential in integration. This means accessing direct sensory experience.

Introducing AIR(s): Applying the i-brainmap

In AIR(s), direct sensory experience involves acknowledging the direct experience and then reorienting to sensory awareness of the *environment*, looking, listening etc. When you are highly activated and alone it is more effective to focus on the environment, orienting to here and now, because it's easy to get stuck and overwhelmed in intense internal states. But in the process of *i-AM (inter-Active Mindfulness)* direct sensory experience is on *body experience*, tracking physiological changes in the body as they arise. How you orient to direct body experience will change through the journey of integration.

- **Repeat, repeat, repeat: it needs to happen more than once**
  Persistently interrupting and reorienting keeps attention moving rather than fixated, giving the brain a different message than alarm. AIR(s), like any new skill, takes practice. Repetition is required to establish the new pathway.

- **Approach with curiosity not a fix it or something's wrong attitude**
  Experimenting to see what you can discover gives the brain the message that everything is okay. Curiosity is an open mind and is at the heart of brain change, because you can't be curious and anxious at the same time. And trying to fix it or change something in the brain is likely to set off an alert/alarm response. Become curious of what is emerging, and changing.

- **Stopping activation isn't the goal**
  Down-regulation of the distress of activation is important to move towards the i-Zone but it cannot be the focus, because that perpetuates the activation cycle as you struggle to stop or avoid activation.

- **Approach as you would a small, frightened animal – with kindness**
  Gentleness soothes the child brain and tells it everything is okay. Your attitude will influence the message you give the brain.

- **The AND pathway**
  This is what I sometimes call being with not in. For instance, 'I feel this discomfort in my chest remembering that dreadful event AND I'm stroking my dog's ears and can see his brown head and smell his doggy smell.' I'm experiencing the distressing memory and I'm also with another experience, one of dog.

AIR(s) is like a guide rail

AIR(s) is like a guide rail you can hold onto when you're on the slippery slope of an activation cycle and find yourself in a spin or wobbly. It helps to have something to orient towards to draw yourself through the experience of activation. AIR(s) is also like trainer wheels until you get your balance and develop your own way to cycle through activation and into the integration Zone. Each brain is unique, and some things will work better for you than others. You need to experiment to find what works best and adapt it to your particular situation and capabilities.

AIR(s), rather than being a *thing* or a set of steps to hold on to or perform, is more like a series or sequence of coordinates for a ship's captain, describing which way to direct the helm. And these coordinates change as you keep the brain orienting and reorienting in different ways through the process.

Using an acronym is helpful for the brain to remember the sequence in AIR(s). Some people complain that they forget what a particular letter stands for during activation. But even trying to remember what 'I' or 'R' stands for means the old neural loop has been interrupted. You are asking the brain a question: 'What does "R" stand for again?' Asking a question is a way of reorienting the brain, and that interrupts and changes the pattern of activation.

Some people familiar with my work will know the AIR(s) technique by other names, including: 'the protocol', AIR-space, AIR-ways, brain map App, the A-I-M (Activation to Integration Map), ANDSO and, now, AIR(s). Just call it AIR: the 's' is silent but never to be forgotten.]

Activation to integration is circular

Like the ensō, the ancient Japanese symbol, or the ouroboros, the snake eating its own tail, activation to integration is circular. The ensō signifies that we are always at the beginning and also that activation is like a cycle, as is integration: we go past where we've been before; the same but different. The important point is that the activation cycle becomes the integration cycle.

In the beginning, you hardly notice the subtle changes because it seems that you're just going around the same old circle, but slowly you begin to realise that you are seeing and experiencing differently and that there is more space in your reactions, or you can orient to things in another way, or you know that you'll come through it instead of being stuck in it forever. In short, you keep moving through the cycle instead of getting stuck in it, and the cycle itself begins to change.

Your brain needs AIR(s) when it's stuck in a neural loop or activation cycle

The most difficult thing to understand in this approach is that there is very little difference between activation and integration except how you respond. Any response that gives the brain the message that there is still a threat associated with a particular trigger or reaction will perpetuate the cycle. But a different response that allows you to move and track what is happening, as it happens, and lean in gently with curiosity to understand the small, soft animal of your body-brain, invites different feedback.

Applying AIR(s)

Applying AIR(s) just once won't give the system sufficiently different feedback to create sustainable brain change. You need to do it again and again, like travelling back and forth along a pathway until it becomes a more defined track. This is how the brain works, back and forth, back and forth, through repetition, changing the action potential and increasing the probability that the new pattern will fire again. The more that neurons fire together, the stronger they wire together. When you've had a neural highway of fear it takes quite a lot of practice to change or loosen the old neural pathway and create a new one.

For a time, the brain will automatically bounce back into the older, more established pathway, especially if you're not mindful. It takes effort and practice to change it and create an alternative route. But if you get too stressed about it and tell yourself something like, 'Oh my god, I have to change this, I can't stand it,' your brain will read the situation as threat and will be more likely to create another activation cycle. So you need to approach it gently yet firmly, just like you would hold a frightened animal or a small, distressed child until they calm down and settle.

What you're doing through this repetition is creating and strengthening an AND pathway – the old map AND the new map – holding them both open at the same time, shifting attention back and forth between them so that the brain can create new connections.

It is this movement, this shifting of orientation, intention and attention back and forth again and again, that weaves a new pathway. Acknowledging AND Interrupting AND Reorienting AND Soothing with awareness builds a new pathway and an integrated map of the old experience interwoven with the new map (i-brainmap) as it becomes your direct experience. You own the map and create your own integrated map.

This is a different kind of mindfulness

While I call this a mindfulness-based technique, it is different to many mindfulness techniques in that I am not suggesting that you sit, observing the experience, but that you use structured ways to move through it. I don't recommend 'just being mindful' of what is happening when you're activated. What I do recommend is a specific focus on external sensory detail during activation, which is embedded in AIR(s). Once the intensity of the activation has passed you can tune into body awareness, but during high states of activation you are likely to feel more overwhelmed and want to run – you're hardwired for that. If you sit and observe those internal states, especially if they are states of terror, it's likely to overwhelm the system and perpetuate the loop.

Mindfulness is an important skill in integration because it teaches you to notice what your attention is doing and how to shift attention.

With practice, you may be able to stay more present to internal states of distress as they happen, but most of us need to focus on the external environment during high levels of activation. This serves two purposes. First, it changes your orientation to here and now: looking, listening, touching and smelling with detailed sensory awareness, like the mother getting the child's attention when he's distressed. Mindful attention on the environment says, 'I'm here now,' not back in the nightmare. You look around and see that there is no current threat. Second, getting and reorienting your own attention interrupts the activation cycle gently and persistently, reorienting to the current context.

In later phases of integration, it becomes easier to stay present and mindful to the internal experience of the body as you develop confidence and skill in riding the wave of activation. This switches on and strengthens the parts of the brain that connect to internal body states. These parts of the brain are affected in trauma, and the body can feel dangerous. So reconnecting repeatedly and gently to these parts of the brain through body awareness establishes new pathways in the brain.

Mary, eating and mindfulness

Mary: Sometimes the eating takes me over.

Rita: What about the mindfulness?

I can eat mindfully when I'm deliberately being mindful. But other times something gets triggered – activated – and I don't even think to do anything mindfully. It's like an auto-switch. The eating is driven by something outside my control.

It sounds like it's driven by lower brain activation, and consciously you don't feel like you have any control.

That's right. Even if I say to myself, 'That's enough.' I don't even want that bit of cake, but it's like I have to have it. Almost like I'm punishing myself. Sometimes I eat till it hurts. Not much anymore, but that's how it used to be. Then I'd purge. I think the purging is worse than anything. I felt disgusting. Ashamed. Ugly.

But you don't purge anymore?

No, I haven't for a long time.

But you still get this drive to eat sometimes, where it seems to take you over? Like another part of you, or something not a part of you? Outside yourself?

Yes, it seems alien, like it's not me. But it drives me.

So we want to change your relationship with this part of you. And the way to begin is to give it some AIR(s) as it's happening.

That's hard, because it's like I'm in it till it's over.

Yes, I agree, awareness as it happens is the hardest part of all of this.

Sometimes I can say I'm activated but nothing changes.

Well, firstly, we're not ...

Yeah, yeah, I know. We're not trying to change the activation. But we sort of are, aren't we?

Well we're trying to create the conditions that allow the brain to respond differently because we're giving it a different message.

Okay, yeah, that makes sense. It's a bit hard to tell the difference sometimes.

Yes, it's about what message we are giving the brain. And it takes repetition, but not with the intention to stop.

Because that tells the brain there is some problem, right?

Right. But back to your comment about awareness. I think there are different kinds of awareness of activation.

Mmm?

Well, often when you think you're aware it's more of a cognitive awareness. Like the concept of activation rather than noticing the direct experience. So it's like split-brain awareness. Your kid brain is still stuck in the activation all alone while your big brain is saying 'Oh, yeah, it's activation.' It may be a subtle form of dissociation too.

I can feel a bit fuzzy come to think of it. I'm saying I'm activated but I can't really get my attention. It's like it's outside the room.

So we might need to experiment with some more challenging add-ons with AIR(s) to make your brain work a bit harder to get your attention.

Like a maths equation?

Well, how's your maths?

Not so hot.

So that'd probably make you more dissociative. But also it's too big-brain. We need something that challenges more of your brain but not so much that it gets all your attention. Rather that it interrupts the existing loop. We might try some nursery rhymes.

That sounds ... different.

What's your favorite nursery rhyme?

'Mary Had a Little Lamb', of course.

Of course. But it mightn't be challenging enough. You might need something that requires more attention, like 'Ten Green Bottles'.

I can do 'Ten Green Bottles'.

Introducing AIR(s): Applying the i-brainmap

Yeah, that might be good, because it needs more attention to keep remembering where you're up to.

So what do I do?

You use it to interrupt the neural loop of activation. You still call it 'activation', give it a number between 0 and 10, and move through AIR(s). But at the moment I don't think you're really interrupting the cycle, so we might need to use more specific techniques.

I prefer not to give specific interrupting techniques to begin with, but invite the person to experiment with AIR(s) to see how they respond; then we introduce more specific approaches once we know what is useful and what isn't. But for people who find it particularly difficult to get their own attention – often because there is some dissociation – I will sometimes suggest nursery rhymes or other specific interrupting techniques.

See more on why nursery rhymes are useful in chapter 18 on interruption, page 218.

Stuckness is a sure sign

The feeling of stuckness is the give-away indicator that you're caught in an old pattern. So any time you feel stuck you could use AIR(s). The challenge is to flick on the light but not get into a struggle or judge your emotional reactions during activation, which would be like beating up on the kid for having a nightmare. This process and technique I'm giving you is about reducing the stuckness, not eliminating emotions. This approach requires learning to accept and move through the moment-to-moment experience, not in a passive way, gritting your teeth when you feel uncomfortable, but seeing it as it is and moving through it, like surfing the wave.

A metaphor for understanding stuck brain and unsticking

Neural loops are like frozen berries in the brain. When you take frozen berries out of the freezer you can let them thaw slowly or you can add water. Water is like attention. If you add water and then let them sit in a strainer for a while, they'll stick to the strainer. This is like shifting your attention once and thinking that's all you need to do to thaw the old frozen pathway; that's what happens with distraction. Instead, you need to keep the attention moving, flowing, otherwise you'll keep sticking. Keep running water over the berries until they soften and thaw – be persistent in shifting your attention. Warm water is even better, the warmth of kindness. The other reason you need to keep attention moving is that fixated attention is consistent with the freeze response of terror and can give the brain the alarm message. Repeatedly and gently shifting attention gives it a different message.

Mary, this takes time to master

Rita: This takes some time, Mary. You're changing patterns that have probably been around for … how old are you?

Mary: Fifty-six.

Probably been around for about fifty-plus years. We need to give your brain a chance to integrate all this new information.

I guess it'll take a while. A long while.

Sometimes it happens more quickly and effortlessly than you might imagine. The main effort is in developing awareness in the moment. As your mindfulness muscle strengthens, you'll be more awake and can see how these habits kick in. Start to notice the body cues when you're activated.

Knowing when to lean into something and when to stand back and how to move between is a profoundly important skill in brain change. If you lean in too close when your attention is unstable, you can fall into the loop and find it hard to get yourself out. If, on the other hand, you always stand back, afraid of coming in close, your brain is likely to read this as avoidance and interpret it as too scary, a current threat, and so perpetuate the activation cycle. The opposite is learning to move between, like an artisan who knows when to use strength or skill to impose something and when to listen and turn with the grain or the fibre of the material. This movement between craft and attunement is 'flow' and is the essence of every work of art and also brain change, which is an art form.

Applying AIR(s)

In the beginning, while you're learning the sequence to move through activation towards integration, it's best to go through each principle. Although it's not always apparent at first, each step has a purpose and is best included when you begin the practice. Some aspects of AIR(s) focus on setting intention rather than doing something, but remember we are dealing with a very sophisticated system where your intention is as important as what you do. How you approach something will affect the message you send the brain.

When you want to create brain change, it's helpful initially to repeat something rather than try a lot of different techniques. This way the brain establishes a stronger new pathway. Once that's established, you can experiment with what works because the learning will be consolidated. You're building a new competing pathway of probability, and if you create a lot of smaller different pathways the brain is still likely to follow the established route, so repeating a new pathway until it is strengthened and familiar is important. Like learning anything new it may feel awkward at first.

Using the sequence as I've developed it helps to name and reconnect the emotions or direct body experience with the impulse to act and recognise current needs. This helps the brain link between felt experience and action, or movement, because these connections are typically disrupted during traumatic and overwhelming events. Therefore in post-traumatic stress, emotions can lose their meaning and become only painful meaningless experiences rather than information coming from the body that gives you a message or impulse to act. AIR(s) invites you to ask the question, 'What do I need right now?' to help consolidate this recognition of emotions and body experience as information rather than meaningless painful experiences.

In the later phases of integration you will be able to adapt or simplify AIR(s) into something that works most efficiently for you.

There are also many twists and turns that can seem like integration but are really dead ends that take you into a maze of distraction – that freeze the berries. They may be interesting or seem like an answer, but often they are just another form of avoid-escape, control or some other sneaky secondary activation.

Chapter 17
AH! = Awareness as it Happens

In the next chapters I discuss each principle of AIR(s) in detail. In this chapter I explain the first essential factor in the AIR(s) sequence: awareness that activation is happening and – importantly – acknowledging and naming what is happening.

AIR(s)

<u>A</u>wareness as it happens AH!
This is activation   0–10

Acknowledge – naming

Recognising activation as it happens

Recognising an experience as activation while it is happening is like flicking on a light in the brain to see the body-memory map, and creating a pause. This is often the hardest part because, typically, your system treats the experience as a current threat and gets *lost in the tunnel*, especially when it's an old familiar feeling. But before anything can change you need to recognise that this experience is activation. This can be tricky because activation is a shape shifter.

Noticing, naming and numbering engage a broader range of brain functions, allowing the brain to make more connections. Making wider connections is like throwing ropes out of the tunnel so the brain can hook on, get some traction on something solid, and draw you through the experience of activation. Switching on more parts of the brain is often described as having more space; instead of being trapped in the tunnel, alone in the dark experience, there is a sense of movement, even if it is only subtle in the beginning.

AH! is also like a pause, a breathing out, that allows a softening of the activation cycle, a small gap of possibility. This slows things down and allows you to begin drawing your attention into the present. Finding the pause is an essential part of mindfulness.

AH! As it Happens – is the only time your brain can change a lower brain pathway; anything else is like standing on the beach and watching the waves or talking about how to surf instead of getting into the water and facing the waves. By acknowledging whatever is happening as it happens, your experience changes from overwhelm and *lost in the tunnel* to 'Oh, this is activation, and I can give it AIR(s).' Your brain can begin to change and integrate old body-memory maps.

It helps to name it

In the beginning it helps to name it as activation. Using the cue word *activation* helps the brain make the association with the i-brainmap to remind you that there is no current threat, but that the lower brain is lost in a body-memory map.

Using a cue word is like giving the child having a nightmare a name for what is happening; giving the brain a cue word means it can begin to recognise activation and name it next time it happens, making it less terrifying. The brain can link this current experience or body-memory map to the rest of the brain with a broader recognition and understanding, adapting the i-brainmap based on your changing experience.

0 to 10 creates space

Giving the activation a number between 0 and 10, what is referred to as a SUDS scale (Subjective Units of Distress), helps the brain make more connections. Trying to come up with a number between 0 and 10 is like a quick-hand trick that requires some contextualising because you have to measure the activation against something. This challenges the brain to have to leap out of the tunnel and remember other experiences; for example, 'Oh, last week it was a "7", today it's an "8".' So instead of being fully in the forever experience, your brain has to subtly access some other experience to measure against.

Take anger, for instance. If you're angry, it can feel as if you *are* the anger; you're completely identified – or over-identified (secondary activation) – with your anger: 'I am angry.' If the anger takes you over, you can't find any space between you and it. But if you notice you're getting angry – 'Oh, I feel angry, my jaw is clenched, and it's at an "8"' – you experience a little bit of space between you, or your capacity to observe, and the experience of anger. It's this awareness, space, or mindfulness of the whole experience of anger that is the beginning of choice, because you start to change your relationship or orientation to the emotion.

Making it your own, and habituation

Activation happens at lightning speed because it is linked to your survival response. So in the beginning people do whatever they can remember of the AIR(s) sequence. Some people find that acknowledging activation is the first thing they do, whereas others name the activation after they have identified the feeling or given it a number between 0 and 10. The order in which you move through the different elements can be flexible, and as you will see they overlap, as long as you begin with awareness as it happens.

When you first start using AIR(s) it's fresh, so most people find that applying AIR(s) during activation helps. They say, 'It works.' But then things change. Because it works initially, you keep using it, but you may secretly begin to use it to try to stop the activation. This gives the brain a different message, a 'stop it' message. And as you know, the brain reads this as a threat and responds by keeping that loop going to protect you from the threat. And around you go again and again, and you come to therapy and complain, 'It's not working.'

It's important to understand that the brain habituates very rapidly. In other words, it adapts to change. You try a new technique like AIR(s), and it seems to 'work', meaning it gives you some relief from the symptoms of activation. Then the brain adapts. That's part of its incredible efficiency. If you had to learn how to drive a car each time you wanted to drive to work, you'd never be able to manage all the demands of life. So when you do something repeatedly the brain starts to adapt and make it automatic; it creates a map that it can use instead of having to learn it again each time. It says, 'Oh, that's just that AIR(s) thing, and we know how to do that,' and it doesn't give it much attention. Then it seems to stop 'working', because the essential aspect of the AIR(s) protocol is to first get your own attention so that you can reorient it.

To keep the AIR(s) fresh and active in the brain, you may need to keep adapting it slightly; anything novel is more likely to get the brain's attention. Once it becomes routine or automatic it won't be as effective at catalysing brain integration.

Defining 'it works' and 'it isn't working'

What most people mean when they say 'it works' or 'it isn't working' is whether it reduces the activation or not. But reducing the activation isn't as relevant as whether you are moving towards integration or stuck in an activation cycle. The important question to ask to know whether the map and techniques are working is, 'Are there signs of integration?' That is really the only question that matters, and that can't be measured by how much activation is occurring but by your response to the activation.

Reaction to activation

Notice any reaction you have to the activation that's like 'Oh no, not this again,' or 'I've gotta stop it and make it go away.' If there is a habitual reaction to the activation, it's usually another activation cycle based on avoidance, stopping or controlling, and that can perpetuate the cycle. Instead, it helps to approach with curiosity. Saying, 'Oh, just this' or 'Oh, hello you, I know you,' and greeting activation as a familiar (though perhaps unwanted) visitor rather than a scary monster, and with as much curiosity as possible, signals to the brain that there's no current threat. Then the alarm brain can put down the guns and let in some fresh AIR(s).

One of the reasons that curiosity is an important part of integration and brain change is that it involves holding something lightly in your attention. The opposite would be fixation, hyper-vigilance, criticising, worrying or analysing – 'Why, why, why?' – which are all likely to trigger some alarm in the brain.

Acknowledge or accept

Acknowledging means noticing and naming the experience, holding it lightly, not analysing activation or letting it grab attention. By acknowledging your experience during activation you have already started to reorient by gently shifting the focus inward and holding it lightly in attention rather than with fixed attention. Acknowledging means, 'Just notice what's happening, this feeling, thought or impulse,' nothing else. You don't have to do anything.

Acknowledging, attending with curiosity, is inherently accepting. But if you tell yourself you *need* to accept this, it can rebound in resistance: 'No, I don't want to.' Just acknowledge what is happening.

Notice trying to stop

Using the term 'acknowledge' also invites you to notice and acknowledge your impulse to avoid or efforts to stop the activation. Acknowledging, just noticing and naming and giving the experience a number between 0 and 10, gives the brain a signpost or flag on the map of experience that potentially allows it to recognise activation and make other connections. This creates a more interconnected map, which encourages integration. By identifying physiological tags (what some people refer to as somatic markers) during activation, the brain can recognise them the next time activation occurs and make the necessary connections.

It is essential to acknowledge and name whatever is happening before doing anything else, otherwise you are likely to create another avoidance or control loop with these techniques. Acknowledging and naming during activation is the foundation for later integration because the brain is building connections to a larger whole-brain map.

It's not just a feeling

The activation is not always a feeling; sometimes it's a secondary reaction such as over-thinking, or you might be remembering something. It may be an old story such as the victim myth or a behaviour or impulse, such as overeating or withdrawal. At times, you'll be more aware of the secondary activation than the feeling response. Don't get too hung up on whether it's primary or secondary activation. I just call it all activation because usually the activation cycle has become entrenched, and it's hard to separate primary and secondary reactions that are all tangled up together.

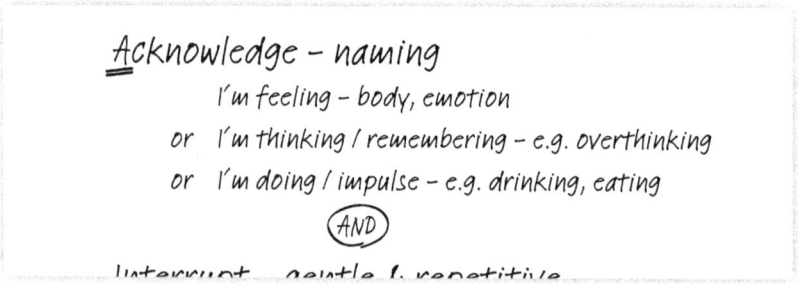

Acknowledge – naming
  I'm feeling – body, emotion
or *I'm thinking / remembering – e.g. overthinking*
or *I'm doing / impulse – e.g. drinking, eating*
  (AND)

You don't need to name them all. Acknowledging what is happening is the first base. If you dash past without touching down here, it won't give the brain the basis for a home run – that is, integration.

The initial acknowledgment validates what is happening. There is only a thin line between saying it isn't current and telling yourself it isn't real, which is why acknowledging is important. Activation feels very real; it's just that your brain is using the wrong map for this place and time. So if you don't acknowledge the experience it can be like saying it isn't real, like saying 'Just get over it!', denying or minimising the experience. Denial or minimising may work in the short term, but in the long term it's likely to create more avoidance of what you know is a real experience, so you end up in a split.

Name the obvious

Just notice and name the most obvious reactions, because it all happens so quickly and you don't want to get hooked into trying to work out exactly what is happening. The idea in acknowledging is to touch down lightly with the most obvious reactions and then move through the AIR(s) sequence. Keep the attention moving, swinging lightly through the AIR(s), making contact then swinging back again. Yes, it can feel like a circus at times!

Often you will have one aspect of activation that grabs your attention most. This is different for everyone and may change over time as your brain integrates old memory maps.

Becoming curious about what is happening as it happens, acknowledging and giving it a score, are all extremely helpful in slowing down the activation; a pause that creates gaps in the cycle of activation. The best thing you can do when you're in a spin is to slow down and not panic. Easier said than done, of course, but the more you practice it the better you'll get.

Mary, growing awareness

Mary: This thing happened.

Rita: Uh-huh?

I had a situation with Sarah, my eldest daughter. She asked if I'd mind the kids because she had some work training, and it was her usual day off. She said it was really important. I was reluctant because I already said I'd take Auntie Maud to an Open Garden in the morning. But Sarah sounded so desperate that I rang Auntie Maud and cancelled. She was very disappointed, poor love. Her two sons never visit her, let alone take her anywhere, and she is the dearest woman. Mum's sister. Reminds me of Gran. Oh! I hadn't thought of that till now.

And the situation?

Sarah didn't show up. By nine I was worried because she said she'd drop the kids off before 8.30 to be in the city in time for the training. So I rang her, and she said she decided to stay home because she was too tired. 'When were you going to ring and let me know?' I asked. 'Mum, I just got out of the shower. I'm dripping wet, don't be so damned impatient. I was going to ring when I was dressed.' Something like that, as if I was such a demanding impatient cow that she had to yell at me. But I hadn't even said anything. Anyway, there was no point talking to her while she was like that so I said 'sorry' and then 'goodbye'.

Uh-huh.

I thought you'd ball me out for saying 'sorry' and not standing up for myself.

No, I'm not going to ball you out for anything, Mary. I'm curious about what sense you made of it.

Phew. So I'm not in trouble?

No, I'm not your sixth grade teacher. I'm working with you so you can create what you want, it's not about what I or anyone else wants.

But here's the weird thing, Rita. I was upset for three days. I couldn't stop thinking about it. I went over and over how she couldn't even be bothered to let me know and I had to ring her to find out. I can't believe I said 'sorry' to her. 'Sorry' is in neon lights now. So I went over and over it. I was sad and angry and stuck. And then it happened …

What happened?

I realised I was activated. Three days later I realised I was activated. A bit slow, huh?

Great that you were able to recognise it as activation, Mary.

Yeah, but three days later. It was like a light went on in my head, and I saw it so clearly. Before that I'd even been looking at the map you gave me and thinking about what you said, but I didn't make the connection that I was activated somehow.

Lights coming on sounds like start-up integration to me.

But it took me three days! Once I got it, it was so clear, but before that I didn't make the connection. It was like I was just trapped in it.

That's because when you're stuck in lower brain distress or activation the parts of the brain that make connections to help you make sense of things and join the dots have gone offline. That's why I give you the map, so your brain has something to help it recognise activation and orient to when it happens – because that's the only time integration can occur.

It's weird that once I got it, it was clear but before that I was just stuck in the spin.

And what did you notice when you realised it was activation, Mary?

That was weird too. It sort of dissolved. Like the fear you have when you hear a noise in the middle of the night because you think it's a burglar. Then you get up and have a look and there's nothing there but the wind making the curtain flap, because your hopeless husband forgot to shut the window.

So, once you saw what it was, the brain was able to put down the fear?

It wasn't really fear. It was upset and anger and something else, like all this stuff about me not being important or I don't matter to them, I'm just their baby sitter, a convenience. It went on and on. I was in one of those loops you talk about.

A neural loop. So when you recognised that it was activation it dissipated?

Quite a bit. Not entirely, but I could think about it clearly instead of going over and over it. It was like I'd had a cracked record in my head, as Auntie Maud would say.

Yes, overthinking is usually very repetitive. So once you named it as activation, what did you notice then?

Just that I got my mind back. I'm not sure what I want to do about it, but I don't like the way my girls treat me, and I would like to talk about that and how I can respond differently. Hello, looks like I'm back to that old issue about saying 'no' again. This is like being on the city loop, but you can't get off.

Okay, let's work on the big N-O.

There's awareness and then there's awareness

Awareness during activation is essential for integration, like switching on the light when the child is in the nightmare. But awareness isn't a one-dimensional experience. To investigate the different qualities of awareness would take another book, so here I will discuss three different aspects of awareness. Imagine them on a continuum with closed or fixed awareness at one end and fuzzy or distant awareness at the other, and open awareness or curiosity somewhere in the middle. Below I discuss how each of these qualities of awareness affect integration.

Closed or fixed awareness

Closed awareness is like recognising or naming something in a way that closes the mind. Like 'Oh, yeah. That's x or y. I've got it,' and the mind closes, because you think you have the right map. Your brain works from an existing map, even the AIR(s) map, rather than the direct experience. This doesn't invite insight or integration.

If you think of awareness like a dialogue with an intimate other, fixed awareness is like the argument that repeats and you stand your ground, take your usual position and follow the same line of argument. It is familiar and repetitive.

Fixed attention, as I've mentioned, is associated with trauma and therefore can alert the brain that there is a possible danger.

Fuzzy or distant awareness

This is like watching from a distance, and can indicate some dissociative experience. Fuzzy awareness is when nothing is really clear, like an out of focus picture or a movie with subtitles, but the action and words are out of sync so it's confusing. This is a bit like saying, 'Whatever. I'd rather ignore it or think about how I'll be rich and famous one day ...' like floating around in a balloon but never coming down to land.

Using the analogy of a dialogue, this is like avoiding the hard conversations or skirting around the edge of them, or perhaps getting lost in the discussion but never really getting to the heart of things; the issue remains unclear or avoided. Or you might spend all your time together partying or planning your next holiday, but never discussing your problems or important matters.

Open awareness or curiosity with attention

This is the quality of awareness that has clarity and openness and could be described as insight. You see what is happening as it happens and your attention moves and discovers other aspects of the experience. In other words, attention isn't fixated on one orientation or a fixed way of seeing things. This is like leaning into the experience gently, and noticing what is really going on – and then the experience opens up. Instead of only seeing what is on the surface you can penetrate the experience, like David Attenborough or a deep-sea explorer. The word that best describes this awareness is 'curiosity'.

In dialogue this is like meeting the other and coming in close even though it may be uncomfortable, and being willing to tune into your own internal experience and also hear the other person. (*Insight dialogue* by Gregory Kramer provides steps for creating this kind of dialogue. See Further Reading.) It is a creative dialogue of discovery and you never know where it will lead you, because it is emerging, and often surprising, as you move in closer and closer to know about your experience and the activation in new ways.

The first two qualities of awareness don't move towards integration, but the third, open awareness, is essential to begin the process. So when I refer to 'awareness as it happens' I'm referring to open awareness, which is like mindfulness. It is the quality of awareness that develops through insight meditation (Vipassana), as you uncover and discover moment-to-moment experience in a new way. While this quality of awareness is easily developed in meditation, for most of us it is hard to maintain as we interact with the world. Inviting curiosity can be a gentle way into this quality of awareness.

Chapter 18
Interrupting the pattern

In this chapter I unpack the second principle in the AIR(s) sequence: interruption.

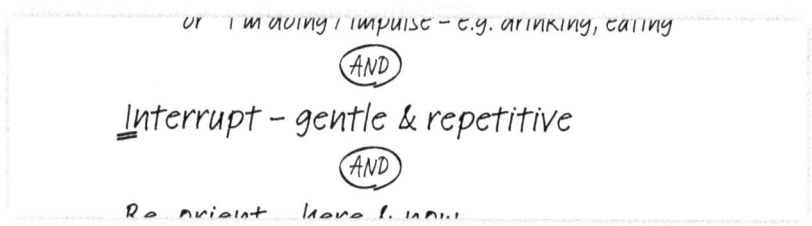

Intention to pause

Interrupting is gentle yet persistent, like a gentle knocking at the door.

Awareness, and acknowledging what is happening, begins to interrupt the activation cycle. You can interrupt it further by deliberately pausing – not doing anything, just pausing. Many people find it helpful to take a breath. As much as possible, slow down the activation cycle to create gaps in the automatic rapid-fire reactions, which are instant and automatic habits of the lower brain in response to perceived threat. Unless of course there is a threat, then you need that rapid fire.

Interrupting is as much about your intention as what you do. You're not trying to fix or change anything, because, as you know, that can kick start the brain's alert or alarm response. Your intention primes the brain, creating an invisible code or hum that gives the brain a message about whether the experience is threatening or safe.

You are getting the attention gently and persistently rather than grabbing attention. Interruption is persistent but not continuous, like a knocking at the door. Usually when someone knocks gently at the door, there is a knock then a break. You stop, look up and listen – 'Is that someone knocking at the door?' – but when you hear nothing you return to your task. Then it starts again. You stop to listen. If this keeps happening, you eventually leave your task (or, in this case, the brain steps out of the activation loop) to go and find out, because curiosity beckons.

This sequence – knock-knock-silence-listening-what's that?-return to task/loop-knock-knock-pause-listen-break-back to task/loop-knock-knock – is what we want to create in interrupting techniques. If the knocking is continuous and uninterrupted, it's like grabbing the attention. Also, when there is an uninterrupted noise the brain habituates quickly and stops taking any notice. But if the knocking stops and starts, is gentle, changes slightly and yet is persistent, it can interrupt the brain's stuck attention.

So interrupt gently and repeatedly, or sometimes more firmly, loudly if the child brain's attention is fixated. Invite the brain's curiosity through gently knocking, again and again, until the lower brain forgets its crying and looks up, listens and wonders who is at the door.

> *Curiosity will conquer fear even more than bravery will.*
>
> James Stephens[3]

Interrupting to notice your intention

Interrupting is the factor that reminds you to notice your intention, which primes the brain. People often forget what the 'I' in AIR(s) stands for. But even asking the question 'What does "I" stand for?' during activation is interrupting, and it engages curiosity.

Adding *Interrupt* is intended to remind you that AIR(s) isn't trying to change, fix or stop anything but to *interrupt* and invite curiosity, which gives the brain the message that everything is okay: 'This is just activation and I'm just moving in for a closer look. Though it may be uncomfortable, it won't bite.'

Intention primes the brain

Priming the brain is like playing background music when you are doing the housework. Playing your favourite music can set the mood or context; it's like cueing the brain to recall similar (happy) contexts or experiences. Music is a great brain primer. Priming is also like prepar-

---

3   James Stephens, *The Crock of Gold*, BiblioBazaar, Charleston [1912] 2006, p. 13.

ing, like prep for theatre or painting a wall. Like the invisible step that goes unnoticed but affects what comes later. Priming cues the brain in a particular way.

Knowing how you are priming your brain is one of the most important aspects learned through mindful attention. You become aware of what's on your mind and begin to have choice about how to focus or orient attention, which primes the brain. We don't tend to consciously prime the brain but instead we let it be primed by past experience or whatever is on our mind, or it's primed for us by our environment (including media and culture). Our brain is always taking cues from the world around us as well as the internal environment of the body.

If you want to encourage brain change, curiosity is the best way to prime the pump because curiosity keeps the brain open to the unexpected, which is the basis of change. On the other hand, if you know what will happen next you have already primed the brain with certain expectations, and that is a limited approach to brain change. It's also what most of us do, because we operate on auto-pilot and have an extreme reliance on big-brain function, technology, and goal-outcome orientation, all of which prime the brain in a particular way.

If you want to prime the brain for whole-brain change, you need to include the language of the body-brain, which is sensory. This is an essential element in brain change and integration because our habits are embedded in the lower brain, the body-brain.

Some people use the i-brainmap to prime the brain. They carry it with them in a bag or coat pocket or stick it on the fridge to remind themselves of what is going on when they're activated and to cue themselves to use the techniques.

Intention can affect why techniques work for some but not others. Also, if your intention changes it can mean that a technique that worked initially may become ineffective. Approaching the techniques in the next section as an experiment will prime the brain for change.

Techniques for interrupting

Initially, when I give a person the i-brainmap I don't usually provide specific interrupting techniques but instead I explain that the AIR(s) sequence is intended to interrupt the activation cycle. I don't want to be too prescriptive when I give people the map; instead I want to give them a rope to hold onto to move through the activation rather than tell them how to get through it. You have to take this journey, that's how you will learn and develop your own map and skills, through direct experience of moving through activation to integration.

Another reason I don't suggest specific interrupting techniques when you first start with AIR(s) is because your brain needs to create a repetitive sequence that you can follow. It's a pathway you walk again and again until it becomes well worn. This is important in the beginning before we add anything that confuses this sequence. It also allows the brain to come up with its own strategies.

Once AIR(s) is established we can introduce specific interrupting techniques. But giving you techniques before you've established the sequence is more likely to result in distraction and avoidance or fixing, as you focus on the techniques to stop the activation.

Internal or external interruption

You can either interrupt the internal pattern of response or the external pattern, including your interactions and behaviours.

If your usual habit is to focus on external events, especially another person, you can interrupt this (and therefore change the experience) by shifting attention to your feet – for example, ask yourself how your feet feel. On the other hand, if you typically focus on your internal feelings or reactions it can be more interrupting to orient to action; just do something rather than stay locked in a frozen feeling. But if you always *do* something it might be more effective to slow things down and tune into yourself, and not get into action, which has probably become an escape plan.

Although some of these strategies are technically reorientation, they also create an interruption. This is why you don't need to follow the sequence once the principles are familiar, because they overlap and interact.

Sometimes people think they have to do something profoundly different for brain change, but if you can just interrupt the cycle and give your brain some space you can reduce your distress, move towards the *i-Zone* and then access your big-brain resources. Once you have done that, you can begin to see things differently and come up with a different response or become curious. Then change is possible. Even though, paradoxically, we're not trying to change anything because that primes the brain in a whole different way.

If the cycle of activation happens in dialogue or a relationship with someone, one of the simplest strategies is to interrupt and then slow things down so you can see clearly what is happening. This may be as simple as looking away, thinking of your feet or suggesting that the two of you go get a coffee and finish the conversation in a different environment, or walk while you talk.

Mary, interrupting the 'yes' habit

Rita: So Mary it might be good to try some interrupting before you say yes.

Mary: How will I do that?

Well, when Sarah asks you to mind the children you interrupt the usual automatic response of pleasing and appeasing –

Or saying 'yes'.

Yes. So under pressure you're likely to automatically respond by saying 'yes'. So we want to slow things down and give you some space or a pause to find a different response. Does that make sense?

Yes. Sounds good in theory but not sure how it will go in reality.

It's best to see it as an experiment, Mary. Even approaching it as an experiment can prime the brain in a different way.

Okay. I'll play Doctor Brain Scientist extraordinaire. I'll need a white coat though.

White suits you, too. We're only interrupting the usual pattern, creating a pause, making some space. We can experiment with your responses later.

So many experiments.

By just interrupting the usual pathway it gives your brain some space to move and change. We don't want you to get sucked into getting it right or fixing it. You know all about that.

Okay, experiment to take the pressure off. I can give it a go. What will I do exactly?

For a start you can just say you'll get back to her on her request.

Okay. That should put the cat among the pigeons. I'm not sure I want to experiment on animals though.

Experiments in interrupting

Internal interrupters

- **Shifting attention**
  This is a profoundly simply and important way to interrupt a pattern, and is often overlooked because we think we have to do something. But the doing is often a continuation of a pattern of avoid, escape or control rather than interruption. For example, focus attention on your feet.

- **Sensory detail**
  One of the techniques I use in session (see my session with Jack in chapter 8) is based on the work of Babette Rothschild. When someone is highly activated, I ask them to count pomegranates or pomegranate seeds in a painting I have in my room. Asking a question about sensory detail is a quick way to get the attention and interrupt the activation cycle.

- **Observing with awareness**
  This is one of the simplest although not necessarily easiest ways to interrupt. Mindfulness practices help to build this skill. Observing with awareness or mindfulness slows things down. Anything that slows down the experience is an interruption because it changes the usual rapid automatic response of activation.

- **Focus on breath**
  Taking a deep belly breath, sighing as you breathe out, and certain rhythmical breathing practices, can be effective. Breathing techniques can be problematic for some people with generalised anxiety, as focusing on the breath can increase anxiety.

- **Shifting the eyes**
  Another effective technique is shifting eye focus. It can be as simple as looking up and looking around, or you can move the eyes from side to side or up and down, around and so on. One reason that this is effective is that when we are frightened the gaze is fixated. So intentionally shifting the focus, softening the gaze and moving the eyes during activation, can help interrupt the pathway and give the brain a different message.

- **Looking up**
  If the mind is going on and on and around and around, look up. It's even better if you are outside walking and look up at the sky, or if you're inside go to a window and look out at the sky.

- **A hint of a smile**
  Another simple interrupter when you feel stuck is to invite the hint of a smile to your lips. Apparently your brain doesn't care whether you pretend to smile or it's real. In fact, all you have to do is put a pencil in your mouth so that the ends stick out either side. This is enough for the brain to respond more optimistically as if it really is smiling. So don't worry if you don't feel like smiling, just try it as an experiment, invite your curious brain to see what happens when you put a pencil in your mouth or put a gentle smile on your lips.

External interrupters

External interrupters focus on changing behaviour or interpersonal interactions. If you interrupt the pattern through changing your usual outward reaction, it's good to consider how you are setting your intention. It's better if it's an experiment: 'I wonder what would happen if I try this?' rather than 'I have to fix this problem', as we did with Mary. By now you know why this intention is important.

More specific techniques when you need more interruption traction

Tapping

Tapping is helpful to interrupt the cycle if it's a thinking or impulse/behaviour loop. (If activation is more emotional or physiological, soothing techniques, such as touch and smell, are usually more effective).

I'm not referring to any specific tapping technique, although some people report that specific tapping techniques are useful. Rhythmical tapping and patting are soothing for the lower brain and are associated with the soothing capacity of music. A mother will instinctively rock a distressed infant, which releases endorphins in the brainstem. Although rocking is a soothing technique it can be used to interrupt. Soothing techniques are more consistently rhythmical than interrupting techniques, which are more effective with a stop-start or slight occasional change to keep the brain engaged. (As you can see techniques overlap, and can be soothing and interrupting or reorienting).

You can tap anywhere and any old time: hands, thighs or side of the face on the cheek bones. Rhythmical is good but with some irregularity, like the knock at the door. Best to keep it simple. Some people find tapping or drumming on the table more effective. Experiment.

While playing music is helpful because it is interrupting, orienting and soothing, try to develop a toolkit of techniques that don't require any equipment, because activation can happen anywhere anytime. And you can always tap your fingers or your tongue (see below). It's also important to add an active element to the process because that primes the brain in a different way than passively listening to music.

Tapping or drumming your fingers is often an automatic response to stress, so if you are a finger tapper link it in with the i-brainmap and the AIR(s) sequence and see if you can do it more mindfully, so it becomes a way to interrupt your stress reaction. You can also recognise it as a sign that you may be activated.

Some people find it helpful to gently tap each finger against their thumb in sequence, and keep repeating, when they are stressed or anxious. It can be done on one hand or both and you can create complex patterns to hold your attention.

Tongue-tip-tapping

I developed this technique specifically to interrupt overthinking. It involves tapping the tongue very gently on the roof of the mouth. The first thing is to relax the tongue, which relaxes the mind. The reason relaxing the tongue quietens the mind is because when we're thinking, the tongue is sub-vocalising; that is, subtly moving and pronouncing. So relaxing the tongue quietens the mind, but relaxing the tongue is very difficult. You can let the tongue hang out of your mouth, which works but is not a good look in a corporate meeting or in front of a classroom full of rowdy teenagers.

So, to begin, soften the tongue until it feels like a big slug in the bottom of your mouth. Then just curl it up so that it gently touches the roof of the mouth. Although the tongue is curled, it is still relaxed and not pushing back on the roof of the mouth. Then you just let it drop a tiny way, less than a centimetre. It just comes off the roof of the mouth effortlessly. And then you tap again. One indicator that you are doing it correctly is that saliva is usually released. This is likely an indication that the parasympathetic system has kicked in. It is a very gentle and subtle movement. The main mistake people make is to press against the roof of the mouth, which engages the strong muscles of the tongue. It should be relaxed and effortless. Experiment.

Rhythmical movement

Simple dance sequences, stepping or swaying, can be effective interrupting techniques, as well as soothing. Sometimes I work with these in a session when a person is stuck in activation and we need a fresh way to interrupt and get their attention. I call it Daggy Dancing because it's playful, and no one can take it seriously when they see me demonstrating Daggy Dancing. If nothing else, demonstrating Daggy Dancing leaves an indelible memory that will usually get a laugh, or at least a smile, which a person can use when they're activated.

Everyone can do Daggy Dancing; no special training is required. Just don't look in the mirror, although that will surely interrupt the usual pathway. (Some of my clients reading this who didn't get the *Daggy Dancing* treatment may be feeling a bit ripped off. But trust me when I say that the image of me doing Daggy Dancing may be disturbing, and leave a permanent memory on your brain that may cause distress or embarrassment.)

In Daggy Dancing, just move the body any way it wants and let it be as *daggy* as you can. In other words, you're not allowed to be cool when you do Daggy Dancing. It can be done to music, but it's even better if you hum and become your own one-man or one-woman band.

Jiggling, swaying or rhythmical rocking can also be helpful. Rocking backwards and forwards on heels and then toes is soothing for some people. Just moving, getting up out of bed or the chair is helpful anytime you feel stuck or frozen. Taking a walk is a good way to interrupt an activation cycle.

Nursery rhymes

Another technique I often suggest to interrupt activation is used by clever little people all the time: nursery rhymes. Nursery rhymes are soothing because they are familiar and repetitive, sequential and musical and usually associated with safety or happy moments from childhood, which primes the brain.

For me and many of my clients, reciting a nursery rhyme works to interrupt the activation cycle as well as to soothe the lower brain. It's likely that nursery rhymes also connect to the playful brain of childhood. So if you're feeling stuck, start reciting your favourite nursery rhyme and keep doing it until the cycle is interrupted. It seems to work best with overthinking rather than feeling reactions.

Because it's associated with childhood it's important to find a nursery rhyme that doesn't have any strong reminders with painful or traumatic memories. Children will often hum or sing when distressed. French Jewish children recited 'Sur Le Pont D'Avignon' together as they were going to the gas chambers.

Some people find nursery rhymes childish. This response is probably from the big brain, more specifically the critical big brain, as the servant of secondary activation. It is child-like because the lower brain is like a child and that's the part that is distressed.

Song snippets

If using nursery rhymes feels childish or somehow minimises your experience then it might be more helpful to find some other lyrical words that feel more fitting. You could use a snippet of a song or a line from a poem, humming a favourite tune, for instance. It's best to keep it simple and use only a line or two, such as the chorus of a song, rather than a whole song, because you are building a tool that is like knocking at the door, short and repetitive. But because the brain habituates, you may need to keep changing the nursery rhyme, song or poem, or use one that requires some effort of attention, to keep your brain engaged.

Other people prefer to use a particular practice such as breathing and counting or a specific meditation or yoga practice to interrupt. Just be mindful of your intention when using these techniques. Often they are hiding a *fix-it* approach, which means they may be helpful in the short term in reducing activation, or helping you get back to sleep, but in the long term keep giving the brain the message that it still needs to be on alert, that something may be wrong.

Jack, uncovering body cues

Rita: Jack, I noticed when you started talking about your boss that your hands were clenched into fists. Then as we worked with the body your hands were open in a pushing-away kind of gesture. Did you notice that?

Jack: No, I was busy grinding my teeth down thinking about what a … um … annoying little man he is.

So notice how you orient attention, Jack. As we said before, the focus is on him. So we want to find some ways to interrupt that if we can, and perhaps orient to something else to change the pattern of experience.

Not sure I'll be able to do that when I'm eye-balling short Pete. I just want to rip his arms off.

And notice your hands when you say that, Jack.

Hmm, yep, fists all right. You can probably guess what I'd like to do with them.

But, as I said, I noticed that when the activation reduced a little your hands were more open, and you made a kind of pushing-away gesture, and I was wondering if we could use that to interrupt.

Not sure how to do that.

I think your hands are a body cue telling you you're activated. But perhaps we can use a different body cue, based on what your body just did naturally when it was less agitated, to interrupt the cycle.

So when I come down from a '9' or '10' my hands unclench and are open – is that what you mean? As long as you're not suggesting I'm gonna stroke my arm instead of making a fist when I'm in his office.

No, Jack, probably not helpful.

That's alright then.

We're not trying to impose something that feels incongruent but step through activation. Use the body to move the mind, you might say. Use the hand thing as cause, not effect.

I need a bit more than this, Rita. I don't know what you mean.

Using the body cue to set the intention, prime the brain and interrupt.

I could give it a go. How would it work?

Well, if you make the pushing-away gesture when you're feeling angry with the boss instead of making a fist, it might interrupt the usual pattern of reaction. Using a body cue or something associated with the body-brain, which as you know is where the activation is happening, gives you more traction than just using words.

Like if I try to talk myself out of it and tell myself he's a schmuck and not to let him get to me.

Yes, but your body doesn't believe your words; so we need to work from bottom up, using the body to change the mind.

Okay, yeah, because I can't talk myself out of the activation 'cos it's Ted brain. Right?

Right, Jack. And you might find it easier to focus on your hands instead of trying to talk yourself out of your anger or applying AIR(s), because I know you haven't found it easy to use the sequence.

So if I do the pushing-away thing with my hands, will that change the activation?

I'm not saying that, Jack. It may help interrupt the old pathway and give you a different body experience, but it's also about intention.

So it's just a way of interrupting the pattern?

Interrupting and reorienting using the body's language.

Talking to Ted brain!

Yep. And if you move from angry fist, which indicates a protective, defence reaction of extreme activation, to pushing away, which is along a continuum but not as extreme, you use a gesture or body cue that your body has given us. A cue that gives the body-brain a different message.

So I'm not aiming for a down-tools kind of shift. I'm just moving in a direction that my body goes to when I'm not at a '9' or '10'. And I'm only trying to interrupt, not trying to tell myself I shouldn't feel angry and should just flap my wrists at Pete instead. Something like that?

Yes, all of that. It is a small, manageable shift that you can focus on as an experiment to interrupt the usual pathway of making a fist. It's a sort of interruption, with a twist. Want to try it?

Anything's worth a try when it comes to the boss.

Remember, I'm not suggesting it as a 'fix it' or 'stop it'. It would still be helpful to keep applying AIR(s). It's an experiment.

Curious brain?

That's the one, Jack.

It's an experiment

Different things work for different people. It's an experiment, and you're the guinea pig. Many of these techniques are what people do instinctively when distressed or anxious. The challenge is to do them with awareness and make them your own to encourage integration.

Different techniques help with different reactions and are effective for different people. There is no one-size-fits-all for interrupting. It is best to think of it as an experiment about what works for you, which is likely to be different with different activation cycles. You can develop your own interrupting techniques, but just a word of caution: check to see if you're using techniques gently to interrupt or trying to escape the experience.

Developing a range of interrupting, re-orienting and soothing techniques that you can use in conjunction with the i-brainmap and AIR(s) will build your confidence through your capacity to move through activation towards integration. Through this, you can develop self-efficacy and choice, which is an entirely different experience to what happened during traumatic or overwhelming events when you felt powerless and trapped. This allows the brain to integrate and change the old maps based on this new experience of agency and choice rather than on powerlessness and overwhelm.

Chapter 19
Reorienting

In this chapter, I unpack the third factor in the AIR(s) sequence: reorienting. The importance of reorienting for the brain was discussed in detail in chapter 15.

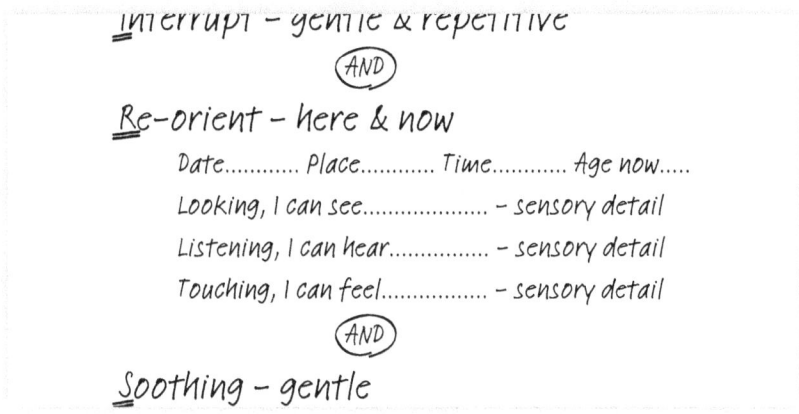

Stay with the experience

Reorienting doesn't mean moving away or distracting yourself, but instead involves being with the experience in a different way. This creates a change in your relationship with the experience, so the brain gets a different message. It holds the experience gently by keeping the body-memory map open and at the same time looking up and checking to see whether the map is relevant or which bits are relevant. Then the brain can update the map based on the current context.

An important element of reorienting is creating an AND pathway: 'I feel anxious, AND I'm looking around and can see that there is nothing here right now that's unsafe or threatening, so I'm okay.' In brief, 'I feel scared, AND I'm okay,' as explained in detail in chapter 15.

Getting your own attention

The first thing is to get the attention of the lower brain during activation. You are like the parent speaking firmly and gently to the child having a nightmare. This starts with interrupting. Then, once you have the child brain's attention, reorient to what feels safe or familiar or okay, usually here and now. How you orient may change throughout the different phases of integration.

The aim is to establish an AND pathway between implicit and explicit, between lower brain and big brain: 'I'm activated and feeling X, AND I'm here now, and noticing that everything is okay.' Orientation is to the present: 'I'm here now, AND I'm remembering X or Y,' replicating the experience of integrated memory.

Ask a question

To orient your attention, it helps to start by saying, 'AND I'm here now.' Asking yourself what is the date, place and time, or your age, can help orient you to the present.

Asking a question orients attention with curiosity, and focuses and directs attention. By asking the question 'What's the date?', or 'What's the time?', you shift attention into the present, because you have to focus on here and now to work out the date and time. Remembering that you're fifty and not five reminds you that you're not that little girl who was terrified when she felt powerless and overwhelmed.

All of these shifts give the brain context, time and place, which are some of the missing pieces when the hippocampus is offline during activation. These techniques establish manually what the hippocampus couldn't achieve when it was overwhelmed by cortisol.

Questions are a way of reorienting attention, although the 'why' question that happens during activation is usually a sign of the secondary activation and overthinking. Asking a question during activation is the same as a parent asking a distressed child something like, 'Where's the puppy gone?' The question engages curiosity and draws the attention to respond, flicking on other parts of the brain. Of course, this can only happen once you get the child's attention through interrupting, and asking a question is also a way to interrupt. The best questions are sensory or contextual like, 'Where's the puppy gone?' or 'How many pomegranates are there in the picture?'

Detailed sensory awareness

Orienting to here and now you need to look and listen as a two-year-old child does, attending to detailed sensory awareness. Lean in close to things, get curious; that's the way a two-year-old experiences things, and that's how you engage the child brain. You can bring attention into the present through the senses. Simply saying, 'I'm here now' is unlikely to do that. Describe what you see, hear, touch and smell in detail.

Looking, I can see ... (sensory detail)

Don't just look around and scan the room. You need to see or look at something closely, curiously. You're trying to get the attention of the child brain, and detail engages the attention, or it's likely to fall back into the nightmare of activation. Naming what you see: 'I can see three lines and another line crossing it. There is a black mark, three, four, five,' and counting, all help engage the attention. Look closely and see that thing as if for the first time.

Listening, I can hear ... (sensory detail)

Listen for sounds around you. You can just notice sounds coming to you or notice and name specific sounds. Experiment with what engages your attention. 'That's a Harley Davidson, and I can hear a magpie, and that sounds like a lawn mower in the distance, no wait, it's a whipper-snipper.'

Touching, I can feel ... (sensory detail)

You might touch something or feel the leather on the chair, or a ring or bracelet, or your bottom against the seat or your feet on the floor, and wriggle your toes or press them into the floor.

Smelling or tasting, I can smell ... (sensory detail)

Smell is the strongest sensory trigger. The olfactory bulb is directly linked to the amygdala and the hippocampus. We can use smell to reorient to here and now or change orientation as smells have such strong associations. How to do this will be discussed shortly.

Specific sensory reorienting techniques

To engage the attention more strongly through the senses, it can be helpful to develop specific ways to focus your attention in the present. Look for red or blue things, for instance. Find three things that are round or metallic. Use a particular scent to reorient gently as well as soothe. Chew a mint and focus on the taste.

Doing something detailed that is itself a detailed sensory experience is a useful way of grounding the attention in the present. People have always done this in various ways, often as a form of distraction, but when done with awareness and an AND intention, not to run away but to allow the distress to be there *and at the same time* focus attention on a detailed task, there is a greater possibility for brain integration.

Some things that people have reported as useful are: contour drawing, sketching, origami, writing (usually a specific writing technique rather than free writing or journaling, because that may keep you writing about the activation), walking, having a shower, following a new recipe, beading, knitting, crocheting or doing any handiwork. All these activities require a particular level of concentration and mindful attention to detail.

Which sense is best?

Many people find that one of the senses can bring them into the present moment more effectively than the others. Finding out which works best to reorient, ground and soothe is part of the discovery of integration. You might carry something, like a small stone or the i-brainmap, that becomes linked to here and now; it can help build another bridge through association and assist the brain to reorient when you feel lost in activation.

As I've said, what most people do instinctively with small children when they are distressed gives us a clue to what helps soothe the lower brain, the child brain. It's why teddy or 'blanky' or a dummy can be so important to soothe a child; it's always sensory.

Using smell to reorient

One woman who was triggered by home, a common trigger for anyone (including Jack) whose first home was unsafe, started to burn lavender oil in the house to help bring her attention into the present. When she'd used other techniques, such as looking and listening, it brought her attention back to the sensory experience of home, which kept her in an activation cycle because home was the trigger. By finding a scent that was linked to feeling safe, and using it in an oil burner, it was a constant reminder (to the child brain) that she was in *this* home not the home of her childhood, which had been dangerous. The lavender was also a soothing smell for her.

Orienting to change or difference

Another way to reorient the brain is to focus on a different time or experience, to remind the brain that time passes and things change over time. Because the lower brain is disconnected from the functions in the brain that orient during activation, you can't recognise that this feeling of activation will pass and change, making it more intolerable.

It can help to say to yourself, 'And this will change too', or 'Things can be different'. This won't usually be enough, because words alone rarely engage the lower brain during intense activation. You also need to tag a specific sensory experience that's different as you say the words. By accessing a memory of a different experience, context, time or place, you tell the brain, 'Yes, things can be different. This will change too.' And then you plug into a different experience (with sensory detail), in this case a physiological tag that's different to the body-memory map of activation.

Cultivating these alternative, resourced states can be done in sessions with a therapist or through writing about times and situations when you felt more okay, integrated, resourced, happier. Or you can create a cache of videos or photos of kids or happy moments to remind you of other times, when you felt different. It is helpful to flag or tag these 'other times' or different experiences when you feel different, okay, happy, and keep them up your psychological sleeve, like a clean hanky you can pull out as needed. This will be discussed in more detail in chapter 22.

Some people use 'safe place' in this way. I prefer to use the term and experience of 'resourced state' or the 'I'm-okay-place' because for some people when there's been a lot of abuse the term 'safety' or 'safe' can be a trigger or have too many associations with painful experience to be useful. It doesn't really matter what you call it as long as you can identify the physiological tags of feeling different, or better in some way, to remind the brain that things can and do change.

Finding other states and experiences becomes easier as you experience more integration, because you can begin to use these experiences of integration. For instance, you might find yourself being able to say, 'Oh yeah, I felt like it would never end that time I was at Fred's house, too, and then I used the techniques and things did change. Yes, things can change.' You tag the thought 'Things will change' with a specific experience, just as you would engage the child to focus on specific details to draw them gently out of the nightmare state.

After you say 'And this will change too' you can add something like:

'**Because (name the experience)**' such as, 'yesterday at basketball', or 'last week when x happened'. Choose a specific experience so the brain can recall it in as much detail as possible. You're creating a re-experiencing or body-memory map of a time when you felt okay.

AND

'**I felt (name the feeling)**'such as 'okay', 'relaxed', 'resourced', 'competent', 'happy', 'present', 'real', 'lighter', 'safe'. Name the different experience.

AND

access the sensory, the physiological, detail of that experience – both its internal and external aspects. Find the different body-memory map of feeling okay, safe or resourced so the brain can remember that things can be different.

Orienting to change and difference is particularly useful if you are somewhere you don't want to be, or where the environment is the trigger, like home. When it's difficult to stay with the here and now or you feel an impulse to avoid-escape, use the orientation for change-difference. People in hospital or prison might find it better to use the second orientation technique – tags to other experiences – because doing 'here and now' might trigger them further.

None of these techniques are intended to help you stay in an environment that is unsafe or scary. If you are currently unsafe your lower-brain alarm system should be activated.

Tune in to the internal or the external

I know I've said this before, but the fastest way to change an experience is to shift attention or change orientation. So if you always attend to the external environment, which often happens if there's been trauma, resulting in hyper-vigilance, then tuning in gently to the internal environment can change an experience.

Many people only tune in to their internal body cues when they are in pain or discomfort, and then they try to stop the pain or escape in some way. So they only ever experience the body as negative and avoid any contact with the internal space. A lot of the work with inter-Active Mindfulness, the technique I developed to use with people in session, is touching in gently, with attention, to direct body experience; it tracks the soft, timid animal of body experience.

>
> **Reminder**
> I don't recommend focusing on the internal physiological experience during activation if you're out of session, as you can easily become overwhelmed or stay stuck in activation. Apply AIR(s) instead.

Jack, reorienting and experimenting with body cues

Jack: Hey, Rita, the hand thing is cool.

Rita: Great. What happened, Jack?

Nothing different with the boss. He's very reliable. Did his thing on Monday morning. I was sitting down, and he was banging on about something, and I noticed my hands were making fists. I remembered what we talked about. So while the boss was still banging on, I tried it. Just the pushing-away thing. It was okay but didn't do much.

Except that you had already started interrupting, Jack, simply by deciding to try it out. Not only that, you were aware of your body reactions during the activation, so you already had a different orientation. There's a lot going on just in that shift.

But then it got interesting because instead of just using the pushing-away in the air, no pun intended, though it was a good one, A-I-R, get it?

Good one, Jack.

Well, instead of just doing that, I pushed against my legs. I don't know what happened, but it made a big difference. I felt calmer straight away. Why did that happen do you reckon?

Very interesting, Jack. Hmm. A couple of things probably changed when you pressed into the thighs. First, it's as if you felt yourself back.

Pardon?

Well, instead of all the attention being outward, you experienced a strong sensation of self: 'my thigh'. Because of the pressure of the flat hand against your thigh, the message 'I'm here now' was stronger, and the feeling of being inside yourself through direct body experience gave you a different awareness of the body during activation. You changed the orientation and experience of the usual body-memory map.

Okay, well, I'm not sure I get that, but yes I could definitely feel it.

The other thing that comes to mind is the work of Peter Levine. He talks about completing the movement or impulse that couldn't be completed during the trauma because of the freezing and overwhelm. Pushing away may have been what you instinctively wanted to do as a kid when your dad was cruel or violent. And in your experiment you did push, completing the movement, and your legs felt it back, so it created a kind of feedback loop. I think you did a lot to give your brain an entirely different body experience, and message, of what happens when your boss is 'banging on'.

Wow, I did all that just by pressing my thighs!

You created a very different experience for the brain in that situation, and it was more active than passive or that defeated feeling you describe.

Yeah, it was good to have something to do. Now that I think about it, the AIR(s) thing isn't enough to grab on to when I'm with the boss.

The thing that impresses me most is that you came up with the idea during activation. That indicates good integration; you were able to access other resources in your brain rather than being dragged along by lower brain activation and feeling powerless.

I don't think I thought about what to do. It just felt right, suddenly.

Like a light going on in the brain?

Yes, exactly.

I think that feeling of a light coming on happens when the hippocampus and other parts of the i-Zone light up. I can't prove it because I can't see inside the brain when you're sitting in the boss's office, but once that light goes on your brain becomes an interconnected circuit and can draw on all its resources, including the left prefrontal cortex.

You know what, Rita?

What, Jack?

I felt really good about it when I left the boss's office. I hardly heard a word he said because I was so interested in this different thing I was doing. I wasn't that fly pinned in a web like I usually am. It was very different.

Great experiment, Jack. You win the Brain Scientist Cup this week.

I felt powerful when I walked out of his office. Instead of him having all the control, I felt in charge. He didn't get to me like he usually does. He doesn't have control over me anymore.

Yes, that's a powerful shift, Jack, learning to not be high-jacked – pun intended.

Keep riding the wave, huh?

Yep. Pressing into yourself, not being pulled into reacting to stuff. But let's not assume it will always work, because then you might get disappointed if you drop back into old pathways. Let's keep experimenting.

Freedom is about choice, including how and where you choose to focus your attention. Being able to shift attention at will offers a great sense of liberation, which is what mindfulness teaches.

Experiment

As always, the best approach is to experiment with different techniques to find what works for you, and don't be surprised if you have to change your reorienting techniques because they lose their currency once you have used them a few times.

Brain Doh

Brain Doh is like a kit of simple knick knacks to give your brain a quick shift. Why 'Brain Doh'? It refers to the currency of the brain, dough, and baking up something different. It also refers to Brain-do, active. But it's hard not to be reminded of Homer Simpson when you add 'Doh', which hopefully makes it more playful because Homer is the ultimate Brain Doh.

A simple way to reorient is to experience something differently. Here are some Brain Dohs.

Record yourself

When your thinking is going around and around and you feel stuck in the loop, speak and record the repetitive statements that are like the *cracked record* in your head. Then listen back. This will give you a different orientation to the statements. Instead of being inside, you will be outside listening in. You can focus on some of the details rather than just the words, which will give you another orientation that is more sensory and of the lower brain. Notice how you sound, the tone of voice and what reactions you have to your own voice saying those words.

Spontaneous writing, drawing or painting, movement (including Daggy Dancing) or expression using sound

These techniques can give you a different perspective on any pattern that you're stuck in. In brain terms, it creates some AND pathways or neural connections: doing the same old thing AND dancing it, drawing it or writing through it.

Humour

Humour is a shift in orientation or perspective, like seeing something in a completely new way. Not only that, laughing and smiling release feel-good chemicals in the brain-body that change the state, so the old adage *laughter is the best medicine* is probably true for brain change too.

Images and videos

Looking at an image or video of something that reminds you of a different experience or another time helps reorient the brain. It's handy to have a cache of these so you can access them easily anytime.

Haiku-e

This is emotional haiku, hence the 'e'.[4*] It also refers to 'cooee', a loud shout used in the Australian bush to attract attention. 'Cooee' is often used to find someone who is lost. In this case you are calling to yourself so you don't get lost in the activation cycle.

Haiku-e begins with awareness of your immediate internal environment, emotions and/or physical experience, then finds words to reflect that experience. Creating a haiku-e requires a new orientation to the direct experience while engaging different parts of the brain, including the creative, curious brain.

You can also use a haiku-e to log other experiences of feeling good, creative or connected. The main thing in haiku-e is to begin by orienting to the immediate experience of your internal environment. Engaging with the experience in a different way is more important than following rules or how good your haiku-e is. Here are some haiku-e:

---

4   I'd like to thank my friend and poet Myron Lysenko for the inspiration for haiku-e.

Sad-sad-so-sad
drown me in this sea of tears,
tears no cry, no cry

                    Dead fish in my skin
                    slip and slide in death cold hands
                    fingers ache my bones

Warm air of jasmine
open heart remember this
to sing my body

Check your motives

Any of the above techniques can also be used as distraction or avoid-escape, so check your intention and see if you can maintain an AND pathway. Remember, you're not trying to capture or change things but discover or see things differently, afresh. What works best will depend on a number of factors including your personality and preferences, your past experience and what you're stuck in, whether it's predominantly thinking, feeling, physiological or an impulse.

What is most comfortable for you may not be the best Brain Doh for you. For example, if you are an artist, drawing or painting may not be the most useful way to reorient, but it could be. If you are a dancer or yoga teacher it may be more helpful to use your voice than go through your yoga routine or a dance movement, because what you do routinely and easily may not get your attention in a fresh way to give you a different orientation that engages the brain to create new connections in the brain. Experiment with Brain Doh to find your own most powerful way to reorient the brain.

Chapter 20
Soothing the lower brain

In this chapter I describe the last, yet essential, aspect of AIR(s): soothing the lower brain, which is where the distress is happening.

Kindness and gentleness

While all of the techniques I describe in previous chapters can help soothe the lower brain, soothing is also about intention. It's important to approach the lower brain as you would a distressed infant, with kindness and gentleness, yet sometimes firmly. It's also helpful at times to use some of the specific soothing techniques discussed in this chapter.

Soothing is very individual: we all feel comforted in different ways, though there are some common experiences of soothing. You may find that a soothing technique that is helpful in the beginning can become avoid-escape, which is more of a risk if you use a soothing technique in isolation and not as part of the AIR(s) sequence. Specific soothing techniques are best grounded in mindfulness, beginning with acknowledging what is happening.

Soothing techniques include anything that soothes the lower brain, the two-year-old. So swaying, rocking, humming, and singing nursery rhymes can all be helpful and may be less addictive than oral soothing techniques, such as eating, drinking or smoking.

Touch is helpful because it releases oxytocin. (We know that skin-to-skin contact releases oxytocin, but I've been unable to find any research on whether this occurs through touching one's own skin.) When a client is activated, I will sometimes invite them to gently stroke the back of their own hand, cheek or forehead when they are distressed or upset or stroke a tight or painful point on the body.

Michael Leunig

Some people find this very difficult if they've experienced interpersonal trauma, neglect or abuse. If you find stroking your own skin too confronting, you can use more focused touch, such as the following variation of a yoga technique that a client shared with me. Slowly and gently stroke the outline of the fingers of your open hand with your other hand. You can include attention to breathing to create a rhythm between the movement of the hand moving up and down the outline of each finger with the in and out breath.

Many people find it helpful to place a hand over the activation point, where the distress is experienced in the body during activation. Often this is somewhere on the torso, such as the diaphragm, chest or belly, or it can be in the jaw or a tightening in the legs. A hand gently placed on the chest or tummy can provide a sense of relief and comfort because it gently meets the distress of the lower brain using its own language, which is sensory. I often invite people to do this in session while we're using inter-Active Mindfulness (i-AM). This gives the lower brain a message of comfort and support, which is a different experience to the usual reactions. And, in some instances, when they become distressed in a particular way, I will sometimes ask if I may place a hand gently on their back.

Mary, self-soothing and sensory soothing

Mary: Is soothing the same as self-soothing? My last therapist did a lot of stuff on self-soothing.

Rita: Self-soothing is similar because it's usually a sensory technique, which as you know soothes the lower brain. What sort of things did you identify as self-soothing, Mary?

Having a cup of tea, or a bath, if I was at home and it was in the evening. Sometimes I'd call a friend. Well, I was meant to, but I never did. While I was upset or angry – activated – I was too upset to talk and I didn't think of it, so I never rang anyone. Then, by the time the upset had passed, I felt too embarrassed and exhausted to ring anyone. I just wanted to forget about it.

So interpersonal contact, although good in theory, may not be helpful during activation for you, Mary?

It was helpful if I was with the therapist but not when it happened at home.

Makes sense that you felt comforted and soothed when you were with your therapist but couldn't initiate contact with anyone during activation. To take considered action requires accessing the big brain, which you're cut off from during high levels of activation. Added to that, during activation it can be difficult to access interpersonal brain functioning because your brain is disconnected. That's the main problem.

I wanted to withdraw and curl up in a ball when it was really bad. I felt stupid when I had to report back to my therapist what I'd done when I was in one of my meltdowns. Usually I'd eat, and that was what we were trying to stop.

Sounds like some techniques resulted in another activation cycle of feeling hopeless or defeated. The techniques made sense when you were calm and your brain was integrated, in session, but during activation you couldn't access those resources, and you felt overwhelmed and powerless. Did anything help?

Going for a walk was the best one. But I couldn't do that at night, and that's often when it happens.

Walking is sensory too. You have to move your body and yet your mind is free to roam when you go for a walk. Plus the fact that certain chemicals are released that change your state.

Yes I always feel better after a walk.

My experience is that walking is inherently integrative. But it sounds like we need to find some other sensory strategies that are soothing when you're activated at night. But before you do specific soothing, it's helpful to apply AIR(s). Then you're giving your brain all the messages required for integration rather than just soothing, which is essential but can easily become avoidance or stopping, as we've said.

Of course! How weird, that I didn't think to use AIR(s) when I got activated at night. I can see now that it's activation. That's so obvious, but ... I just didn't make the connection when it happened.

That's because you were *in* it, not *with* it. But even beginning to recognise it as activation now can kickstart brain integration, because when it happens again there's already the thread of a pathway that's been created with this conversation. Your job is to strengthen that new pathway.

So eating chocolate cake is okay to soothe myself? [*Laughing.*]

That depends on your attitude, Mary. Are you eating to avoid-escape or mindfully, saying 'I'm okay and I'm just eating this piece of chocolate cake'? Eating is an instinctive way to ground yourself in the present through the senses, soothing. But sugar and carbs aren't the best way to stabilise the brain. You can create another cycle that replicates activation or anxiety by eating sugar. Eating some protein with the carbs is probably more helpful when you're upset.

Like snacking on a tin of tuna? Doesn't have the same appeal, Rita. Sorry. Oops.

Fair enough. But think about the value of choice, and make the best one you can at the time. Even taking care of your body-brain a bit more, by choosing something with a bit more protein and a bit less sugar and a bit lower GI, higher fiber, would be helpful – like making something with eggs and almonds instead of a sugary, flaky, highly processed cake.

Okay, I like that. Perhaps I can cook a cake when I'm activated at night, using eggs and almonds or some other nuts.

It would be good to experiment, Mary, because that could help focus your attention, reorient your brain and give you something to eat at the end, something healthier and more balanced. There may be things, such as chocolate almond balls, that you could make fairly quickly because waiting for a cake to cook might be too slow. Low sugar, of course.

Of course. I've got a recipe I could try.

Great experiment, Mary. Keep me posted. Whatever you do it's better if it is somewhat familiar, yet complex enough that it engages your attention.

Soothing or self-soothing?

'Self-soothing' is a term often used by therapists to refer to techniques used in self-care or self-comfort to assist in regulating difficult emotions. Suggested techniques can include having a bath, calling a friend, taking a walk, eating some good brain-food, or anything else the person finds comforting. Although self-soothing is similar to what I refer to as soothing – that is, soothing the lower brain – it is only one aspect.

Soothing the lower brain can also occur through interrupting and re-orienting to the present, as used in AIR(s). Soothing as I refer to it here always has a sensory dimension because that's the language of the lower brain. I make this distinction because if you are using what are called self-soothing techniques you may overlook a whole range of others that aren't usually part of the self-soothing repertoire yet are useful and important, especially mindfulness-based techniques.

Another distinction is attitude. Self-soothing can hide a message to the brain that you have to make the feeling go away, that you *should* feel different, better. It may seem like a useful message, but this attitude can give the brain the message that it's not okay to feel this way, that something needs to be fixed or avoided, which as you know perpetuates the reaction. Saying to yourself, 'I just need a nice cup of tea,' or 'Settle down, you need to self-soothe and not be so reactive,' gives the brain a very different message than 'Oh yeah, there's my lower brain activated by that old thing, and I feel scared, and I need to help the kid brain through it.' The first response may be hiding a 'Stop! This experience is not okay. I have to change it.' The second message says, 'This is the brain doing that old trick that isn't helpful anymore, and I have a choice here, and it's okay because there's nothing happening right now that is threatening,' a change in attitude-intention that is more soothing than the first.

Of course, self-soothing can be done with an attitude of self-care so that it's inherently soothing and encourages brain integration.

In addition, when there has been early and severe trauma or neglect you may have extreme difficulty with the idea of self-soothing but can usually work with mindfulness-based techniques or interrupting-reorienting techniques to soothe the lower brain.

'What do I need right now?'

Part of soothing can be to ask yourself, 'AND what do I need right now?' This can be helpful because, as you know, asking a question can reorient the brain, changing the experience. It also invites an active response, which is very different to the powerlessness that usually accompanies activation.

It's important to ask yourself this question towards the end of the AIR(s) sequence when the whole brain is more connected and moving towards integration. If you ask yourself this before you've moved through the preliminary sequence of AIR(s), you're more likely to respond with a secondary activation such as 'To get out of here!' or 'To eat chocolate cake!' So, first give the brain AIR(s): acknowledge, interrupt, reorient and soothe. And then ask, 'And what do I need right now?'

This question may need to be adapted for anyone whose needs weren't met as a child, because asking for what you need can be a trigger for activation.

Mary, asking what she needs

Mary: That's tricky. If I ask myself what I need, I might answer, 'Chocolate!'

Rita: Yes, the most immediate and instinctive way to soothe the lower brain is through food, and we want you to have other options for soothing the child brain. It can help to say, 'What do I need right now to soothe myself?' or 'What do I really need right now?' We can work on variations that might be more helpful.

I think I'd still say chocolate, or food anyway.

Yes, but remember that when you go through AIR(s) and have your attention in the present, eating mindfully, the brain is getting a very different message. Over time, the brain learns that this activation pattern, or the feelings under it, are no longer a threat.

And then I can get to enjoy the chocolate more.

Yes, and you will also have more choice about how much chocolate you eat.

That'd be different. Choice about chocolate. Hmmm. I can't imagine that, but I'll try to keep an open mind.

We can also talk about things to do when you still feel overwhelmed once you've applied AIR(s) to get your own attention gently.

But wouldn't that be distraction or avoidance again? I'm getting confused.

Good point, Mary. Perhaps, 'gently holding attention' is a better way to say it. Behaviour can look like distraction or avoidance, but isn't if you're orienting differently AND you have an intention to interrupt rather than distract or avoid AND you're approaching with kindness. These are all the things embedded in AIR(s) that we want to help you develop over time in response to activation.

And I'm here now, aware of what is happening and letting it be what it is instead of struggling with it or trying to make it go away.

That's right, Mary. No struggling. But we don't want you to get into a struggle to stop the struggle either.

Okay! That's good because I've already got enough to struggle with, or not struggle with ... I mean ... Oh, whatever!

Getting on with things is a common way people use to orient themselves during distressing or overwhelming events, such as during grief. It's probably what got most of our grandparents through tough times. It focuses the brain on getting things done. The problem is that it can become an avoid-escape reaction. But it can also be co-opted to help us remain grounded in practical routines, which for most of us will have some soothing and reorienting value.

Chapter 21
Finishing i-brainmap with AIR(s)

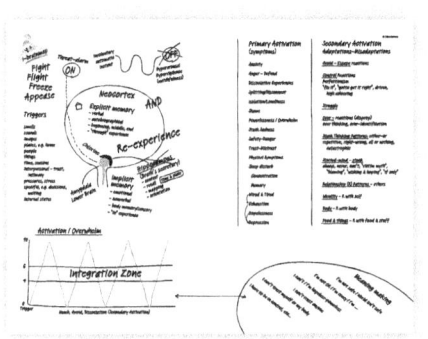

In this chapter I draw in any loose threads in i-brainmap and highlight important points that are easily overlooked or forgotten. I discuss some specific issues that arise, in association with integration, with Jack and Mary.

Create the conditions

Learning what works for you during activation takes time and practice, like learning any new skill. You are working with the brain's innate process of integration, and it is a fluid process, like surfing or swimming in currents and tides. An essential part of creating the right conditions for integration is to go gently, approach with kindness, as you would a frightened animal.

Because activation happens so quickly we need to get the brain involved, because we can't override the lower brain via the big brain during activation. We need the whole brain to get involved for generalised integration to occur. Although I've said it before, it's important to remember that we can't *do* integration, but instead we create the conditions and reduce inhibitors so that the brain can integrate. It's more like gardening or surfing than producing a building from a plan.

It also helps to find an embodied metaphor that makes sense to you; a visual and visceral map of the dynamic of activation into integration. Having a larger sense, like having a map, helps orient you when you feel lost in the dark tunnel or dumped by a wave. The more it's based on your unique experience the more effective it's likely to be.

Mary, what if I open a can of worms?

Mary: I'm not sure if I want to get into too much of this integration, Rita. What if I dig up all my old, stinking skeletons and I can't bury them again? I don't want to live in a zombie movie.

Rita: We're not suggesting that you make anything happen like digging up the past. These techniques give you something to orient to during activation to help you move through the distress.

But old things have been coming up. How do I stop that?

The brain will integrate whatever is necessary. We can't predict what it will do because your brain is unique, so your process of integration is also unique. But we don't want to stop it. Your job is to keep moving through it and not get too caught up in it.

Easier said than done.

That's why it's good to have a map, Mary, and some guiderails to grab hold of when you feel lost. In integration, it's as if the brain sifts and sorts through your old patterning to find what is no longer significant, then packs it away in the basement rather than leaving it scattered around the bedroom floor so that you constantly trip over it.

But can't I just do what I'm already doing? It all feels a bit overwhelming sometimes.

Of course, if it's helpful. This is about whatever works for you. The only thing to be aware of is whether your response is perpetuating the activation cycle in the long run or giving the brain a different message that it can switch off the alarm now – put down the unhelpful response – because the danger has passed, allowing it to integrate.

How will I know if it's helping or making it worse?

If you start to feel like you have a bit more space as it happens then you're probably getting some integration. But if you just feel stuck it may be that your response is perpetuating the activation cycle. It can be hard to distinguish in the beginning. Integration happens subtly and spontaneously, from inside out, so often you may not notice it in the beginning. That's why the best approach is experimental, curious, finding out what works for you.

Go gradually

In the beginning, using the i-brainmap with AIR(s) may feel precarious, but as you practise the skills you can begin to feel some sense of mastery, like learning to surf. One of the hardest things is to let go of old coping strategies that may have become *mis-adaptive*. They worked in the beginning; in fact they were probably all you *could* do. It can feel hard to trust that this new approach will work, and for a while you might flip-flop between the old map of coping strategies and the new map, the i-brainmap.

It is therefore important that you do this gradually and gently. As children learn to swim, the first step is paddling and learning to be less afraid of the water. And while they learn they want their floaties on; but once they learn to swim, those floaties are going to get in the way of improving their swimming. Similarly, i-brainmap is intended to keep you afloat as you learn what works for you and grow your confidence.

We don't want you to leap in from a high cliff; it's not a sink-or-swim program. In the beginning, that means doing what gives you comfort and soothes, yet also being willing to take small risks to try something new. We want to soothe the child brain, not freak it out, so you need to go gently to teach it that everything's okay. Eventually you'll be able to swim out into deep water.

Orientation to integration not activation

Sometimes people think i-brainmap causes activation, but they are usually becoming more aware of how often they are activated or how often avoid-escape reactions are happening.

As you begin making sense of activation in a different way, your avoid-escape strategies sometimes become transparent and you realise that they are no longer helpful. We don't want you to focus on activation – just deal with it when it's arising. There's no need to go looking for it. The focus/orientation is on integration and moving towards the *i-Zone*.

Once you enter the *i-Zone* you have increasing choice about how and what you orient towards.

Jack, naming and owning emotional experience

Jack: Katie reckons I slap around my inner child.

Rita: Does that label, 'inner child', work for you, Jack?

Hmm, not really. I've been calling it the 'big kid'. 'Ted brain' works.

Yes, 'inner child' doesn't work for everyone. But the reason I use 'child brain' is to give you an embodied metaphor linked with the gesture of integration. Knowing it's neurobiological and that this is the way the brain develops and behaves, bottom up, gives you a different, sometimes softer, orientation, because functionally it is like a child. Maybe there's some softening happening towards Ted brain, Jack?

Hmm, maybe. I'd still rather it left the building.

It sounds like there are other shades of emotion creeping in, Jack, rather than extremes of all or nothing, like anger or withdrawal, as your only options.

Yeah, there hasn't been much on the emotional menu. Mostly anger, rage, fury or hitting the wall.

That's often how emotions are experienced when there's been trauma, because it's all driven by lower brain activation. It's like your system hasn't developed any experience, language or expression of softer or more complex emotions.

You betcha. You sure didn't want to cry around Dad. He hated boys being sissies. He said a lot worse than that. He could see a chin trembling at 100 paces. 'I'll give you something to cry about, boy', was a favourite.

So emotions are like a tsunami coming at you.

Yep, tsunami fits. I don't get a little bit angry, I get mad as hell. I try to stay away from anything that makes me mad.

So it can feel unsafe to explore or even feel the full range of emotions because your system reads emotions as dangerous. And your early experience told you it was dangerous to experience and express softer emotions.

Yep, emotions are dangerous, like rogue waves that tumble me and drag me out to sea.

And you can't learn to surf when it's extreme. All you can do is run for cover. So you're either swimming for your life or keeping out of the water.

Boy, no wonder I don't like getting wet. All that slippery emotional stuff makes me cringe.

So until you started having less extreme emotional reactions, especially anger, it hasn't felt safe to explore any emotions. Your system reads emotions as threatening, because that's been your experience so far. But now that's changing and we're seeing some softening and more varied emotional responses, not just activation associated with threat-alarm.

And I've learnt that there are words for this stuff. I can give them a name. That helps somehow.

Yeah, we could probably write a book on why naming emotions is helpful, and why it's different to analysing emotions. But let's just say that in the principles of i-brainmap, naming acknowledges as you experience a feeling, which validates without going into the feeling. And naming flicks on other parts of the brain to name the feeling, making connections ...

And whalla – integration!

Jack, from sink or swim to floating possibilities

Rita: Up until now your brain's been in survival mode, Jack, with an armed burglar constantly casing the joint. There hasn't been room to notice any of this or to access other resources.

Jack: Maybe it explains why sometimes I think I'm smart and clever and other times I'm an idiot.

Just notice how you talk to yourself, Jack – remembering that you were just trying to survive and the Ted part of the brain is like a frightened child and we need to be gentle with a frightened Ted.

Yeah, thanks Rita. Sounds good but I have been an idiot sometimes.

Sometimes it's good to do an audit of things past and then let it go, so you can turn towards the present to move forward. You did what you could to survive, Jack. That's all you had to work with.

Yeah right, Rita.

Notice that toughness, that unforgiving-ness, Jack. Notice that hardness towards yourself. Would you be willing to work with that?

[*Jack draws in his breath between his teeth.*] Yeah ... I don't know, Rita.

That reaction against it is probably protection. Might be a way of keeping away from your vulnerability?

Ouch! That hit the mark.

Well, we don't need to go there just yet. What this has shown us is that part of you doesn't want to forgive yourself.

Try all of me, Rita.

There's a lot of resistance to self-forgiveness.

To be honest, Rita, I hate all that crap. Sounds like the stuff Katie reads.

Okay, let's use some other term. What if we just call it 'letting go'? Letting go the past to free yourself ... to the future?

Hmm, that could be a book title. I reckon Katie'd buy it.

But this is about you, Jack. Could we talk about letting go as a possibility? Or putting down that toughness and instead being curious.

Hmm, that sounds more likely, putting it down.

Not doing it but just floating it as an idea? Because this big kid was doing the best he could with what he had, and mostly he was just surviving and trying to protect himself from the fear and pain of his father's brutality.

Let me sleep on it. [*Hums Meatloaf song.*]

Well sleeping on it is good, Jack. There's a lot of research to suggest that the brain integrates during sleep. But let's not rush it, because we're likely to hit that wall of resistance or defence that protects you. At some point we might want to work with that through the body. It's like a protective skin, and we certainly don't want to rip it off, because it could leave you feeling raw and vulnerable.

Hmmm.

I notice your shoulders relaxing a little bit, Jack ... did you notice that?

Nope, but I don't feel quite as tense as when I thought you wanted to work with that stuff.

We don't want to do anything that you don't feel ready for, Jack. That is only likely to result in resistance or struggle.

Aka activation.

Yep, that's the one, Jack. I just want to invite you to turn towards the idea of putting these reactions down and meeting them gently, whatever is there. We don't want to make it wrong. It's not wrong. It's just how your brain put up your defences to survive and protect you, to get you through. And now you don't need it anymore. That's all.

Yeah, that's all! [*Jack laughs.*]

Things to remember when applying the i-brainmap with AIR(s)

- If you are currently unsafe you need the fight–flight system 'on'. The i-brainmap is about learning to switch it off when there's no current or immediate danger.

- One of the hardest things to learn is that this is all about integration and not trying to stop the activation. There needs to be some activation for integration to occur.

- It isn't helpful to get into a new struggle trying to control the symptoms of activation.

- Sometimes people get caught in the secondary activation of *I gotta get it right* using i-brainmap. This is like trying to assimilate i-brainmap into existing maps or schemas instead of using it to catalyse integration as intended.

- If you find yourself getting into a struggle and trying to control symptoms, it would be better, once you have named the activation, to ask yourself, 'What do I need right now?' By asking this, you shift your attention to your internal need in a way that's active (not the passivity of overwhelm).

- Shifting your attention, intention or orientation changes the experience, and changing the experience changes the brain.

- Think of i-brainmap as an experiment or a journey rather than a destination – not because we don't know *if it will work* but to reduce secondary activation of *trying to get it right* and focusing on outcomes, which is a top-down approach.

- Invite curiosity, which is a specific orientation and a good antidote to stuck attention or a brain knot.

- The most important question to ask is *'What message am I giving the brain?'* Then ask whether this response will perpetuate or interrupt the activation cycle.

- A common pitfall is intellectualising the map in a top-down way. That can perpetuate a split-brain system. Instead of focusing on getting the right map or working it out intellectually, i-brainmap is intended to be used as a dynamic, working map; like a field map that you scribble on and change when you see that it doesn't fit with the current context. It is continually being upgraded and changed to fit with current experience.

- The first step is to give your brain a whole-brain map and then develop techniques that gently interrupt, reorient and soothe the brain.

- The techniques you develop need to be usable wherever you are – because activation can occur anywhere, anytime – and they need to be something you can initiate yourself. Being able to respond in an active way rather than feeling defeated tells the brain you have some choice. Active doesn't necessarily mean *doing* something.

- Remember that activation is a signal that the brain is trying to integrate something.

Expect the unexpected – approach with curiosity

Your experience of integration, like your experience of activation, is unique. Although there are some common principles that encourage brain integration, which are embedded in i-brainmap, how and what your brain integrates is up to you, and your brain.

As you create the ideal conditions to grow brain integration, the brain starts to mop up the spillage from old wrecks that still skulk in your psychological dungeons, only to emerge at some inopportune moment on a dark night or in the boss's office. Once you let the brain know that a body-memory map is no longer dangerous or relevant it can start the mopping up, pulling out old fragments of maps, dusting them off, and upgrading them to create a more useful map, one that includes all your resources and wisdom.

Integration is not always an easy journey, because you can come face to face with the yellow-eyed wolf. It can make your heart quiver, as every cell in your body screams 'Run!' But you hold your hand, turning towards the wolf and see that you're in a child's game and there is nothing there, only your own hard breath of fear. And you breathe out and smile with relief. But then the tears come. All the uncried tears of a lifetime ooze out of you. All the grief that was dammed up behind your fear can rise up like floodwater, drowning your resolve. You think you will never stop crying.

But then, through your tears, you hear something and look up. You hold your breath and listen – 'Was that music?' You wait and listen, but there is only the wide silence and your rough breath and the tears keep coming. You look up and there it is again ... 'Is it chiming?' You listen. Ah, yes, a Currawong in the distance. And you stretch out your hearing, your lips soften into the hint of a smile and your eyes leak more tears, but now they are different, tears from some other place that you'd forgotten.

Jack feels

Jack: Something weird happened, Rita. I cried.

Rita: Do you want to tell me about it?

Not really.

But you wanted me to know that you cried. How is it significant for you, Jack?

Well, apart from the obvious, that I never cry, I mean *never*, and that I'm telling you – *that's* significant – and Katie was with me. Big, huh?

Yeah, that's big, Jack.

Katie cuddled me and I cried like a baby. I couldn't stop it. I don't even know why I was crying. Nothing out of the ordinary happened. It was Saturday. We just had a day at home, working around the house. I felt happy, Rita. It wasn't the big buzz of happy I can get when I achieve something but ... I can't explain it ...

More peaceful? At home in yourself?

Yeah maybe, I don't know. I can't explain it. But then I cried.

It's not unusual, Jack, for people to cry when the brain is integrating.

But why? I feel happier than I've felt in all my life. Well, a different happy. But I think this is happiness. And then I cry! Weird, huh?

Sounds like integration to me. When you're afraid you focus on the threat. But once your brain can put down the guns and resume peace, often the brain will process old pain, like it's trying to heal old wounds. And you can feel again – a range of emotions, not just self-protection. It's like giving the child-brain permission because it's safe to release whatever is there. And for many people there's a lot of sorrow, for what was lost, or never was, for how hard it's been or what they longed for, regret ... But this crying sounds like release and part of integration. A good crying, you could say. How was it for you to cry?

It's not my favorite thing, it just felt weird, awkward ... but ... Katie was so gentle. I think that's why I kept crying. She just stroked my hair and cuddled me and let me cry. In the past, with her so close I would have seen it as an opportunity ... well, you know ... but this was different. I can't explain it.

So you allowed it to happen and trusted that it was okay, Jack? You didn't need to protect yourself from your deepest feelings?

Okay, okay. I think that's enough talking about it. I'd like to talk about something else now.

Okay, Jack. Something's changing though, integrating. I think it's really profound, reaching out to Katie when you felt sad or vulnerable instead of pulling away.

Yes, it's different. I don't know what to call this stuff ... Integration doesn't seem a big enough word for it.

That's fine, Jack. We don't need to analyse and label it. That feeling quality sounds more connected to body experience, a softening of reactions, softer emotions.

Yes. Like these feelings are mine ...

Your feelings belong to you. Aha.

Yeah, they belong to me. When I felt things before it was like the tsunami; like activation or the beach in cold togs. Or when I felt good it was like I was watching a movie; they weren't my feelings but someone I was watching go through their routine.

Disconnected?

Yeah, disconnected.

Can you describe this new feeling in your body, Jack?

Well ... it's lighter. I feel lighter.

Aha. I still call it integration. That's why I call all of it integration, because sometimes it's indefinable.

Yeah, well, if this is integration I'd like more of it. Not the crying part but the after part. Now I get why you didn't give me the low-down on integration, because this isn't what I expected.

No. And if you had expected it, if I'd said you might cry and cry, you may have resisted. But we can't predict how each brain will integrate. It's a unique experience, different for everyone.

Yeah, if you'd said I'd be crying like a baby I think I would have ... I don't know what, but probably resisted. But this was okay, even though I can't explain it.

Yeah, integration is hard to articulate sometimes.

Hey, it's more like surfing than therapy, because there are no words when you're out there riding the waves.

You're right, Jack. Just ride those waves, huh, and forget about the words or even the books on surfing?

Yeah, just ride the waves. Sounds like a hell of a lot more fun than therapy.

Developing the integration muscle

As you develop the integration muscle you can ride the waves of integration, with i-brainmap and AIR(s) as the ground or board (with trainer wheels) that give you direction and security until you can body surf unaided. As your capacity to move towards integration strengthens you have more choice about how you respond to whatever experience arises. Central to this increased capacity to choose is the ability to orient attention, especially the unique state of orientation at the heart of integration – the *AND pathway*.

Instead of attention being hijacked by the lower brain through terror, you learn to orient in new ways, based on the direct experience of moving through activation to integration. This choice starts from the bottom up and is based on your growing capacity to recognise activation as it arises and not become caught in its sticky web no matter how it presents. This frees your attention, so you can choose how you orient to an experience. Do you focus on your boss's behavior, over which you have no control, or on your internal reactions to manage your distress until you can reconnect with your resources to decide how you want to respond?

This process of brain integration isn't neat and often it's not nice. You will fall off your board and get dumped by waves more times than you can count. But the only thing that matters is climbing back onto your board and riding the next wave and the next. It's this that tells the brain that everything is okay. It's just another wave and you can handle it, even though you might be scared. Besides, you're tired of sitting on the beach and missing all the fun.

The many faces of integration

Integration has many forms and many faces. Given the right conditions the brain will do what it needs to do to remap the past. One common experience many people report is a feeling of space and freedom as the brain integrates. It's as if you've been living inside a brain-body-mind with many locked and barred rooms and now you can open them. And not all of them have wolves and demons; many have held precious parts of you that you had lost or forgotten. Reclaiming these lost parts offers new ways to respond to what life holds in each moment. At the heart of this discovery (or recovery) is curiosity, because when it's safe, the brain is intensely curious, and playful.

Mary, finding the beautiful in herself

[*This dialogue takes place after Mary has described a recent experience of activation.*]

Rita: Do you want to work with that through the body, Mary?

Mary: Okay, let's do it.

[*Mary closes her eyes and settles into the chair and sighs.*]

So, just notice that, Mary. How it is to sink into the body, the sigh as you come into yourself … Uh-huh … hmm … Noticing whatever's there, Mary … What are you most aware of?

The feeling in my chest.

Can you describe it to me, the sensations?

It's like a tight ball.

How big is it?

About the size of an apple.

Uh-huh … Does it have a texture or quality, anything else about it?

It's kind of dark and heavy …

Is it like that all the way through?

It's dark, maybe a little movement in deep …

Just notice whatever's there, not trying to change it … is it alright to move in closer and deeper inside it?

Yeah, I can move in closer but there seems to be something blocking … I can't see. It's too dark.

And as you come in closer, curious, is there anything new you discover?

… hmmm … the block's dissolving … it's moving, like a vibration … now there's light coming from it. Like it's alive.

Can you describe the light to me?

It's like the light after rain when the sun comes out.

It sounds beautiful, Mary.

It is … it's beautiful.

So notice the beautiful inside you, Mary … hmm … just notice that …

[*Tears start rolling down Mary's face, an almost hint of a smile on her lips.*]

Hmm … I'm here if you want to speak any of this, Mary. I'll just stay here with you as you experience the beautiful in you …

[*Long silence*]

It feels strange for someone to see this part of me … No one has seen that before. I don't even see it much.

I see you, Mary, I see … the beautiful in you.

There's lots of beautiful colors: indigo, and white, blue … it's lovely. [*Tears continue to trickle down Mary's face.*]

[*Silence*]

I'm just here. Mary, if there's anything you want to share as you meet the beautiful in you.

[*Long silence*]

I don't have any words for this. [*More tears*]

No need for words if there are none, Mary. We can sit in silence with this beautiful in you.

[*Long, long silence*]

Anything you want to say before we start to come back to the room, Mary?

Just that it reminds me how it was to sit with Granny. Like she saw something beautiful and special in me. I still miss her. [*More tears*]

Yeah, your Granny saw the beautiful in you and met it … and now you miss her … hmm …

I still feel her with me, but it's not the same as climbing into her lap. I can still remember her smell and her funny white hair that would never sit down.

Yes, she's still in your heart, there's still a connection to the love you had for your Granny, and the way you felt close to her. Remember this feeling. You can come back to this place in your body-memory, like a garden to rest in, a beautiful resting place.

[*Mary sighs loudly.*] Yes it's like resting.

Beautiful, Mary. Let yourself rest …

Mmmm … She feels close, the feeling I always got when she was around. It's still there. I'd forgotten how this felt.[*Mary sighs loudly.*]

Yes, let yourself feel that, Mary. That safe resting place in your body remembering your Granny … hmmm … resting into that …

I feel so grateful that I had her in my life. She was … is like a precious gift …

And you can connect into that feeling of peace and gratitude, Mary. It's still there in you … notice how it feels in your body … how you hold this space inside … this resting place of gratitude in your body … Where do you notice it most, or is it a general feeling?

It's sort of a softness, I can breathe … it's mainly here [*points to the lower abdomen*] and my heart feels open, warm … like I'm accepted, loved just as I am … [*tears again*]

Just notice that feeling, Mary, and the tears … whatever's there …

These are glad tears, like the coming home feeling you get when you've been gone a long time and you smell the smell of home …

[*Mary cries quietly for a while and then opens her eyes.*]

How do I keep this place with me, Rita? I don't want to lose it again.

Ritual is a language of the lower brain, an action with feeling. Children create and enact rituals all the time in their play, like tagging something and giving it meaning, a remembering through the body's actions. A ritual can help consolidate a feeling, like a re-enactment, especially of something precious that we have lost or to help let go of something painful and inexpressible that we've been unable to release.

Well, the first important thing you've done is to remember it, and how that memory of your beloved grandmother is embodied. Tagging the physiology will help your body remember, and coming back to this place in the body, like watering a garden, can help sustain it.

Yes, but as soon as I open my eyes I can feel it leaving again.

Yes, that's why it's good to come back slowly to keep the thread alive. But the other thing you might want to consider is some kind of ritual.

What sort of ritual?

I'm not sure yet. What sorts of things remind you of your grandmother?

[*Together we create a ritual for Mary to practise frequently to nourish and remember this feeling of love and gratitude associated with her grandmother.*]

i-brainmap doesn't tell you where to go

By giving you whole-brain understanding, i-brainmap provides a map you can use to travel to new territories in your brain-body-mind, rather than follow the old rutted pathways that take you back to the same old endings. But it can't take you where you long to go. It doesn't suggest where you should go, that's for you to decide.

While many people, once they know how to make new tracks in their brain, go off happily on their adventure of integration, some people need some strategies for remembering happiness and gratitude and other experiences of wellbeing. This will be discussed in the next and final chapter.

Personalised map of integration

Hopefully by now you've developed an understanding of integration based on your experience. A personalised map of integration is like an upgrade in your computer system: it changes everything, refreshing what is useful and discarding what is outmoded; the system is made congruent and works optimally. That's integration.

And so ...

When you wake up with that old, familiar feeling of dread or defeat sitting on your chest, like a stinking blanket left in the dog kennel; and when you start scanning your life for potential causes for the feeling with a whole-hearted, 'What's wrong with my life?'; and when you take out a magnifier to examine possible cracks in your relationships, health, finances, current job, asking yourself 'Why am I like this? What's wrong with me?' over and over ... perhaps instead you can experiment by orienting with curiosity to the experience in your head, chest or belly.

It may be that your brain has been trying to integrate something in your sleep that left a residue of dread or defeat in your body as it tried to update the body-memory map of when your teacher ridiculed you in third grade. Just in case, before you start to dissect everything that ever went wrong in your relationship, and before your partner has rolled over and said 'Good morning, my love,' or grunted on their way to the bathroom, why not give this experience some AIR(s), invite in some curiosity. Put a hand on your chest where it hurts and hold your heart in your hand like a small, frightened animal, and see what happens next.

Chapter 22
Sustainable happiness

In this final chapter I introduce you to a particular orientation, sustainable happiness, which is like the bright star that some brains orient to spontaneously once integration becomes established. But for those brains that need assistance to remember happiness, you will find some suggestions in this chapter on how to turn towards the ordinary happiness in each day, until you can find your personal formula or compass for sustainable happiness.

And we say goodbye to Jack and Mary.

Happiness lost and found

The only place you can fully experience your birthright of happiness is inside your own skin, through your child brain. But to go there is to face, and move beyond, the demons of your past, held in frozen storage, and free them, because they are covering the vulnerabilities you buried when you were three years old. But you are not three now, and behind that dark door at the back of the dungeon you may find the beautiful in you, the exquisite innocence that is fascinated by a butterfly wing.

When there is nothing within you that makes you tremble or turn your face away, you can rest inside yourself.

Remembering happiness

When the brain is integrating (present tense, not past tense, because it is ongoing – like weeding, it never ends) and interconnected, it's like a big, happy kid and just wants to play. Sure, it gets sad and lonely, angry or disappointed, but when it's interconnected and integrating, it moves through each experience as it arises, and then it recovers, moving back into integrity, like waves rolling onto the beach.

Many brain-faces, aka people that I've worked with, rebound (and reorient) to this state of psychological flexibility, or homeostasis, and a general feeling of wellbeing, once the brain's integrative process is kickstarted and the integration motor is humming – the *humming brain*. In other words, once the integration process is underway, most brain-faces find their own bright star, or version of happiness, peace, love, the beautiful, or whatever is meaningful for them, to orient towards. I'm not pretending their lives, or mine, don't have many ups and downs, but there is a confidence in the process of integration, riding the waves of experience and knowing you'll come back to ground, to humming brain – or peace brain, not pea brain.

Sometimes, when there has been very early trauma or disruption to the interpersonal connection with mother, the brain may need some help to develop specific strategies to orient towards sustainable happiness. This is like rewiring the brain to look where you want to go and not at the bumps and cracks (or boulders in the road) that you want to avoid.

Sustainable happiness

By sustainable happiness I mean a quality of feeling that is not dependent on external events. In other words, it's an inside-out orientation of happiness that you can uncover and ultimately create using memory maps inside your body, rather than chasing happiness out in the world, which is an external orientation of happiness, and a cultural addiction of the West.

It's easy to be happy when you have everything you want, but this *having* orientation to happiness is a very precarious kind of happiness. An orientation to *having* as happiness can keep you always in a loop chasing the next *must have* item, or experience, because there is always something else to want, to wish for. This *having* version of happiness is the foundation for consumerism and all advertising.

The challenge is to know how to orient when things don't go your way or you can't get what you want, and still find peace, or rebound to happiness.

Sustainable happiness is large enough to include whatever experiences arise. It's like an ever-widening circle that lets in all experience of the world (both inner and outer). Like surfing a wave, integrated happiness means trusting that you will be able to move through and recover (or maintain) your connection and integrity through each wave of experience.

There are two sides to sustainable happiness. One is to develop the resources to manage and move through difficult and painful emotions as they arise. This is everything I've been writing about and is the essence of i-brainmap, AIR(s) and i-AM.

The other part of sustainable happiness is to recognise and cultivate qualities associated with happiness that you can return to, or orient towards, like a bright star or still point on the horizon. You can build a repertoire of personal and direct experiences of happiness, what I call *Catch yourself happy*.

Catch yourself happy

Catch yourself happy is an orientation to the experience of ordinary happiness as it arises. Recognising happiness in your everyday life, instead of chasing happiness by wishing things were different, is the orientation of sustainable happiness. Following are some suggestions for cultivating this kind of happiness. Also, have a look at the work of Rick Hanson and what he calls *taking in the good*.

Jack, a precious moment remembered

Jack: We took Ted to the beach for the first time since he was tiny. Wanna see the video?

Rita: Sure.

[Jack takes out his phone and moves to kneel beside me.]

Check out the look on his face … laughing … That's Katie laughing in the background … Now he's getting it …didn't take long … look at him go … He's a funny little guy.

Gorgeous, Jack.

Funny, huh? *[Jack goes back to his chair and puts the phone in his jacket.]*

Yeah, the look on his little face is priceless. Would you be willing to work with this a bit, Jack?

I don't get what's to work with.

Well, for the last few weeks we've been working with difficult internal states to help you learn to move through them –

Activation.

Yes. activation … and not get lost in them. But now we want you to start to orient towards, and cultivate, feeling good as it happens. It's like the other side of the integration coin. The brain tends to rebound to happiness, but it helps to give it some cues.

Sure, if you can give me a bucket of that feeling I got the day we were at the beach I'll buy a truckload.

Trouble is, Jack, it's not for sale.

Bummer.

It's free. For everyone.

Right.

When the brain is functioning optimally, that's what it rebounds to. In other words, brains in the wild are incredibly playful, in the moment, enjoying the waves.

Like Ted.

Exactly like Ted. And when Ted brain is scared or overwhelmed it forgets to play. But once those old maps have been integrated, or *are* integrating, the brain just wants to play again, and it's flexible and creative.

Yeah. I get it. Just watching Ted play and how he learns is amazing. He blows me away.

Well, every brain has that capacity, Jack. So, getting back to cultivating happiness …

Yeah, let's.

The trick to this is to notice happiness, or feeling good, as it arises in your day and give it a physiological tag. It's like we're building body-memory maps for happiness that you can come back to when you need to remember that things can be okay. As you repeatedly come back to these body-memory maps of feeling happy, glad, playful, inspired, creative etc. you're strengthening the pathways and changing the brain. Using exactly the same principles we used to allow the brain to rewire the body-memory maps of distress, overwhelm and so on.

Yeah, I know those ones.

And because they are the more established maps we need to strengthen the new maps and give them a physiological tag, or body-memory map, as they arise spontaneously in your day – what I call 'catch yourself happy'.

I like it, Rita.

So, what if we practise it now?

[*I invite Jack to take out his phone and watch Ted discovering waves again. Then we track the feelings in his body and move in close, like a close encounter with a small, wild animal, bending in and watching and listening to the delicate sensory experience, and shifts in his body, as they arise.*]

Catching yourself happy is as simple as orienting to feel-good experiences. Not trying to *make* them happen but *noticing* the simple things that bring pleasure or delight. And then becoming curious about your internal experience, zooming in to track the subtle physiological changes associated with feeling good.

When the brain has been battered by pain or stress it can forget how to play and take delight, so it may need some re-tuning into what flushes synapses with dopamine and splashes serotonin through your neuronal pathways, like a giggle erupting from a small child discovering the waves at the beach.

Like everything about brain change, it takes practice if you want to make sustainable change.

Physiological tagging

Physiological tagging of a feel-good experience creates an anchor that you can return to later as required, strengthening a body-memory map of that enjoyable experience without having to pursue the trigger event. In other words, you feel like you're at the beach without going to the beach (though a trip to the beach is always good for body and brain). Detailed sensory awareness builds a stronger map than just thinking about what makes you happy, or pretending you're at the beach, because it uses the language of the lower brain.

All the principles for brain change that we discussed in relation to activation and integration apply to cultivating happiness – or any other quality you want to develop, such as gratitude, compassion, serenity, creativity, beauty, trust or balance. Just remember to tag it in the body-brain, because that is where you can build the strongest, most sustainable memory maps.

The bedrock of sustainable happiness

The bedrock of sustainable happiness is gratitude. Gratitude is an orientation to *what is*, what you have, the glass half full, instead of an orientation to what is wrong, missing, or wished for. Because the human brain evolved in a cave surrounded by saber-tooth tigers, it needed to be wired for and oriented to threat, or finding the problem. And then – as the preceding chapters explain – once these maps of threat were engaged, your system oriented to the old maps of survival even when circumstances changed. But once your brain has some new maps, and you can orient the brain any way you like because your happy hippo (that would be the hippocampus) is on the job and your brain is integrating, then you can choose to orient towards what sustains happiness.

Gratitude is at the other end of the spectrum to 'What's wrong with this picture?' or 'Where's the threat?'. Reorienting to what is precious, what you appreciate about your life, your partner or your body, instead of what is wrong, grows some happy maps. You can use these maps of experience as a point of reference to orient towards when you feel at sea because you've been dumped by a wave of activation or rough experience. This is your point of orientation, like a bright star to guide you on a dark night.

Priming the brain for gratitude or what you value needs to include the body-brain because, as you know, that's where those earliest body-memory maps of survival are buried. If you just do a big-brain audit of what is good in your life now it won't change much, because your old body-memory maps are more established and likely to kick in when you're vulnerable or not mindful. The physiology of gratitude is what gives your brain traction for appreciation.

If you want to cultivate any quality in a sustainable way you need to develop it through the body, or the old memory maps will prevail.

Daily book ends for sustainable happiness

Orienting to gratitude, or any other quality you want to cultivate, at the beginning and end of each day grows your gratitude map. This increases the action potential of the brain or the probability that the brain will use the gratitude map instead of the survival map or the *What's wrong in this picture?* map, throughout the day.

Three suggestions for growing some gratitude maps are given below.

Priming for gratitude

You can prime the brain for gratitude each morning by spending a few minutes eliciting experiences and qualities of gratitude. This isn't just thinking about gratitude – it's orienting to the *body experience* of gratitude. You can either recall events or focus on things in your life, or this day, you're grateful for at the moment and, at the same time, check in with how it feels in the body. This primes the brain for gratitude throughout the day, especially if you practise it regularly. Build a gratitude map.

Gratitude soup

At the end of the day, in the evening (it can be done at bedtime), you can recall what happened during the day that you are grateful for. By setting this as a date in the evening you invite your brain to orient to gratitude throughout the day, because you are looking for ideas for what we call gratitude soup.

Together, my niece Kellie and I created the recipe for *gratitude soup* for her family, who now have it most nights at dinner; it's become a family favourite. There are no rules for making *gratitude soup* except to share something you're grateful for. Each person throws his or her scrap of gratitude, things they are grateful for right now or that happened during the day, into the pot of gratitude for everyone else to share.

Kellie, her husband and the boys usually throw three (sometimes more) things each into the pot at dinnertime – even Ethan, who is only three, throws something in. It can be anything from feeling glad Odin joined the family, even if he does sneak onto the couch at night and leave his hair as evidence. Or feeling lucky that you had a 30-cent cone after school, or a perfect Saturday with the kids playing in the pool and an oven-fired pizza for tea. On Sunday night someone might throw in a thick clot of gratitude that can nourish you for weeks: 'You're the best mum in the whole world, and I'm so lucky you're *my* mum.'

Gratitude soup makes a rich and hearty meal that the whole family can enjoy.

Brain love

Brain love is something you can try any time, but is particularly soothing at the end of the day.

Gently close your eyes and imagine the space between your ears and behind your eyes, where the universe of your brain sits. Imagine each neuron like a star blinking in the vast galaxy of your inner being, humming in harmony with your body and mind, like a symphony playing the music of the spheres in a velvet night sky that stretches into infinite possibility.

From this space of vast awareness recall all the things your brain has done for you today: walking, talking, eating, laughing, seeing, smelling, tasting, sleeping ... And recall the range of feelings that you experienced throughout the day: curiosity, frustration, satisfaction, sadness, delight, anger, joy, pain, appreciation ...

And now consider some of what your brain does for you that you don't notice: beating your heart, breathing your body, giving you goosebumps when you're cold, growling your hunger, firing up your immune system to fight off a bug that someone sneezed over you, constantly trying to protect you and keep you safe.

Opening into the feeling of awe and gratitude for your brain, as you remember all that it does for you in every moment of every day, awake in the vast awareness of your brain's potential ... and notice how it responds to your gratitude, whether it smiles back at you.

Mary, what's different?

Mary: I feel lighter. In fact I think I've lost a few kilos. Even though I haven't weighed myself for ages, some of my clothes feel looser.

Rita: Yes. I think when you can relax around food you begin to listen to what your body needs, rather than eating to soothe the lower brain.

I wouldn't say I'm relaxed about food exactly, but it isn't always on my mind like it was before.

The other thing to remember as you integrate is to begin to notice the difference, or occasionally how far you've come on this adventure of integration. It's easy to keep using the same orientation of threat, or looking for the problem even when things have changed significantly.

Like instead of looking to see if I've lost weight, that's the old way, I notice ... what? How do I orient instead?

Well, you might orient to wellness in your body or regular exercise that you enjoy, and eating food that's good for the brain. It's easy to forget that the brain is a physical system, not just a mind, and it needs to be fed, watered and given a good supply of oxygen for it to function optimally.

Yes, but I did some of that when I hated my body too.

Okay, true. But this time it's more about doing it for its own sake, to take care of your brain because it's such a precious and amazing system, rather than doing it to change your body. The intention is different.

You really love the brain don't you, Rita?

I really do love the brain. How can I not? It's funny, curious, smart, can take in new ideas in a wink, is creative, takes care of all the housekeeping without even needing my attention, unless something is wrong. It protects me, keeps me healthy … I include the body in the brain too, so it also manages to direct things so I can get around, lets me feel pleasure –

And pain.

Yes and pain, as a warning that something could be wrong. Which is good, as long as we know how to listen to the signals and know when it's a false alarm and how to tone it down when it's not relevant to the current situation.

Like in the i-brainmap?

Yes. That's what the i-brainmap is all about. But we need a functioning alarm system to escape danger. The trouble is when a fear system that was designed to help us escape from lions is driving our behaviour, or when we're locked in a split-brain system of either–or that stops us as a species from shifting gears to the next evolution of the brain – that is, integration.

Integrated brain?

Yes, integrated brain. I think integrated brain is the next evolution of the brain. It includes lower brain and big brain, instinct and intellect, body and mind. We need both, but our obsession with the mind and intellect, top down, as we try to override the body, doesn't encourage integration.

Mary, sorry again

Mary: 'Sorry' is in neon lights for me now. I've noticed how often women say 'sorry' and how rarely men do.

Rita: Hmm, interesting. Might be a PhD in that.

Funny you should say that. I'm thinking of going back to study. I always thought I would study again once the kids were off my hands and I had more free time. Ha! What a joke, I've got less time now than ever.

That's great, Mary. What do you think you'll study?

Not sure yet. There are a couple of Master's degrees I'm interested in. All this stuff you've been teaching me has got me really interested in the brain. And I feel like my brain is working better now. I don't think I had the confidence before. I might do something in Gerontology.

Fabulous.

I don't just want to be the baby-sitter. I feel like I've got more to contribute. I've got more energy and want to use it. But something else happened that I'm still reeling from.

What's that, Mary?

Well, it's Don. He's been so supportive about me going back to study. I told him it could cost upwards of $30,000. And he said, 'If that's what you want to do, love, then you do it. Don't worry about the money.'

Is that unusual for him, to be so supportive?

Well, no, that's what's strange. He's always been supportive, Rita. That's what's shocking.

Hmm. Curious.

It's as if I always think I have to stand up for myself and argue to get what I want. But he never questions it when I say I want to do something. It's like I've been fighting a battle with him, but he didn't even know there was a war.

Interesting.

He's always been supportive and gone along with what I wanted. I don't think I've really seen that before. I've spent my whole married life noticing all the things about him that irritate me, and getting annoyed at him. But, really, he's very supportive. I feel like crying when I think about how mean I've been to him sometimes.

Just be gentle with yourself, Mary, as you see what you haven't been able to see before.

It's like a curtain has dropped and I'm seeing him differently – probably the shower curtain that he didn't put up properly. [*Laughs.*] Seriously though, he's no different. Don doesn't change, but I've changed a lot. It's not that he doesn't irritate me sometimes, but it feels different.

Yes, it sounds more integrated that you can feel irritated but you don't disconnect and get stuck in the experience, or overwhelmed by it. There's more balance now, with this new insight that he has some qualities that you appreciate.

Yes, it's softer, more peaceful. There's a new comfort in our relationship, like an old blanket with all the stains and holes, and patches. Sure it's a bit scratchy at times, and no matter how many times you wash it you can never get that musty smell out of it from the time you left it damp in the boot after camping at the river ... well, you know what I mean.

I do, Mary. And I love the metaphor. Have you thought about becoming a writer?

Well, funny you should mention that ...

Goodbye Jack and Mary

It would be nice to offer you a neat ending for Jack and Mary, but that's not how integration works. Although i-brainmap and the work we do in session kickstarts the integration process, it doesn't end when a person walks out the door for the last time. There are no bells and whistles, because integration is a quiet coming home to self that is so personal it's often hard to describe – like trying to write about love or catch a butterfly – let alone celebrate. It happens incrementally, like spring coming gently: one morning you look up from your desk and realise the air is warmer and you can smell the blossom. But the earth has been warming, quietly thawing, unnoticed for weeks. *That* is integration.

Epilogue

When I have a terrible need of – shall I say the word – religion. Then I go out and paint the stars.

Vincent van Gogh[5]

When I set out to write this book I didn't understand how interwoven i-brainmap was with my own story, or what an intense personal journey the book would become. This book has been my pilgrimage. Coming to the page each day and facing myself alone is the deepest pilgrimage I have undertaken. As I unearthed old shames and torments my lips trembled and I wanted to turn away. But I grabbed those old bones and shook them, washed them with curiosity and a good scrub of honesty, until they shone white and I could write them down.

At times, coming to the page was like stroking a quivering wild horse; at other times it blindsided me – and then I stared into the yellow eyes of the wolf. But I've also cradled 'new knowing' like a babe until she took her first teetering steps, and I wrote her down. I wrote it all down. So much has been discarded, but first I met it all, and wrote it down.

Along the way I've had to face my own pain, loneliness, anger, stuck habits – oh, and of course my ego – bursting with envy and pride, judgments, criticisms and cynicisms. I've watched them all arrive and sit fat and churlish on the page.

When Mary faced the turmoil of standing up for herself – I met that in me, stepping into the intimate terrain of my own brain-body-mind to know it so close it was hard to breathe, and write it down. When Jack struggled with anger and disconnection – I sat down with those beasts in me, sitting through the long night until in the morning I could look them in the eye and write them down.

---

5   As quoted in *An Examined Faith: Social Context and Religious Commitment*, James Luther Adams and George K. Beach, Beacon Press, Boston, 1991, p. 259.

This has been my pilgrimage, tramping through the wild, sometimes impenetrable terrain, until I reached the ends of my universe through the desolate, and sometimes wonder of my inner geography. And I have mapped it down with my primitive tools: curiosity, attention, honesty and my words. As I faced myself in writing I uncovered more and more. Writing is my teacher, mentor and friend.

My most startling uncovery in writing this book has been to come face to face with the gaping hole of my spirituality[6], a deep longing for the peace I found and lost in the monastery. And this is the first time I've been able or willing to admit that to myself, and I cry for it, the quiet crying of something small and precious lost to me or hardly remembered.

Until I wrote it, I hadn't understood how losing the Dharma and my teacher tore me away from my connection to spirit. I only see it now, fully, in this moment. My head throbs, tears leak from my eyes and snot drips from my nose as I write it down. The pain in my chest feels like someone is crushing a rock into that place and grinding it into my heart. It's hard to breathe.

With this painful body-memory map wide open I can see why I've cried and cried whenever I've been on meditation retreats. When I've tried to meditate since the monastery, more than twenty-five years ago, I've usually been unsettled, disconnected and frustrated, or cried. With this new, wider, integrated map I can see from here to before, and how everything that reminds me of that time is like a trigger that activates all the experience that swept through after the monastery. Back to when I was alone in India and lost, before I found my skins again and pulled them back over me to keep out that sharp sting of crowding reality. I guess my brain is trying to integrate it now, right now as I write it down, but it's hard because the tears are blinding me.

I don't know what to do with this new insight. Perhaps it's enough to see it clearly, and there is nothing to do. Isn't that what I've been saying for the past hundred pages? Fixing or changing will tell my brain it's still a problem. But allowing myself to know it quietly and to cry for what I've lost is the beginning of integration.

---

6   It's hard to define what I mean by spirituality, because mine is a spirit connected to my flesh, not separate from it. It is in the ordinary, not outside it. It is in my breath and bones and skin. My spirituality is like a haiku that laughs at the Pobblebonk or holds the soft light of dawn to my cheek. It is not an ode to some unknown god that sits in high clouds.

Epilogue

Now my stomach is full of butterflies; I think they're the big blue ones. I don't know if it's fear or excitement, perhaps it doesn't matter which. And who knows if I'll dare to include this in the final pages of the book, for now it's enough to write it down and cry.

As I look up, out the window from where I write, the sharp-edged late autumn morning is bright from last night's rain. The tightness in my chest is opening to the beauty of gold and vermillion, with the shy blush of pink on the powder puff clouds in their blue blanket of sky. A crow caws slowly as if he holds eternity, and a crimson Rosella waddles like a drunken old man along a branch amongst the speckled green and gold and brown oak leaves. The sun pierces through and lights the last golden leaves of Liquid Amber, ablaze in its own glory. And for now, this is enough. This is my version of the beautiful, and it pierces through to my heart, and the ache dissolves as I watch the drunken parrot.

In a flash of insight, I glimpse – in this moment of integration, as my old memory map lies open *and* I look out at this bright day – that this is my personal practice of presence, an everyday spirituality. Where body, mind and spirit come together: inner and outer, old and new, concentric circles spinning in harmony. In this moment it's as if my brain is alight and everyone in there, neurons, synapses, glial cells, waves and particles, all align and something fresh emerges as they sing to each other, a humming brain.

Yes, this moment of integration is very like those spaces in the monastery when I felt my mind and body and spirit as one, released from bondage, like an eagle gliding on a warm current of air, alive to the moment. I sigh and breathe again.

So this is goodbye. Thank you for coming along with me on this journey. I hope you found your own pilgrim brain-heart and will continue to travel your intimate geography with some new maps of that greatest mystery of all – You – and of course your brain!

I hope you love your brain just a bit more, because that squishy mass between your ears rules your universe. It is the mystery beyond our comprehension. It makes us all the same, even in our difference, because it is the only way we can know the world.

May your brain be happy and may your curiosity never fade.

Further reading

Books, researchers, authors, sites or video clips mentioned in the book or that influenced the development of i-brainmap are listed below. Also included are authors whose teachings affected me personally, rather than influencing the development of i-brainmap directly.

There are more resources and links available that you may find insightful or useful on my website; www.ibrainmap.com.au

Books

Assagioli, Roberto, *Psychosynthesis, A collection of basic writings*, Viking Press, New York, 1965

Csikszentmihalyi, Mihaly, *Flow: The psychology of optimal experience*, Harper & Row, New York, 1990

Damasio, Antonio, *Descartes' error: emotion, reason and the human brain*, Putnam, New York, 1994

Damasio, Antonio, *The feeling of what happens: body, emotion and the making of consciousness*, Vintage, London, 2000

Damasio, Antonio, *The self comes to mind: constructing the conscious brain*, Vintage, London, 2012

Feldenkrais, Moshe, *Awareness through movement*, Harper One, New York, 1990

Ferrucci, Piero, *What we may be: Techniques for psychological and spiritual growth through psychosynthesis*, Jeremy Tarcher Inc, Los Angeles, 1982

Gendlin, Eugene, *Focusing,* New York, Bantam Books, 1981

Hanson, Rick, with Richard Mendius, *Buddha's brain: The practical neuroscience of happiness, love & wisdom,* New Harbinger, Oakland, CA, 2009

Kornfield, Jack, *A path with heart: A guide through the perils and promises of spiritual life,* New York, Bantam Books, 1993

Kramer, Gregory, *Insight dialogue: The interpersonal path to freedom,* Shambala, Boston & London, 2007

Kurtz, Ron, *Body-centered psychotherapy: The Hakomi Method,* Life Rhythm, Mendocino, CA, 1990

LeDoux, Joseph, *The emotional brain: The mysterious underpinnings of emotional life,* Phoenix, London, 1998

Levine, Peter, *Waking the tiger: Healing trauma,* North Atlantic Books, California, 1997

Ogden, Pat, Kekuni Minton & Clare Pain, *Trauma and the body: A sensorimotor approach to psychotherapy,* Norton & Co, New York & London, 2006

Perry, Bruce & Maia Szalavitz, *The boy who was raised as a dog: And other stories from a child psychiatrist's notebook, what traumatised children can teach us about loss, love and healing,* Basic Books, New York, 2008

Perry, Bruce & Maia Szalavitz, *Born for love: Why empathy is essential – and endangered,* Harper Collins, New York, 2010

Rose, Steven, *The 21st century brain: Explaining, mending and manipulating the mind,* Random House, London, 2005

Rothschild, Babette, *The body remembers: The psychophysiology of trauma and trauma treatment,* Norton & Co, New York, 2000

Siegel, Dan *The developing mind: How relationships and the brain interact to shape who we are,* Guilford Press, New York, 2012

Siegel, Dan and Mary Hartzell, *Parenting from the inside out : How a deeper self-understanding can help you raise children who thrive,* New York J.P. Tarcher/Penguin, 2004

Articles

Fehr, B. and J. Russell, 'Concept of emotion viewed from a prototype perspective', *Journal of Experimental Psychology*: General 113 (1984): 464

van der Kolk, Bessel, 'The body keeps the score: Memory & the evolving psychobiology of post traumatic stress', *Harvard Review of Psychiatry*, 1994, 1(5), 253–265

Wylie, Mary Sykes, 'The limits of talk: Bessel van der Kolk wants to transform the treatment of trauma', *Psychotherapy Networker*, 28 Jan/Feb 2004: 30–41

Video

LeDoux, Joseph, neuroscientist, delivers the Copernicus Center 2011 lecture 'Our emotional brains', www.youtube.com/watch?v=tjhCPhhzBqQ

Brown, Brené, 'The power of vulnerability', 2010, http://www.ted.com/talks/brene_brown_on_vulnerability.html

Brown, Brené, 'Listening to shame', 2012, http://www.ted.com/talks/brene_brown_listening_to_shame.html

Websites

childtrauma.org (The ChildTrauma Academy was founded in 1990 by Dr Bruce Perry as the Center for the Study of Childhood Trauma)

johnbriere.com (John Briere's Self-Trauma Model was presented at a conference I attended, and it is embedded in his work – which can be accessed through this website.)

metta.org (Gregory Kramer is the founder and guiding teacher of Metta Programs, which offers Insight Meditation. Kramer developed the practice of Insight Dialogue.)

mindsightinstitute.com (Dr Dan Siegel is Director of the Mindsight Institute, the home of the interdisciplinary field of Interpersonal Neurobiology.)

somatictraumatherapy.com (The website of Babette Rothschild, body-psychotherapist and specialist educator in the treatment of trauma)

Further reading

traumacenter.org (Dr Bessel der Kolk is founder and medical director of the Trauma Center, an initiative of the Justice Resource Institute of Boston, Massachusetts.)

traumahealing.com (Peter Levine is the originator and developer of Somatic Experiencing® and the Director of the Somatic Experiencing Trauma Institute.)

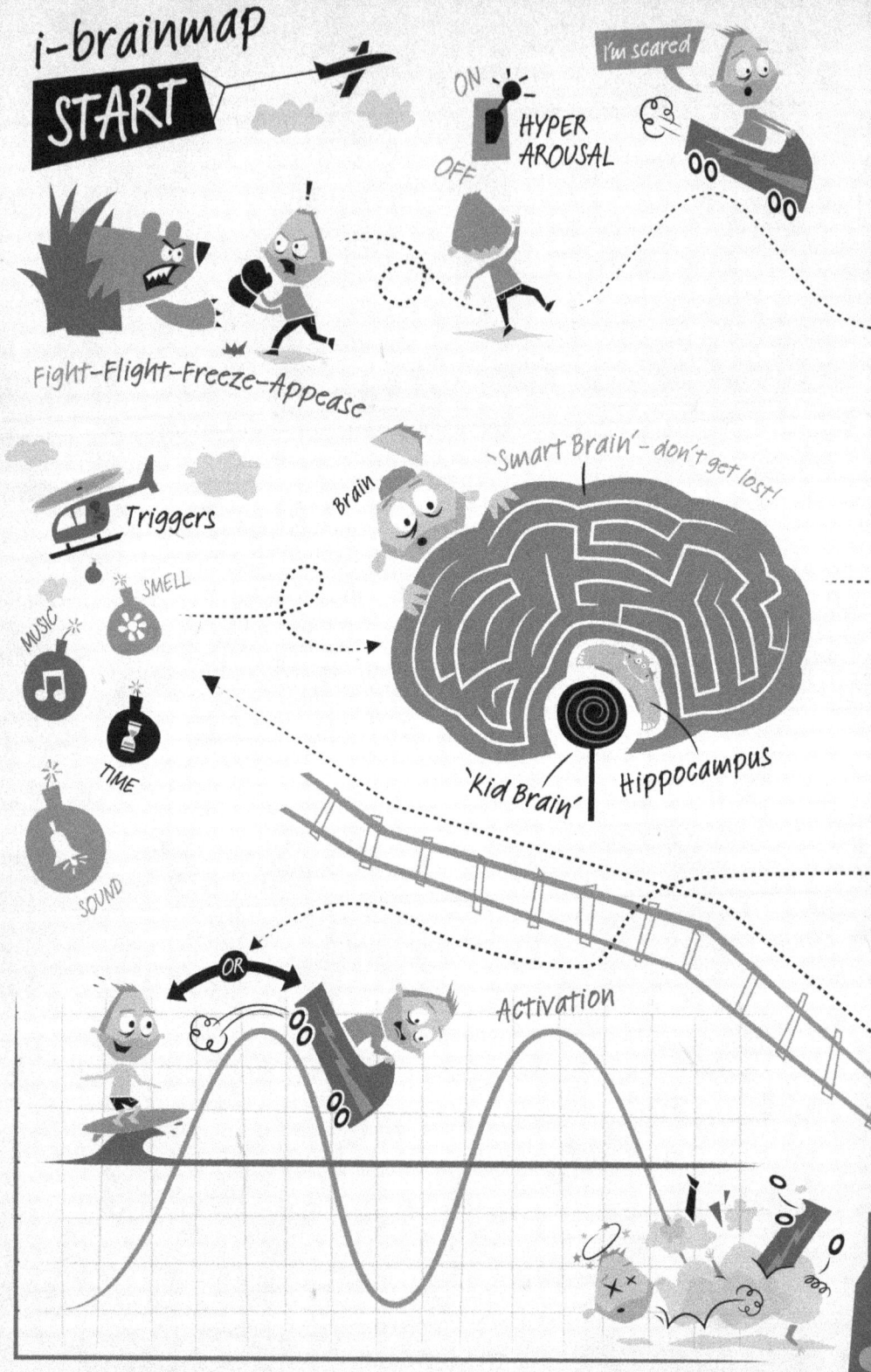

Acknowledgements

Firstly I want to thank the small and extraordinary team of people who worked with me on this book. To my editor Fran Macdonald for your clarity and consistently high standards that called me to step up and give my best, and so much more, I bow to you in gratitude for making it possible. To my fabulous illustrator/designer Sam Harmer who knows how to translate ideas into images, always a delight and inspiration to work with, I thank you. To Carol Goudie my copy editor for your dedication to detail and generous efforts to guide us at the end, thank you.

To my dear friend Sue Walker for your constant support and encouragement, especially on those dark nights when the finish seemed so far away, thank you. To my good friend Helen Young for your encouragement, reading and feedback, thanks old friend. For my dream group, Donna, Sue and Mary Rose for your love and support always, thank you.

To all those who read the early rough drafts of the book and offered feedback, thank you. To the final readers Maggie O'Shea, Mariagrazia Bellio and Fiona Newton, thank you for your generous feedback.

To my mother who showed me 'unstoppable', I wish you were here to celebrate with me, Mum. And to Dad for your generous support that made this book possible, thank you.

To all those who have inspired me – brain scientists, practitioners, and writers and especially Barbara Turner-Vesselago for the gift of *freefall* that opened up my writing like a silver blade through a sweet ripe peach, thank you.

To all my clients through whom I discovered much of what is between these pages, thank you for allowing me to see your brain up close and curious. And lastly, to my own curious brain for calling me, wide-eyed in wonder, to stand before the greatest mystery, the human brain, as it revealed itself, especially how it can heal when it's been wounded, I bow deep in gratitude.

Michael Leunig's artwork on pages 33 and 235 is reprinted with the permission of the artist.

www.ingramcontent.com/pod-product-compliance
Lightning Source LLC
Chambersburg PA
CBHW050242170426
43202CB00015B/2883